GENERATION IN
WAITING

GENERATION IN
WAITING

The Unfulfilled Promise of
Young People in the Middle East

NAVTEJ DHILLON

TARIK YOUSEF

editors

BROOKINGS INSTITUTION PRESS
Washington, D.C.

Library of Congress Cataloging-in-Publication data
Generation in waiting : the unfulfilled promise of young people in the Middle
East / Navtej Dhillon and Tarik Yousef, editors.
    p.   cm.
Includes bibliographical references and index.
Summary: "Portrays young people's plight, urging greater investment to improve
their lives. Perspectives from the Maghreb to the Levant address complex challenges: education, employment, housing and credit, and transitioning to marriage and family. Presents policy implications and sets an agenda for economic
development to create a hopeful future for future generations"—Provided by
publisher.
  ISBN 978-0-8157-0314-3 (pbk. : alk. paper)
1. Youth—Middle East—Social conditions. 2. Youth—Middle East—Economic
conditions. I. Dhillon, Navtej. II.Yousef, Tarik.
  HQ799.M628G46 2009
  305.2350956—dc22   2009030944

              1 3 5 7 9 8 6 4 2

            Printed on acid-free paper

              Typeset in Minion

        Composition by Oakland Street Publishing
                Arlington, Virginia

            Printed by R. R. Donnelley
              Harrisonburg, Virginia

Contents

Foreword

STROBE TALBOTT
President, Brookings Institution

The 2009 inauguration, and leadership transition in the United States, has brought with it the promise of new energy and a change in U.S. foreign policy in the Middle East. Under President Barack Obama, U.S. policy in the Middle East is no longer dominated by the "war on terror." Instead, a new relationship is being defined on the basis of mutual respect and partnership, as the president outlined in his speech to the Muslim world at Cairo University in June 2009. Along with the traditional focus on diplomacy and defense, this partnership promises to elevate economic development in the Middle East, promoting education, employment, and economic growth.

At Brookings, we believe that this approach holds the potential to both further prosperity in the Middle East and secure U.S. strategic interests. One of the least understood features of the Middle East is that it is the youngest region in the world, with a majority of its population under the age of thirty. Unfortunately, too many young men and women remain trapped by low-quality education and unemployment, growing vulnerable to poverty and exclusion. As these challenges grow, the United States should reaffirm its commitment to promoting economic development across the Middle East.

The convergence of American and Middle Eastern interests in social and economic development is not new. The export of American higher education to the region, for example, has contributed to the rise of prominent academic institutions—such as the American Universities of Beirut and Cairo—which have produced many of the region's leaders. Today, strong demographic pressures and an increasingly competitive global economy call for deeper and sustained cooperation between the United States and the

Middle East in building human capital and expanding opportunities for ordinary people.

Generation in Waiting, edited by Navtej Dhillon and Tarik Yousef, is the latest demonstration of our commitment at Brookings to playing our part in charting this course. This book provides a comprehensive analysis of the economic challenges confronting Middle Eastern societies and their young citizens. The work of the Middle East Youth Initiative is part of an ambitious and progressive portfolio of research advanced by the Wolfensohn Center for Development at Brookings and the Dubai School of Government. The Initiative focuses on promoting the economic and social inclusion of young people in the Middle East.

As policymakers in the United States establish new strategies of American engagement in the Middle East, *Generation in Waiting* brings a number of important and timely issues to the fore that often are left out of foreign policy debates. For example, in Iran, understanding the pressures that young people exert on the education system and labor markets helps us gain a better picture of the internal dynamics between the country's current regime and its citizens. In the Palestinian Territories, we can recognize that a solution to the conflict must entail a viable economic plan that responds to the needs of a growing young population. Finally, this volume's stark depiction of life in Yemen, one of the poorest countries in the Middle East, reveals a population on the brink and one that is in severe need of greater development assistance.

The Middle East Youth Initiative's in-depth research on the state of young people in the region must be taken into careful consideration in our quest to preempt future security risks in the region and to seek peace in the Middle East. By working with our partners in the Middle East, the United States can help create a brighter future for current and future generations and begin to restore those invaluable qualities of leadership, credibility, and compassion to the American image in the Muslim world.

Foreword

H.E. DR. ANWAR MOHAMMED GARGASH
Minister of Foreign Affairs and Federal National Council Affairs,
United Arab Emirates
Chairman of the Board of Trustees of the Dubai School of Government

JAMES D. WOLFENSOHN
Chairman and CEO, Wolfensohn & Company and
former World Bank President

Successful and progressive societies are defined by their ability to improve the quality of life for every successive generation. The Middle East faces a momentous challenge to ensure that today's youth and children, the largest segment of the population, have more opportunities than their parents and are able to contribute fully to the region's stability and prosperity.

Over the last four decades, many countries in the region have made impressive human development gains, paving the way for healthier and more educated generations. However, rather than emerging as an empowered generation, too many young lives in the countries discussed here are locked in a frustrating state of dependence on their families and governments. *Generation in Waiting* captures these trends. As this book argues, the quality of education in the region is often low, leaving young people unprepared to compete in the global economy. Young job seekers endure high rates of unemployment and long periods of waiting before securing employment. Furthermore, young people are experiencing deteriorating job quality as many of them start their careers in informal, low-wage jobs. In turn, young people are unable to allocate enough financial resources to marriage, family formation, and independent living.

Over time, policymakers across the region have come to recognize these problems, and many programs and policies have been established to target such obstacles. Higher education in the West Bank and Gaza has adapted creatively to a difficult security environment. Al-Quds Open University, for example, now provides distance learning to approximately 46,000 Palestinian students, making it the largest higher education institution in the West

Bank and Gaza. In Jordan, education reforms are changing curriculum and teaching methods to equip young Jordanians with a broad range of skills. In Egypt, early evidence shows that housing policy reforms have made it easier for young men to afford rental apartments and, therefore, cover one of the principal costs of marriage.

While such initiatives demonstrate real achievements, no country in the Middle East, despite unprecedented recent economic expansion, can claim to have sufficiently addressed the fundamental challenges facing its young citizens. Middle Eastern countries need to reform the basic institutions, which all too often work against the interests of young people. These reforms include: modernizing education systems so students gain relevant skills; expanding the private sector as the engine of job creation; curtailing and reducing the appeal of public sector employment so young workers avoid spending years waiting for government jobs; improving financial markets so young people can access credit to start businesses or purchase homes; and encouraging young people to contribute to society through civic participation.

Today, as Middle Eastern economies are coping with an ailing global economy, we fear that young people will bear the costs of the current downturn. The region's youth unemployment rates are already among the highest in the world, and with the slowdown in growth, young people's employment prospects risk worsening. While a tough economic environment might make reforms more difficult, policy responses pursued by Middle Eastern countries during the downturn will determine whether their young citizens will be able to exploit opportunities when the global economy recovers. Thus, it is critical that countries double their efforts to create a skilled and entrepreneurial work force and to expand the role of the private sector while reducing the appeal of public employment.

Given the changing economic landscape and the need to better understand the lives of young people, this volume, edited by Navtej Dhillon and Tarik Yousef, makes a timely contribution. Since 2006 the Middle East Youth Initiative, a joint program of the Wolfensohn Center for Development at the Brookings Institution and the Dubai School of Government, has collaborated with some of the best scholars across the region to illuminate the complex economic challenges faced by young people.

By bringing together perspectives spanning the Middle East, *Generation in Waiting* provides a truly regional picture of how young people are coming of age. It not only portrays their current plight, but also makes the case for better policies if the Middle East is to avoid squandering its most valuable resource.

ABOUT THE MIDDLE EAST YOUTH INITIATIVE

The Middle East Youth Initiative (MEYI) is a joint project of the Wolfensohn Center for Development at the Brookings Institution and the Dubai School of Government. The first policy research program of its kind, MEYI is devoted to promoting the economic and social inclusion of youth in the Middle East. The initiative's main objective is to accelerate the regional policy community's ability to better understand and respond to the changing needs of young people in the region. By creating an international alliance of academics, policymakers, and youth leaders from the private sector and civil society, MEYI aims to develop and promote a progressive policy agenda.

The Middle East Youth Initiative has embarked on a new partnership with Silatech—a regional initiative funded by Her Highness Sheikha Mozah bint Nasser Al-Missned of Qatar—that seeks to promote large-scale job creation, entrepreneurship, and access to capital and markets for young people. The Middle East Youth Initiative and Silatech will work toward generating solutions in critical youth areas by promoting new knowledge, innovation, and learning across borders.

The Wolfensohn Center for Development at the Brookings Institution was founded in July 2006 by James D. Wolfensohn, former president of the World Bank and a member of the Brookings Board of Trustees. The Center analyzes how resources, knowledge, and implementation capabilities can be combined toward broad-based economic and social change.

The Dubai School of Government is a research and teaching institution focusing on public policy in the Arab world. Established in 2005 under the patronage of H. H. Sheikh Mohammed bin Rashid Al Maktoum, vice president and prime minister of the United Arab Emirates and ruler of Dubai, the school aims to promote good governance by enhancing the region's capacity for effective public policy.

Acknowledgments

This volume has emerged from the research sponsored and supported by the Middle East Youth Initiative. We would like to thank all of the authors of the chapters included in this volume for their excellent research and their contribution to a greater understanding of youth issues throughout the region.

We would also like to express our appreciation to Minister Hala Bseiso Lattouf, John Blomquist, Lael Brainard, Maria Correia, Wendy Cunningham, Samar Dudin, Jean Fares, Ahmed Galal, Heba Handoussa, Barbara Ibrahim, Rami Khouri, Santiago Levy, Rick Little, Cynthia Lloyd, Minister Mahmoud Mohieldin, Caroline Moser, T. Paul Schultz, Amartya Sen, Hilary Silver, Diane Singerman, Tamara Cofman Wittes, Adam Wolfensohn, Elaine Wolfensohn, and Naomi Wolfensohn for their intellectual contribution in shaping the direction of our research. We would also like to recognize the Education for Employment Foundation, Save the Children, and the Syria Trust for Development for sharing their work on youth in local communities around the Middle East.

In addition, we would like to thank our colleagues at the Brookings Institution for offering their support, insight, and suggestions during this process, especially Raj Desai, Raji Jagadeesan, Homi Kharas, and Johannes Linn. Thanks also go to Bob Faherty and the staff at the Brookings Institution Press, especially Chris Kelaher and Janet Walker, for patiently guiding us through the publication process.

Finally, we would like to thank our team at the Middle East Youth Initiative: Samantha Constant and Paul Dyer, for kindly reviewing the text and providing sound advice and direction; Mary Kraetsch for her dedication and diligence in managing the research portfolio and coordinating the various stages of writing and editing; and Diana Greenwald and Amina Fahmy for their excellent research assistance and attention to detail. We would also like to thank our interns—Nour Abdul-Razzak, Krystina Derrickson, and Jamil Wyne—for all their hard work.

GENERATION IN
WAITING

NAVTEJ DHILLON *and* TARIK YOUSEF

Introduction

The Middle East has been characterized as being in the grip of two great games.[1] In the first game, the interests of Middle Eastern nations and western powers intersect to shape geopolitics. The second game—less visible in our daily headlines—involves people and governments trying to advance economic development. But today, a third game, even less well understood, is being played out in the Middle East. This is the *generational game* in which the largest youth cohort in the Middle East's modern history is striving for prosperity and thereby shaping politics.

In recent years, the Middle East has come to be defined by a series of dichotomies: democracy versus authoritarianism; Islam versus secularism; and economically successful versus stagnant. No matter what the fault lines, they all share a generational dimension. It is the young who are pressing against existing economic, political, and religious institutions and norms and forging new ones. This generational game is unfolding in a competitive global economy where young people in the Middle East seek the affluence and openness enjoyed by their peers in other parts of the world.

Over the past two decades, the demographic transition in the region has resulted in a young working-age population that is now the most important resource for Middle Eastern economies. Generally, a large working-age population, and proportionally fewer dependent children and retirees, can free up resources and increase savings, creating better economic and social outcomes. In this regard, there has been tremendous progress: the high mortality and illiteracy rates of past generations have given way to a gener-

1

ation that is healthier and more educated. There have been large gains in more equitable distribution of education between women and men.

However, development in the Middle East is proving uneven, bypassing the majority of young people. Previous generations benefited from free education, public sector job guarantees, and strong state support in the form of subsidies and entitlements. But for those born in the 1980s and later, these institutions, which once ensured intergenerational equity and social justice, are no longer working. The severity of demographic pressures have strained public sector employment and subsidized education systems. Even if these institutions could accommodate the youth bulge, they are not well suited in a world where innovation and entrepreneurship are the drivers of economic growth. As a result, young people in the Middle East are falling further behind their peers in other parts of the world, such as East Asia.

Today in the Middle East, education systems are failing to provide relevant skills, and labor market prospects for young workers are deteriorating. Young women are gaining more education but face widespread exclusion from the labor market. Delayed marriage is becoming a common phenomenon in some countries as young people face obstacles to family formation posed by unemployment, high costs of marriage, and lack of access to affordable housing. Together, these deficits are weakening economic mobility for current and future generations.

With this book, it is our objective to promote a better understanding of the material struggles of young people, which are bound up in larger questions about the Middle East's economic development and politics. This volume brings together perspectives from eight countries to analyze how young people are transitioning to adulthood and to elucidate how institutions are shaping these transitions. Our hope is that this volume will be viewed not within the narrow context of demography or security but rather within a larger agenda of inclusive development in the Middle East. The ultimate goal is to convince policymakers that reforms that tackle the disadvantages of younger age groups can potentially reduce the inequities that exist across income and gender.

Choosing a Framework to Study Young Lives

A number of theoretical frameworks have been used to analyze the lives of young people in different countries and regions. The most common are the neoclassical economic framework of human capital formation and the sociodemographic framework of life course.[2] The former stresses the importance of education and skills of young workers and their contribution to productivity and growth. The latter considers individual transitions and trajectories and their relationship to institutions and historical periods.[3] In addition, the concept of *social exclusion* has been adopted to understand the factors that prevent certain groups from fully participating in the normatively prescribed activities of the society in which they live.[4]

More recently, international organizations have put forth policy frameworks. The World Bank's *World Development Report* of 2007 highlights the opportunities for accelerated economic growth and poverty reduction that can occur when policies and institutions that influence the human capital development of youth are strengthened.[5] A report by the National Research Council in the United States focuses on the extent to which rapidly changing global forces affect youth transitions in developing countries, specifically the transitions to five key adult roles: adult worker, citizen and community participant, spouse, parent, and household head.[6]

In this volume, we build on these frameworks, taking the most relevant aspects of each and applying them to the Middle East. Three major features of our framework are as follows. First, we depart from the traditional approach of studying facets of young people's lives, such as education or employment, separately. Instead, we assess three major interdependent transitions: education, employment, and family formation. Here we pay special attention to marriage where possible, given the availability of data, because social norms in the Middle East make the transition to family formation critical to full social inclusion.

Second, we recognize that individual transitions and trajectories are part of a life course, which is often shaped by the history, economy, politics, and culture of Middle Eastern countries. Events, time, and geography, as well as the agency of individuals, modify and influence transitions. This realization leads us to recognize how life courses have varied across historical periods and national contexts.

Finally, throughout this volume, we stress the importance of institutions and the incentives they generate in influencing young people's transitions. We define institutions as rules and regulations that govern the education system; markets for labor, credit, and housing; and nonmarket institutions such as social norms.

Through this framework, it is our hope that policymakers and future researchers will see the lives of young people in a more interconnected way and recognize that young lives are institutionally patterned. In using this framework, this book marshals the best available data and evidence to elucidate the lives of young people. While it contributes to a better under-standing, it also exposes the limitations of our knowledge given the lack of high quality and available data in the Middle East.

Generation in Waiting: Structure of the Volume

This volume contributes to the growing interest in young people as they relate to development policy and practice. The chapters that follow attempt to provide a comprehensive assessment of the three major transitions of young people in eight Middle East countries.

In chapter one, Navtej Dhillon, Paul Dyer, and Tarik Yousef place the transitions of young people in a larger historical context, arguing that the challenges facing young people today in the Middle East did not exist a gen-eration ago. They argue that previous generations faced a *traditional life course*, prevalent in mostly rural Middle Eastern societies, where the transi-tion to adulthood was mediated by family and the community. An expanded role of state institutions between the 1950s and the 1980s paved the way for the *welfare life course*, where governments provided education, employment, and protection for citizens. Young people born since the beginning of the 1980s have faced a weakening welfare life course while at the same time a new life course has not yet fully emerged.

The authors provide a synthesis of how young people's transitions have become more complex and uncertain. While high demographic pressures and volatile economic growth have undermined the prospects of young people, Dhillon, Dyer, and Yousef emphasize the central role that existing institutions have also played in hindering economic development for the young.

In chapter two, Djavad Salehi-Isfahani and Daniel Egel posit that the dis-content of young Iranians is receiving much attention from outsiders but that the understanding of the economic and social environment shaping their lives is limited. They present a detailed picture of Iran's fertility boom and bust from the 1970s to the 1980s that has paved the way for a youth bulge. In 1995 Iran had 13 million residents aged 15 to 29; this population is set to peak in 2010 at 20 million. Iran's reduction in fertility now presents the country with a "demographic gift" that can drive economic growth.

A foundation for human capital development is already in place in Iran. Salehi-Isfahani and Egel show that average years of schooling have doubled in a generation. However, young Iranians confront a highly competitive and exclusionary education system, where students compete to win the "univer-sity lottery." Once out of school, young Iranians confront unemployment and long waiting times for a first job. Transitions to employment are hampered by a rigid labor market that is ill prepared to absorb a labor force expanding by 3 to 4 percent a year. Faced with bleak employment prospects and high costs of marriage, young Iranians are forced to delay marriage and remain dependent on their families.

Salehi-Isfahani and Egel argue that the postrevolution "social contract" must be reformed and that the most severe necessity for this reform emanates from the large youth population and its continued exclusion. Some steps in this direction have been taken: the size of public sector employment has declined; public sector payroll freezes have been implemented; and recent changes in the 1990 labor law exempted small and medium-size firms from restrictions on hiring and firing. But there is still a way to go before Iran's education, labor, and marriage institutions can change to take advantage of the country's demographic gift.

In chapter three, Ragui Assaad and Ghada Barsoum show that the transitions of young Egyptians are being shaped by the recent changes in Egypt's economic and social environment. Starting in 2004, an economic revival led to a drop in unemployment rates. However, poverty levels remain unchanged because of the rapid growth of low productivity and nonwage employment. Young workers have been most affected by these changes, enduring the lowest earnings and the slowest increase in real earnings.

Assaad and Barsoum identify access and quality as two major challenges facing the education system. Young girls in Upper Egypt and youth from low socioeconomic backgrounds are highly vulnerable to early school dropout and nonenrollment. They identify the Egyptian labor market as grappling with three trends: it is increasingly young, has more females entering the labor market, and is made up of highly educated job seekers. As the youth bulge peaks, the number of new entrants in the labor market increased from 400,000 per year in the late 1970s to around 850,000 per year in the early 2000s. Assaad and Barsoum conclude by assessing the effectiveness of recent education and labor market reforms.

In chapter four, Edward Sayre and Samia Al-Botmeh turn our attention to the acute rupture between demographics and development in the West Bank and Gaza: a rapidly growing youth population with diminishing economic prospects. Sayre and Al-Botmeh posit that in the past Palestinian workers had two main sources of employment. Israel once provided a third of all Palestinian jobs, but in recent years the Israeli labor market has been closed to Palestinian workers. In addition, Palestinians once migrated to the Gulf States for work, but those jobs are now dominated by South Asian migrant workers. As a result, young Palestinians face a protracted transition to employment. Highly educated Palestinians face diminishing prospects: the unemployment rate for 20- to 24-year-old university-educated men stands at 36 percent in the West Bank and 64 percent in Gaza.

Sayre and Al-Botmeh conclude that the public sector and international aid cannot create sufficient opportunities to absorb the burgeoning youth population. Fiscal strains will eventually force the Palestinian Authority to curb the expansion of its already large public sector, and no amount of aid can single-handedly stimulate growth and development. The authors underline the importance of lifting restrictions on the Palestinian economy and allowing freer movement of goods and labor into and out of the Palestinian Territories. In the absence of these preconditions being met and maintained, young Palestinians will be confined to a grim future.

In chapter five, Jad Chaaban focuses on Lebanon's post–civil war generation—a million strong between the ages of 15 and 29. He argues that Lebanon takes pride in its human capital, which is the only comparative advantage it has over its resource-rich neighbors. After the end of the civil war in 1990, Lebanon embarked on ambitious reconstruction efforts and record spending on education and health. However, these investments have not resulted in improved outcomes for the young. Educational inequities are large, with youth in poorer regions having lower enrollment rates than those in the cities; unemployment for young people is higher compared with adults; and emigration rates are alarming, with one-third of youth reporting a desire to emigrate.

Chaaban contends that political instability and the proliferation of conflicts, including the 2006 Hezbollah-Israel war, have created an unpredictable environment for young Lebanese. Persistent expectations of future conflict breeds apathy among the young, who see little point in setting long-term goals. Lack of opportunities has resulted in high levels of migration, perpetuating the vicious cycle of underdevelopment by draining the country of its human capital. In this context, Chaaban makes several recommendations for promoting greater economic and political inclusion of youth, such as improving access to education for students from poorer regions and encouraging public-private partnerships that employ young people.

In chapter six, Taher Kanaan and May Hanania provide a compelling analysis of the state of young people in Jordan. Kanaan and Hanania remind us that Jordan's recent history is characterized by sudden changes in territory, population, and economic shocks emanating from conflict in neighboring countries such as Iraq. They illustrate how the 1991 Gulf War, the second Palestinian intifada of 2000, and the U.S. invasion of Iraq in 2003 have led to an influx of migrants into Jordan. This coupled with an average population growth rate of around 2.7 percent among Jordanians has endowed the country with a major asset—its human capital. To tap into this asset, Jordan must create over 50,000 new jobs every year just to maintain current unemployment levels.

However, Kanaan and Hanania point out that Jordan is far from meeting this challenge. The recent period of positive GDP growth has not only failed to create enough jobs, but the jobs created have not been of sufficient quality to meet the expectations of an increasingly educated labor force. The majority of new jobs have been in the construction sector, and these have largely been taken by foreign workers. Women remain marginalized, experiencing high levels of unemployment. Bleak employment prospects are having an impact on prospects for family formation: the median age of marriage is increasing for both men and women, especially since access to independent housing has become more difficult during the recent real estate boom.

Kanaan and Hanania provide extensive analysis of recent reforms in the education and employment sectors. They argue that despite these reforms, Jordan's political, social, and economic institutions still must evolve considerably to meet the needs of its large youth population. An education system that continues to prepare youth for public sector employment must be fundamentally changed. Furthermore, to cope with high labor market pressures, the economy must invent new engines of job creation given that the public sector and migration are insufficient.

In chapter seven, Brahim Boudarbat and Aziz Ajbilou paint a portrait of a young generation in Morocco coming of age as their country grapples with three major challenges. First, the arrival of the youth bulge coincides with poor macroeconomic performance and sluggish economic growth, which has limited the opportunities for young citizens. Second, Morocco has undergone rapid urbanization during the last four decades, putting pressure on urban labor markets. Finally, persistent poverty continues to affect the young, especially in rural areas.

Through better education and access to decent employment, many young Moroccan men and women in this generation are more empowered to break the trap of poverty and social exclusion. Access to education has significantly improved, and the gender gap in primary education has narrowed. Even unemployment has been slashed in the past few years. But these improvements also mask new disparities. According to Boudarbat and

Ajbilou, repetition rates in primary education are among the worst in the Middle East. Despite more investments in secondary education, Morocco's secondary enrollment rates remain low compared with countries with similar income levels. Transitions to work are defined by high unemployment and long durations of unemployment, especially among secondary and higher education graduates.

Boudarbat and Ajbilou argue that youth unemployment can no longer be seen as a business cycle phenomenon. While the spike in unemployment among educated youth results from the contraction of the public sector in the 1980s, it has mutated into a structural problem and a source of growing social tensions. The Moroccan government has responded with a proliferation of initiatives, such as the reform of the Moroccan labor code, to promote investment and the creation of special development zones. Still, according to Boudarbat and Ajbilou, the government's responses have been piecemeal and seldom evaluated to measure impact.

In chapter eight, Nader Kabbani and Noura Kamel focus on Syria's transition from a public sector–led economy toward a "social market" economy as the country becomes a net oil importer in the near future. Young people and their growing education, employment, and housing needs are an important impetus for these economic reforms. But because they prefer public sector jobs, they are also the source of resistance.

The challenge for Syria, argue Kabbani and Kamel, will be to build and sustain support for market reforms among members of the young generation who will be the benefactors of this change. What is first needed, the authors say, is reform in the education system. The mismatch between the skills of job seekers and the needs of employers is reflected in exceptionally low returns to education. In Syria, an additional year of schooling is associated with a mere 2 percent increase in wages compared with an average 10 to 15 percent increase globally. As part of the economic reforms, labor market outcomes for young workers will need to improve. Kabbani and Kamel show that youth unemployment has declined from 26 percent in 2002 to around 19 percent recently. Although many employed youth have found jobs in the private sector, the lure of public sector employment remains strong, especially among young women.

These employment preferences have an economic and social rationale: young women earn higher wages in the public sector; for men public sector jobs provide the stability and prestige necessary for marriage and family formation. While the Syrian government has reduced public sector employment and allowed private sector competition in many sectors, a number of recent initiatives may reinforce the appeal of government jobs. Public sector wages have increased repeatedly since 2000. Unless retrenchment policies accompany efforts to better align public sector wages and benefits with a thriving private sector, queuing for government jobs will continue and support for economic reforms will weaken.

In chapter nine, Ragui Assaad, Ghada Barsoum, Emily Cupito, and Daniel Egel concentrate on Yemen—the poorest country in the Middle East and one that faces deficits in both human development and natural resources. Given the continuing high fertility rate of over six children per woman of childbearing age, Yemen's population is one of the youngest in the Middle East: over 75 percent of the population is under the age of 25. The authors argue that with a dwindling supply of natural resources, low levels of human development, and high levels of poverty, Yemen risks losing a generation to poverty.

The authors show that Yemen has some of the poorest education indicators in the world with low enrollment and widespread illiteracy. Poor educational attainment, low retention, and poor standards in education quality are pervasive throughout the country, but they have a disproportionate effect on young women in rural areas. The Yemeni labor market is defined by limited employment opportunities in the formal sector. Youth employment is primarily confined to informal employment, which offers limited job security and few opportunities for career advancement. A high incidence of migration to urban areas within Yemen and internationally reflects the extent to which youth and families must travel in search of gainful employment.

In response to these challenges, the Yemeni government has undertaken a series of reforms designed to increase school enrollment and promote job creation in the private sector. Adoption of the National Children and Youth Strategy in 2006 reflects the government's commitment to improving the status of youth in Yemen. However, these efforts are constrained by a severe shortage of resources and limited institutional and administrative capacity. To begin to redress these shortcomings, the authors call on the international community, both in the West and among Yemen's richer neighbors, to increase aid and assistance to Yemen.

In the concluding chapter, Navtej Dhillon and Djavad Salehi-Isfahani focus on how Middle Eastern countries are responding to the problems of their young citizens and draw attention to major gaps in the current approach. They argue that more investments in schools, training programs, and subsidies targeting young people, while well-intentioned, do not address the underlying causes of social exclusion. They interpret the difficulties faced by young people as a consequence of failures in key market and nonmarket institutions. Transitions of young people are influenced by several interconnected markets such as education, labor, credit, housing, and marriage. For a new life course to emerge for Middle Eastern youth, institutions and key markets must be reformed.

Dhillon and Salehi-Isfahani outline ten institutional features of Middle Eastern economies and societies that hold the potential for furthering prosperity and equity for the young generation. They argue that reforms can happen and that demographic pressures are already serving as a major impetus. They also propose principles for guiding future policies and programs. In this sense, the book ends with a meditation on not only the plights of young people, but also on ways in which public policy can improve their lives.

Notes

1. Alan Richards and John Waterbury, *A Political Economy of the Middle East* (Boulder, Colo.: Westview Press, 2007).

2. Hilary Silver, "Social Exclusion: Comparative Analysis of Europe and Middle East Youth," Middle East Youth Initiative Working Paper 1 (Wolfensohn Center for Development at the Brookings Institution and the Dubai School of Government, 2007)

3. Glen H. Elder Jr., Monica Kirkpatrick Johnson, and Robert Crosnoe, "The Emergence and Development of Life Course Theory," in *Handbook of the Life Course*, edited by Jeylan T. Mortimer and Michael J. Shanahan (New York: Springer, 2004).

4. Silver, "Social Exclusion: Comparative Analysis of Europe and Middle East Youth."

5. World Bank, *World Development Report 2007: Development and the Next Generation* (Washington: 2006).

6. Cynthia Lloyd, ed., *Growing Up Global: The Changing Transitions to Adulthood in Developing Countries* (Washington: National Academies Press, 2005).

NAVTEJ DHILLON, PAUL DYER, *and* TARIK YOUSEF

1

Generation in Waiting: An Overview of School to Work and Family Formation Transitions

Representing the largest birth cohort in the history of the Middle East, the young men and women born between 1980 and 1995 are now coming of age and entering adulthood. Today, more than 100 million individuals between the ages of 15 and 29 live in the Middle East, up from less than 67 million in 1990. They make up 30 percent of the region's population and nearly 47 percent of its working-age population. Much has been promised to this generation in terms of better quality of life and greater prosperity; however, many of these promises remain elusive.

As the Middle East's youth population has grown, young people have increasingly struggled with securing critical milestones in their transition to adulthood. Across the region, education systems have failed to prepare young people for changing roles in the economy. Labor market outcomes have remained poor, with young people enduring high rates of unemployment and low-quality jobs. Delays in marriage and family formation are now common in many countries. Moreover, with limited progress in improving the quality of education and job creation, the challenges that afflict today's young people now risk being passed on to future generations.

Young people in the Middle East experience different economic, political, and social realities depending on where they grow up. Obvious distinctions include the extent to which countries rely on hydrocarbon rents, their integration with the global economy, and their levels of stability and peace. Furthermore, youth is not a homogeneous social category: gender and family income significantly influence young people's transitions. This heterogeneity is captured well by the eight country studies presented in this volume.

11

In this chapter, we provide a framework for understanding the common challenges facing the Middle East's young generation and how institutional reforms can lead to substantial improvements in their lives. The chapter begins by analyzing how life courses within Middle Eastern societies have been transformed in response to economic and social changes in the twentieth century. It then focuses on the interrelated challenges facing young people in their education, employment, and family formation transitions. Next, we illustrate how the institutions that govern education systems, the labor market, and family formation have failed to mediate young people's transitions, leaving them in essence as a generation in waiting. In the final section, we outline guiding principles for improving transitions for young people across the Middle East.

The Middle East's Three Life Courses

One useful way to understand the lives of young people in the Middle East is to place the temporal phase of "youth" in a larger life course framework. A life course comprises critical transitions and trajectories such as schooling, career, family, and retirement. This framework recognizes human development as a lifelong process that is shaped by individual agency, the time and place in which individuals come of age, and the opportunities and constraints of their environment.[1] Furthermore, success in one's life is cumulative: opportunities are amplified or diminished by development outcomes in early life, especially during adolescence and youth.

The life course perspective, as it applies to young people in the Middle East, focuses largely on the school-to-work transition and the work-to-family formation transition. It draws attention to the prevailing institutions in the education system and to markets for labor, housing, and credit as well to social norms, all of which shape young people's life course.[2] To understand the exclusion of young people, it is critical to assess how life courses, and the key institutions that support these life courses, have evolved over time in the Middle East in response to demographic pressures, and periodic prosperity and economic downturn.

Today, the Middle East is characterized by three major life courses: the traditional life course, the welfare life course, and the post-welfare life course.[3] These life courses coexist, undergoing ebbs and flows in response to external and internal changes over time and with increases in population. The traditional life course has declined as a result of economic advancement; the welfare life course remains dominant though increasingly inadequate and the post-welfare life course is underdeveloped. The growing incongruity between these life courses, and the related failure of existing institutions to mediate the transitions of young people, have paved the way for a generation in waiting.

The Traditional Life Course

In the traditional life course, found mostly in rural Middle Eastern societies, individuals move directly from childhood into adulthood, a transition mediated by family and the community and one that presents young people, especially women, with few economic opportunities. This traditional life course still prevails in poorer, more rural parts of Middle Eastern countries though is less widespread as a result of economic development and modernization.

Access to formal education is often a privilege of the few because of a lack of schools in local communities and because of poverty, which pushes individuals into employment at a young age. Where primary education is available, it is largely taken up by boys rather than girls. Young men seeking jobs are limited largely to the family farm or trades in the local community; long job searches are rare because families pass on vocations and skills from one generation to the next. Young women experience different transitions: they marry early, and their roles are confined largely to family and household responsibilities, occasionally accompanied by some wage work to supplement household income.

This traditional life course characterized much of the Middle East at independence. It has been estimated that in 1950 nearly 85 percent of the region's population lived in rural areas. Educational attainment was low and illiteracy prevailed. In 1939, for example, adult illiteracy in Egypt was estimated at 99.5 percent and only 23.3 percent of 5- to 19-year-olds were enrolled in school.[4] Even today, in countries like Morocco and Yemen, the education transitions associated with the traditional life course continue, particularly in rural areas. The adult illiteracy rate is still 47.7 percent in Morocco and 45.9 percent in Yemen.[5] Overall, however, investments in education, poverty alleviation, and improvements in macroeconomic conditions over the past five decades have made the traditional life course less pervasive, replaced largely by the welfare life course.

The Welfare Life Course

The economic development of the Middle East following independence paved the way for the welfare life course wherein state institutions emerged as the dominant transition structures. States provided a growing population with free education, stable employment in the government and public sector enterprises, and expanding social protection mechanisms. These institutions enabled the postindependence generation to secure higher levels of socio-economic welfare, institutionalizing stable transitions for many individuals.

In the context of the welfare life course in the Middle East, educational access increased dramatically. Net enrollment in primary education expanded from 62 percent in 1970 to 85 percent in 2003, and the gender inequalities in education inherited from the traditional life course were gradually erased.[6] Moreover, public sector employment guarantees for high school and university graduates in countries like Egypt and Morocco encouraged young people, especially from modest backgrounds, to stay longer in school.[7] Strong job protection provided security and steady incomes for workers and their families.

The ability of governments in the region to provide these resources was bolstered by oil production, whether directly by export revenues or indirectly by the return of workers' remittances, investments, and direct aid. However, the oil price crash in the mid-1980s and the subsequent decade-long period of economic stagnation led to a retrenchment of state institutions. At the same time, the Middle East experienced the initial increase in youth population (figure 1-1). This growing youth population imposed rising pressures on the region's education systems and led to an unprecedented growth of labor supply.[8] Together, economic stagnation and rising demographic pressures diminished the capacity of governments to sustain the welfare life course.

Many Middle Eastern countries responded to these pressures by embracing structural adjustment and economic reforms designed to scale back state-led institutions and to stimulate private-sector-led growth. However, these reforms have been uneven and selective, retaining the embedded institutions and interests that developed under the welfare life course. Even today, Middle Eastern economies are still defined by highly centralized, government-subsidized education systems that are proving inflexible in providing skills to prepare young people for the changing global economy. Despite some contraction, the public sector continues to dominate many economies in the region and remains the workplace of choice for graduates. The ability of the private sector to grow and create jobs has remained limited, in large part because of restrictive regulatory environments.

In the context of changing demography and globalization, the welfare life course and its institutional arrangements are advancing the interests of some incumbents (adults) while excluding the majority of young citizens. As the Middle East faces a competitive global economy and huge numbers of

Figure 1-1. *The Youth Bulge and Regional Economic Performance,*
1980–2010[a]

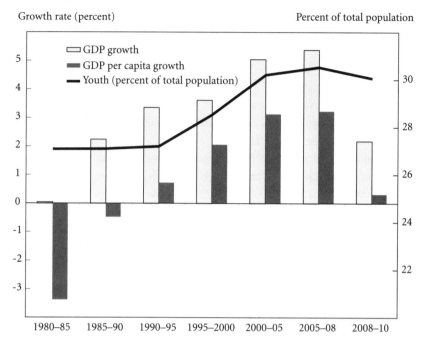

Source: International Monetary Fund; United Nations, World Population Prospects: 2008 Revision.

a. Data are for Algeria, Bahrain, Egypt, Iran, Jordan, Kuwait, Libya, Morocco, Oman, Saudi Arabia, Syria, Tunisia, and United Arab Emirates.

unemployed graduates seeking salaried jobs, these institutions provide the wrong incentives and hinder economic development.[9] To date, the economic performance of Middle Eastern countries has been poor and volatile, and the region lags behind other regions such as East Asia.[10] This poor economic performance can be attributed partly to the lack of reforms and the related failure to move beyond the welfare life course. As a result, even the recent period of economic renewal between 2002 and 2008 did not sufficiently improve the transitions of young people.[11]

The Post-Welfare Life Course

In the post-welfare life course, young people's transitions are based on choice, better information, and the right signals from institutions. The education transition is built on acquiring a broad range of skills as opposed to simply the degrees necessary for public sector work. Work transitions are flexible and provide productive careers in the private sector rather than government jobs. Access to capital allows young people to build credit reputations that can be leveraged toward marriage and family formation. These critical transitions are mediated by well-functioning markets, the private sector, and governments.

Because the Middle East is still transitioning from state-run to market economies, this new life course has yet to fully emerge. As a result, young people's transitions have become more complex, even stalled. They are increasingly moving from primary to secondary and higher education, but with weak skills formation. The emergence of the informal sector and the decline of the public sector have paved the way for more uncertain and unstable transitions. This is especially the case for women, who are gaining more education but participating less in the labor market than their male counterparts. Family formation is involuntarily delayed, and young people are likely to reside longer with their parents.

This leaves young people in the situation of waiting to become full adults—a state of *waithood*—struggling to resolve uncertainty on a number of interrelated fronts: attaining the right education, securing a quality job, and finding ways to afford the costs of family formation.[12] Failure in one transition spills over into the next. Aside from waiting for these varying opportunities, young people are also waiting for a larger change: for a different set of institutions to emerge that can support a new life course. Most young people do not want a traditional life course; they desire the stability and certainty of the welfare life course that is no longer available to many of them; and public policy and institutions have not sufficiently evolved to help forge a new life course.

The Stalled Transition to Adulthood

In the transition to adulthood, young people are engaged in multiple, interrelated searches: for education and training that will improve their job prospects; for employment that will bolster their income and long-term career prospects; and for personal happiness and success through establishing their own families and independent lives, aided by access to housing and credit. However, young people face several obstacles in securing these critical transitions.

Figure 1-2. *Net School Enrollment Rates in the Middle East, 2007*[a]

Enrollment rate (percent)

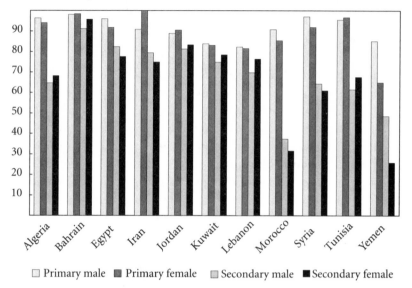

Source: World Bank, *World Development Indicators* (Washington: 2008).
a. Data are for 2007 or most recently available data.

The Education Transition: Greater Access, Lower Quality

As part of the legacy of the welfare life course, the countries of the Middle East have invested heavily in education and human capital development. Over the past five decades, the free provision of education has contributed to a massive expansion in educational access. In recent years, investment in public education has amounted to nearly 5 percent of GDP and 20 percent of government expenditure regionally, comparing well with other developing regions.[13] In turn, the region has seen considerable advances in educational attainment: primary education is now nearly universal across the region, and secondary enrollment has risen to nearly 75 percent on the whole (figure 1-2). Importantly, educational attainment for women has improved, even surpassing that of men in several countries.

Despite these investments in educational attainment, high dropout and repetition rates remain a concern, especially among low-income students, and low enrollment rates are common in rural areas. Further, deep inequities remain in access to higher education. Students from low-income backgrounds are more likely to end up in vocational education and training (VET) than in the academic tracks. In Jordan, 95 percent of those in the academic secondary track are from middle- and high-income backgrounds.[14] This suggests that the region's educational systems are failing to promote equity in access even as they expand investments in underlying infrastructure.

Educational systems in the Middle East suffer in regard to the quality of education, as illustrated in the accompanying chapters in this volume and reported by international institutions.[15] Evidence of the low quality of education in the region can be found in the low average scores for Middle Eastern students on international standardized examinations such as the Trends in International Mathematics and Sciences Study (figure 1-3).[16]

Although most countries in the region have engaged in efforts at educational reform, many key features of regional school systems—the extent to which they are centralized, the level of accountability, the curriculum and pedagogy, and tracking mechanisms—have not been reformed sufficiently to create more fulfilling and productive education transitions. Continued dependence on rote methodologies places little emphasis on teaching critical and analytical skills. A lack of computers and other technology in the classroom means students do not learn needed technology skills. Moreover, teacher quality is limited by inadequate training in modern pedagogy, low salaries, and a lack of performance incentives, especially at the secondary education level.

High investments in expanding secondary education have proven ineffective because standards have been poor.[17] These quality concerns extend beyond the traditional academic track to vocational education and training, despite an increase in government investment in this alternative to academic education. VET programs across the region, mostly operated by government entities, are highly fragmented in their administration. For example, in Egypt, there are 1,237 vocational training centers operated independently by 27 separate ministries or authorities.[18] Training remains largely divorced from the needs of the private sector; not only are curricula outdated, but there are few instances in which private sector representatives play a role in curricula or program design. Thus, VET programs have developed a reputation across the region as a poor alternative to traditional education.

The low quality of education in the region has undermined the ability of young people to successfully transition to adult life. Faced with more complex pathways to employment and family formation, youth have been disempowered as future citizens, parents, and workers by the poor quality of

Figure 1-3. *TIMSS Results from Participating Middle Eastern Countries, Plus United States and Singapore, 2007*[a]

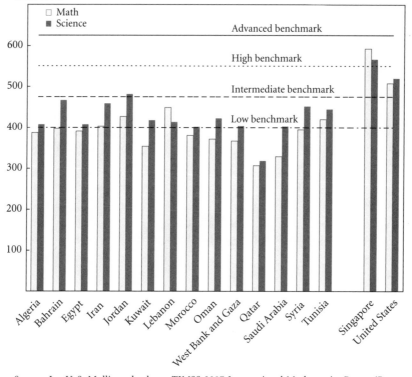

TIMSS score

Source: Ina V. S. Mullis and others, *TIMSS 2007 International Mathematics Report* (Boston College, Lynch School of Education, TIMSS and PIRLS International Study Center, 2008); Michael O. Martin and others, *TIMSS 2007 International Science Report* (Boston College, Lynch School of Education, TIMSS and PIRLS International Study Center, 2008).
a. The scale international average for TIMSS results is 500.

the educational system. This imposes costs on Middle Eastern economies: poor quality of education is associated with lower earnings for workers; a shortage of skilled workers undermines economic growth; and policy failures to improve educational quality are likely to reinforce existing inequities across socioeconomic background and gender.

The Transition to Work: Poor Labor Market Outcomes and Worsening Job Quality

The incongruence between the welfare life course and the post-welfare life course is experienced most severely by young people in the labor market.

Figure 1-4. *Youth Unemployment Rates in the Middle East, 2006*[a]

Unemployment rate (percent)

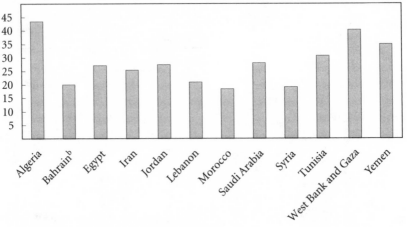

Source: Authors' calculations based on official data.

a. All figures reflect unemployment rates for those aged 15–24 for 2006 or most recently available year.

b. Data for Bahrain include nationals only.

Poor labor market outcomes—unemployment, underemployment and stagnant wages—have imposed themselves persistently on regional economies since the early 1990s.[19] Such outcomes are demonstrated most boldly by regional unemployment rates. By 2000 total unemployment had reached a peak of nearly 15 percent of the region's labor force. Despite a return to high rates of growth in more recent years, unemployment has remained high, estimated in 2008 at nearly 11 percent.

The worst outcomes have been experienced by youth, reflecting specific problems in the ability of young people to gain a foothold in the labor market. Currently, the youth unemployment rate (for those between the ages of 15 and 24) in the Middle East averages between 20 and 25 percent, while rates higher than 30 percent occur in several countries (figure 1-4). In fact, unemployment is largely a youth problem; young people make up more than 50 percent of the region's total unemployed workers, a rate that goes as high as 77 percent in Syria. Many of these unemployed, often first-time job seekers, wait for years to find a position. In Egypt, for example, average unemployment duration for new entrants is nearly two and a half years; in Iran and Morocco, it is closer to three years.

Education provides no guarantee against unemployment. In fact, in several countries unemployment rates are highest among youth with relatively

Figure 1-5. *Youth Unemployment by Educational Attainment, Various Years*

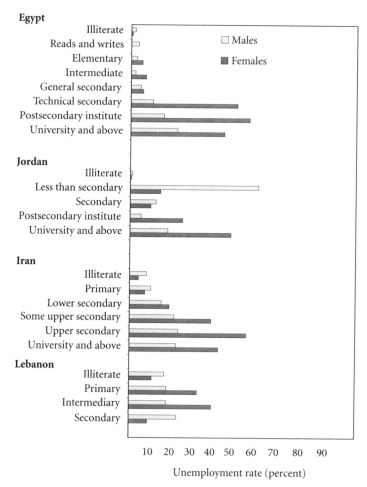

Source: Authors' calculations based on official data. Data for Lebanon and Iran are from 2004. Data for Jordan are from 2007. Data for Egypt are from 2006.

high levels of educational attainment (figure 1-5). In total, those with secondary degrees and higher, who make up the majority of young labor market entrants in several countries and who understandably hold higher expectations in regard to employment and job quality, tend to have higher unemployment rates and unemployment durations than those with less education.

Even as young people's labor market prospects have worsened in the Middle East, hardly any research is available on the short-term and long-term effects of early unemployment. Evidence from developed countries, however, shows that experiencing unemployment early in one's life has two major effects. First, it undermines immediate well-being through the loss of income. Second, early unemployment may adversely affect long-term economic prospects, with those facing long spells of unemployment at an early age experiencing depressed future wages or repeated incidences of unemployment.[20] In the Middle East, these effects might be deeper given that labor markets in the region are more rigid and that jobs are harder to find than in Europe and the United States. Once they secure employment, young workers are more likely to be confined to low-wage and low-skill jobs. Opportunities in the public sector—the traditional source of "good" jobs—have been compressed because of budget constraints, reduced rates of hiring, and the lack of turnover of older workers in the sector. Meanwhile, the formal private sector accounts for a relatively small share of total employment even in the context of higher rates of economic growth seen in recent years.

The lack of secure opportunities in the formal public and private sectors means that a majority of new entrants in the labor market are finding employment in the informal sector. For example, nearly 32 percent of jobs for new entrants in Egypt in 2005 were found in the informal sector, up from 21 percent in 1990. This is particularly the case for those youth who have not secured higher education. Often informal jobs are of poor quality. They generally offer low pay in micro- and small enterprises and tend to be short term or seasonal in nature. Moreover, they provide little in the way of training or on-the-job skills development that can be leveraged by young people toward the development of stronger career paths or to gain access to the formal sector. In addition, such informal jobs provide little in the way of job stability or protections that are offered to contracted workers in the formal sector.

The informal nature of one's first job can also have a lasting impact on future employment prospects. In Egypt, for example, only 11 percent of young Egyptians who find their first jobs in the informal sector are able to secure formal second jobs.[21] Conversely, only 7 percent of those with formal first jobs move on to informal second jobs. Well-educated, urban men who start out in the informal sector show some mobility and are most able to secure better jobs in the future. On the other hand, young men with low levels of educational attainment and those living in rural areas are less able to transition to better jobs. Similarly, young women have lower mobility in their transitions between jobs and are more likely to be trapped in the informal sector once they have started an informal job.

The increase in informality has been matched by a strong deflation of the value of academic credentials across the Middle East. While young people have been gradually securing higher levels of education, returns to education—the measure of an individual's wage gain from investing in more education—have declined significantly.[22] Past returns to education had been quite high across the region, a factor most likely driven by the strong role of the state in employing secondary and university graduates within the welfare life course. With the withdrawal of public sector employment guarantees, the partial deregulation of formal private sector employment, and rising informality, returns to education have been minimized. Thus, young people in the Middle East have seen their personal investments in education decline in value as they enter the labor force.

Importantly, young women face the most difficult school-to-work transitions in the Middle East. While female labor force participation rates are rising, they are the lowest of any region in the world: only 30 percent of 15- to 29-year-old women are participating in the labor market. The high rate of inactivity is partially driven by cultural norms and women's own choices to focus on their roles as caretakers; however, the choice to stay out of the labor market is often the result of frustrations at poor labor market prospects. Those who do choose to enter the labor market face difficult prospects: female unemployment rates in the region are generally double those of men, and waiting periods to secure a job are longer for women. When they do find work, women face intense competition in a more limited number of sectors. This competition depresses their wages, giving rise to the region's well-documented gender wage disparities.[23]

Transition to Family Formation:
Delayed Marriage and Housing Constraints

With poor labor market outcomes, young people in the Middle East are finding that other steps toward adulthood, especially those related to marriage and family formation, are becoming more difficult. While early marriage persists in poorer, rural areas where the traditional life course is more prevalent, the general trend is toward a delay of marriage. Contrary to common assumptions, young men in the Middle East have the lowest rates of marriage in the developing world. Only 50 percent of Middle Eastern men between the ages of 25 and 29 are married.[24] Although the average age of marriage for young women in the region is lower than that of men, similar trends prevail in regard to delayed marriage.

Figure 1-6. *Wedding Costs by Income Quartile in Egypt, 2000–04*

Months of earnings

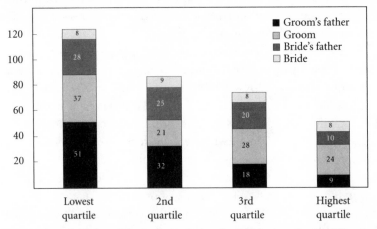

Source: Diane Singerman, "The Economic Imperatives of Marriage: Emerging Practices and Identities among Youth in the Middle East," Middle East Youth Initiative Working Paper 6 (Wolfensohn Center for Development at the Brookings Institution and the Dubai School of Government, 2007).

In part, the delay in marriage stems from young people staying longer in education. This has had positive development effects, especially for young women, and has contributed to declines in fertility. However, marriage remains an important rite of passage to adulthood, and an involuntary delay in marriage is a barrier to full social inclusion. This may be particularly true in the Middle East, where the continued cultural emphasis on family marks marriage as a social expectation. That sexual relations outside of marriage remain strictly taboo in the region adds to the sense of frustration among youth in regard to delayed marriage.[25]

THE HIGH COSTS OF MARRIAGE AND HOUSING. Among the most important barriers to marriage are its high cost and the related rise in expectations of independent living upon marriage. For example, one estimate puts the average nominal costs of marriage in Egypt (including housing, furniture and appliances, dowry and gifts, and celebration costs) at 32,329 Egyptian pounds ($6,800).[26] Traditionally, the groom bears the weight of these costs; given average incomes among young men, the average groom in Egypt must save all of his earnings for twenty-nine months to be able to afford marriage. In addition, the groom's parents contribute the equivalent of fourteen months of income. The savings burden is significantly higher for those with lower incomes (figure 1-6). Among the poorest quartile of the

Table 1-1. *Housing Costs and Mortgage Lending in the Middle East,*
Various Years

Country	House price-to-income ratio	Rent-to-income ratio	Housing credit[a] (percent)
Algeria	8.1 (2002 est.)	10.0 (1998))	6.5 (2001)
Egypt	4.9 (1998)	20.0 (1998)	7.4 (1993)
Iran	9.0 (2002)	20.0 (2002)	n.a.
Jordan	6.5 (1998)	16.7 (1998)	19.0 (1999)
Lebanon	9.0 (2002)	n.a.	9.0 (1995)[b]
Morocco	9.2 (1998)	5.0 (1998)	13.0 (2001)
Tunisia	5.2 (1998)	20.3 (1999)	10.4 (2000)
Yemen	10–17 (2000)	25.0 (2000)	n.a.

Source: World Bank, *The Macroeconomic and Sectoral Performance of Housing Supply Policies in Selected MENA Countries: A Comparative Analysis* (Washington: 2005).

n.a. = not available

a. Housing credit ratio of total mortgage loans to all outstanding loans in both commercial and government financial institutions.

b. Includes credit for construction.

population, marriage contributions for the groom and his parents are equal to an average eighty-eight months of income, meaning that young men in this category must save for at least seven years in order to afford the costs of marriage.

Housing is one of the largest costs related to marriage, and as a result its high costs drive trends toward delayed marriage. Purchasing a home in the Middle East is expensive. Whereas individuals in developed countries spend an average of thirty months of income to cover the full cost of a home, costs for a home in the Middle East range from about sixty months of wages in Egypt to as much as two hundred months of wages in Yemen (table 1-1).[27] The lack of availability of low-income housing and starter homes in the region adds to the pressures on younger people as they are just starting out. Further, individuals have few means to leverage future earnings to purchase housing. Mortgage-based lending is not widespread in the region, and the credit bureaus needed to support a viable mortgage industry are only just being established.

In many countries in the region, the rental market does not provide an affordable alternative to the purchase of housing because there is a marked shortage in the supply of rental properties. This shortage has been driven by regulations that control the ability of landlords to increase rents at the conclusion of a rental contract. In Egypt, for example, rent control laws put in place in the 1960s fixed rents in nominal terms to rates prevailing at the time and guaranteed indefinite occupancy rights for tenants.[28] As a result, landlords began keeping properties vacant or requiring large, up-front payments from new tenants. For young prospective renters, renting a property requires significant amounts of start-up capital, the same problem they face in trying to purchase a home.

The lack of marriage opportunities and housing options leads many young people to continue living with their parents well into their adult lives. This parental support provides a valuable social safety net in the context of poor labor market outcomes, but it reinforces a relationship of economic dependence for emerging adults. It may raise the reservation wages of young people seeking jobs, leading to higher levels of voluntary unemployment. For those youth unable to afford the time costs of waiting for a good job, familial support may be subsidizing low wages and poor job quality. At the same time, delayed household formation can itself become a barrier to employment and labor mobility because youth are confined to live where they have the support of their families rather than where the most optimal job opportunities may be found.

NEW SOCIAL CHALLENGES STEMMING FROM THE DELAY IN MARRIAGE AND HOUSEHOLD FORMATION. As the transition to marriage and family formation slows in the Middle East, new challenges are emerging related to alternatives to marriage. Dating has become more common, although most of these relationships are maintained secretly. There has also been a rise in controversial alternative forms of marriage such as *'urfi, misyar,* and *mut'a.*[29] Like dating relationships, such marriages are often entered into without the knowledge of family members or the community, and they are generally temporary by design.[30] While such relationships increase the opportunity for young people to form adult relationships with members of the opposite sex, they are posing new public policy challenges.

One issue of increasing concern is the sexual health of young adults in the region. While the incidence of HIV/AIDS and other sexually transmitted infections remains relatively low in the Middle East, evidence suggests that these diseases are becoming a growing public health concern. According to the United Nations, an estimated 380,000 adults and children are living with HIV/AIDS in Arab countries, with nearly 40,000 persons newly infected with the disease in 2007.[31] The number of new cases suggests a growing problem. The risks are compounded by the secretive nature of sexual relationships among young people in the Middle East and by the fact that youth remain ill informed about sexually transmitted infections, contraception, and reproductive health.

Alternatives to traditional marriage also pose particular problems related to family law and the economic welfare of women entering these relationships and the children that may be born to them. Children born to traditional marriages are provided economic support and legal status as dependents of the father and mother. For those born to nontraditional marriages or outside of a legal marriage, this is not necessarily the case. Until recently, for example, children born to *'urfi* marriages in Egypt were not eligible for Egyptian citizenship or government benefits.[32] The growing incidence of such relationships and the increasing number of children that result from such unions are posing challenges to the legal institutions that govern family law and legal status.

Institutions: Impediments to the Post-Welfare Life Course

The critical transitions for youth described above are embedded in the institutions that govern related markets. These include formal institutions such as education tracking mechanisms and regulations that govern relationships between employers and employees, as well as informal institutions such as cultural norms and social and familial expectations.[33] Together, these institutions generate the signals and incentives that shape individual decisions and choices. They serve as the "transition structures" that mediate the movement of individuals from one stage of life to the next.[34]

In the Middle East, the prevailing institutions in the education system and labor, housing, and credit markets have not sufficiently adapted to demographic changes and globalization. The institutional structure with which young people now engage in the Middle East is not that of the post-welfare state but reflects the norms and regulations of the welfare life course. In this section, we describe how particular institutional arrangements are working against the welfare of young people and impeding the emergence of a post-welfare life course (table 1-2).

The Nature and Impact of Labor Market Institutions

The behaviors of economic actors in the labor force—including new entrants, older established workers, firms, and the government—are determined largely by formal labor market regulations and dominant institutional structures. Most important for the Middle East, these include the continued dominance of the public sector in employment and the restrictive regulatory environment imposed on private firms.

Table 1-2. *Institutional Impediments to a New Life Course in the Middle East*

Transition	Institutional feature	Effects on young people
Education	Highly centralized education system	Contributes to low educational quality (in terms of curricula and pedagogy) and skills mismatch
	University admission policies	Promotes rote memorization over investment in skills
	Tracking mechanisms	Undermines value of vocational education
Work	Dominant role of the government in employment provision	Contributes to long durations of unemployment because youth wait for government employment
	High employment protection	Protects older workers and reduces opportunities for young workers
		Makes firms less likely to hire new, younger employees (lower turnover)
		Contributes to an increase in informal enterprises where young people have fewer opportunities for human capital development
Marriage and family formation	Marriage contracts and high marriage costs	Contributes to phenomenon of delayed marriage among young men who cannot afford the high costs of marriage
	Rent controls	Limits access of first-time renters to affordable housing
	Absence of mortgage facilities	Prolongs dependency on parents and failure to accumulate physical assets (for example, housing)

The public sector continues to play a significant role in structuring work transitions. Governments across the region have reduced the size of public sector employment, but they still employ a significant share of the region's workforce, particularly secondary and university graduates (figure 1-7). Given the relatively high wages, job security, attractive benefits, and pension coverage that come with public sector employment, young new entrants

Figure 1-7. *Government Employment as a Share of Total Employment among Secondary and University Graduates, Selected Countries, Various Years*

Share of total employment (percent)

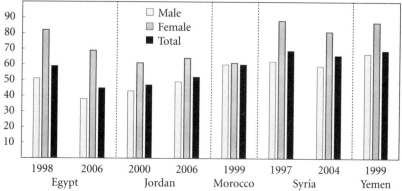

Source: Official sources.

continue to queue for public sector positions despite the creation of fewer new positions in this sector and a lack of turnover among older workers.

Formal private sector employment has failed to emerge as a strong alternative for young workers, largely because of the restrictive regulatory environment imposed on formal private sector firms in the region. Although indexes measuring labor market rigidity show that some Middle Eastern countries have made improvements in recent years, the region as a whole maintains higher levels of labor market regulation than other regions (table 1-3).

The rigidity of these regulations in the formal private sector affects young people's work transitions in several ways. Mostly notably, rigid regulations on hiring and firing workers raise labor market costs for private firms. In response, companies prove resistant to the perceived risks of hiring young, untested new entrants who lack a record of work experience and productivity. Rigid regulations also lower job turnover among established workers, limiting the number of job openings for young people to those created through economic growth. This lower turnover means that young workers are unable to compete with incumbent workers.

Labor regulations also adversely affect youth employment through the link between severance payments and tenure. As severance pay increases with tenure, and tenure increases with age, older employees are more costly to dismiss than younger workers. During negative shocks to the economy and

Table 1-3. *The Rigidity of Labor Market Regulations in the Middle East, 2008*[a]

Country/region	Difficulty of hiring index	Rigidity of hours index	Difficulty of firing index	Rigidity of employment index
Algeria	44	60	40	48
Egypt	0	20	60	27
Iran	11	60	50	40
Jordan	11	20	60	30
Kuwait	0	40	0	13
Lebanon	44	0	30	25
Morocco	100	40	50	63
Saudi Arabia	0	40	0	13
Syria	22	40	50	37
Tunisia	28	40	80	49
United Arab Emirates	0	60	0	20
Yemen	0	60	40	33
Regional averages				
Middle East	21	43	46	37
Africa	40	35	37	37
East Asia	19	19	39	26
Developed economies	22	26	21	23
Latin America	54	51	29	44
South Asia	14	20	62	32

Source: World Bank, *Doing Business 2008* (Washington: 2007).

a. Indexes are on a scale of 0–100, with higher values reflecting more rigid regulatory environments. Regional averages are population-weighted means of scores for the countries for which data are reported.

labor markets, young people bear the brunt of adjustment, increasing the overall gap between employment rates for young and older workers.[35] In this regard, several Middle Eastern countries maintain significant severance payment requirements. In Egypt, for example, mandated severance packages for established workers amount to 132 weeks worth of their final salaries.[36] The average is 80 weeks in Syria, 91 weeks in Iran, and 85 weeks in Morocco. The regional average is 53.6 weeks, compared to an average of 25.8 weeks for developed countries and 38.6 weeks for the East Asia and Pacific region.

Excessive regulation also drives firms into the informal economy, which means initial jobs for young people are increasingly found in the informal sector and work transitions take place therein. Informality is often associated with high tax burdens on formal private firms, the costs of which keep small firms from scaling up their operations or formalizing their relationship with the state. In the Middle East, however, informality is more often related to the regulation of labor. Adhering to the costs of labor market regulations and faced with the burdens of high dismissal costs, smaller firms largely choose to operate outside of the regulatory environment.

During the 2002–08 period of renewed economic growth across Middle Eastern countries, a number of reforms to reduce job protection and bolster labor market flexibility in the formal sector were implemented. Egypt relaxed its labor laws in 2003 to allow firms to hire workers on temporary and renewable fixed-term contracts.[37] In Iran, the government passed legislation in 2003 that exempts small firms (with fewer than ten workers) from its rigid labor laws, giving them a degree of flexibility in hiring and firing.[38] While these reforms are meant to encourage private firms to hire more young new entrants, they often do not contribute to stable work transitions. Older, established workers enjoy the protection of open-ended contracts and stronger protections against dismissal, and young workers entering the labor market through these temporary contracts endure job insecurity.

Short-term and temporary contracts often mean less investment in training and human capital development of young workers, as well as protracted transitions to family formation. Furthermore, introducing greater flexibility in the private formal sector while maintaining job protection measures in the public sector has made the latter more attractive, reinforcing the incentive for educated youth to remain unemployed while waiting for public sector positions.

Institutions of the Education System Reinforce the Skills Mismatch

The institutions that govern the labor market play an important role in perpetuating the common problems of skills mismatch between what students learn and what employers want. Most important, the combination of a large public sector and a highly regulated private sector (both in education and employment) distorts incentives for learning and skills formation. Regional education systems continue to be geared toward providing the skills needed for public sector employment, with a focus on creating secondary and university graduates that can play functionary roles in the bureaucracy. At the same time, the influence of the private sector in driving skill formation remains limited. Not only do businesses have a minimal role in informing curriculum design, but high levels of regulation force the private sector to act like the public sector, valuing ex ante signals such as qualifications rather than ex post signals of productivity.

Furthermore, the lure of public sector employment drives the choices that students and their parents make in regard to skills formation and educational investments. The result is that nearly all students who go beyond primary education pursue the university track even though relatively few can expect to gain access to university or to secure public employment.

The design of university admission policies themselves reinforces distorted incentives for learning and skills development. Often university admission is based largely on students' scores on cumulative examinations that are designed to assess knowledge of memorized facts. This, in turn, has a disproportionate effect on school curricula, both in public and private schools; understanding the importance of this examination, these schools focus their instruction not on skills development but on the knowledge needed to succeed on the examination. Similarly, it affects how parents invest in their children's education. For example, to make up for weaknesses in the public education system, many parents invest in private tutoring, but this tutoring often entails prepping for standardized tests rather than developing a broader range of knowledge and skills.[39]

In the presence of these institutional arrangements, efforts to develop alternative transitions of learning and skills development have proved unsuccessful. For example, despite high investments, vocational education has yet to emerge as an effective institution to mediate school to work transitions. Students resist the vocational track, preferring to secure a slot at a university. Moreover, private firms, understanding the institutional incentives that push capable students toward the university track, view vocational graduates as being the least capable youth. Moreover, private firms, understanding the institutional incentives that push capable students toward the university track, view vocational graduates as being the least capable youth, reinforcing the reputation of vocational education and training as a dead end.

Institutions of Family Formation are Inflexible and Exclusionary

Young people's transition to marriage and family formation is shaped by formal and informal institutions. Marriage contracts, which are embedded in tradition to promote the welfare and bargaining power of women, stress financial security. Marriage contracts are forward-looking agreements, with dowry and other marriage costs acting as a way of institutionalizing the exchange of resources between the two families. In the traditional life course, where kin marriages were common and families shared resources, the imperative for up-front financial assurances was weaker. In the welfare life course, however, as marriages outside kinship became more common, education and job security emerged as critical signals of future earnings.

Today, marriage contracts continue to place high emphasis on economic security, particularly for the bride. But in the absence of clear career trajectories, young people lack the means to amass the resources needed to demonstrate the ability to provide future financial security. The response of the marriage market to this increased uncertainty has been to use up-front marriage costs as a device for screening grooms. In addition, with family laws and social customs providing men the exclusive right to divorce their wives, high dowry costs (*mahr*) paid by the grooms act as a disincentive for unilateral divorce.[40]

One way young men could cope with the onerous costs of family formation is through better access to credit and housing. The role of credit markets is to allow individuals to smooth their consumption against future earnings; however, in the Middle East, underdeveloped credit markets fail to play this role. Limited access to mortgage finance means that housing is increasingly out of reach for young people.

Where young people have received assistance aimed at reducing the burdens of the costs of marriage, it is often through the welfare life course institutions. These have included the provision of government subsidies in the form of marriage grants or loans, as well as legislation that limits the size of dowries. But these interventions fail to recognize the complex social rules of the marriage market wherein high dowry costs are driven by prospective brides (and their families) trying to assess the suitability of grooms and to ensure financial security.[41] In the long run, smoother family formation transitions need better credit and housing institutions and reforms to family law that provide more financial security for women, rather than assistance through more restrictive legislation or the provision of grants and low-interest loans.

Toward a New Life Course

Caught in a bind between two life courses, young people in the Middle East are struggling to build a foundation for successful lives and contribute to the development of their societies. Across the region, there is a growing recognition of the urgency of expanding opportunities for and investments targeted on young people. Efforts by governments and nongovernmental organizations offer the potential for resolving some of the long-standing youth challenges. However, if implemented without regard to the institutional context, such programs may prove no more successful than past interventions.

To effectively improve skill formation, the cultivation of work experience, and the formation of successful new families, three principles should guide policy and program design.

First, many of the challenges facing young people are associated with high demographic pressures. A natural extension of this outlook is to treat these problems as passing and transient. This leads policymakers to focus on short-term and input-driven solutions, such as expanding training programs and improving educational infrastructure. Instead, policies should be long term and treat the youth bulge as a window for reform that benefits the whole of society. The goal should be to use the large youth population to prepare Middle Eastern economies for the competitive global economy.

Second, policy reforms should recognize links across sectors and the role of signals and incentives in shaping a new life course. Outcomes in education, employment, housing, and family formation are interconnected. Failure to build on these connections often undermines policy efforts. For example, many governments are promoting the role of the private sector in education while at the same time instituting above-inflation wage increases for government jobs. This has the effect of reinforcing aspects of the welfare life course in the work transition while trying to move toward a new life course in the education transition. This conflict can undermine the effectiveness of interventions or, worse, can be counterproductive in resolving youth-related economic issues.

Finally, a long-term, integrated policy reform agenda can be implemented more effectively when based on an understanding of the sequencing and interdependence of steps in the reform process. Reforms are difficult, requiring costly steps both economically and politically. However, policymakers can start at the least controversial changes and build momentum. For example, before relaxing employment protections, it is important to first create a system of income and social protection, such as an unemployment insurance program, that would provide protections for workers without imposing restrictive job protection regulations on private firms.

In addition, a number of other policy initiatives can be pursued that are politically more feasible in the short run. These include reforming university admission policies to test a broader range of skills; changing public sector hiring policies to encourage investments in skills over credentials; creating incentives in education and employment by taking experience through volunteerism into consideration when reviewing applications; and developing credit and mortgage finance targeted at young entrepreneurs and first-time homebuyers. Together, these small steps can improve the institutional environment needed for a new life course.

Through this new life course, young people can have access to better education, enabling them to make a larger contribution to economic growth. Expanding employment opportunities can reduce poverty. As more women enter the labor market and secure quality jobs, gender inequality can diminish over time. In turn, the post-welfare life course can not only end the waiting of the current generation but also ensure that future generations are better off.

Notes

1. Glen H. Elder Jr., Monica Kirkpatrick Johnson, and Robert Crosnoe, "The Emergence and Development of Life Course Theory," in *Handbook of the Life Course*, edited by Jeylan T. Mortimer and Michael J. Shanahan (New York: Springer, 2004).

2. Reinhold Sackmann and Matthias Wingens, "From Transitions to Trajectories: Sequence Types," in *Social Dynamics of the Life Course: Transitions, Institutions and Interrelations*, edited by Walter Heinz and Victor W. Marshall (New York: Aldine Transaction, 2003); James E. Rosenbaum and others, "Market and Network Theories of the Transition from High School to Work: Their Application to Industrialized Societies," *Annual Review of Sociology* 16: 263–99.

3. Navtej Dhillon and Daniel Egel, "Life Courses in the Middle East," Middle East Youth Initiative Working Paper (Wolfensohn Center for Development at the Brookings Institution and the Dubai School of Government, forthcoming 2009).

4. World Bank, *Unlocking the Employment Potential in the Middle East and North Africa: Toward a New Social Contract* (Washington: 2004).

5. United Nations Development Program, *Fighting Climate Change: Human Solidarity in a Divided World.* Human Development Report 2007/2008 (New York: 2007).

6. World Bank, *The Road Not Traveled: Education Reform in the Middle East and North Africa* (Washington: 2008).

7. World Bank, *Unlocking the Employment Potential in the Middle East and North Africa.*

8. Over the past ten years, labor force growth has averaged 3.5 percent a year, driven both by the influx of young new entrants and rising female activity rates.

9. Djavad Salehi-Isfahani, "Microeconomics of Growth in MENA: The Role of Households," in *Explaining Growth in the Middle East,* Contributions to Economic Analysis, Volume 278, edited by Jeffrey B. Nugent and M. Hashem Pesaran (London: Elsevier, 2006).

10. Marcus Noland and Howard Pack, *The Arab Economies in a Changing World* (Washington: Peterson Institute for International Economics, 2007).

11. Navtej Dhillon, Djavad Salehi-Isfahani, Paul Dyer, Tarik Yousef, Amina Fahmy, and Mary Kraetsch, "Missed by the Boom, Hit by the Bust: Making Markets Work for Young People in the Middle East" (Wolfensohn Center for Development at the Brookings Institution and Dubai School of Government, 2009).

12. Navtej Dhillon and Tarik Yousef, "Inclusion: Meeting the 100 Million Youth Challenge," Middle East Youth Initiative Report (Wolfensohn Center for Development at the Brookings Institution and Dubai School of Government, 2007).

13. World Bank, *The Road Not Traveled.*

14. European Training Foundation and the World Bank, "Reforming Technical Vocational Education and Training in the Middle East and North Africa: Experiences and Challenges" (Luxembourg: Office for Official Publications of the European Communities, 2006).

15. World Bank, *The Road Not Traveled;* United Nations Development Program, *Arab Human Development Report 2002: Creating Opportunities for Future Generations* (New York: 2002); United Nations Development Program, *Arab Human Development Report 2003: Building a Knowledge Society* (New York: 2003).

16. Ina V. S. Mullis and others, *TIMSS 2007 International Mathematics Report* (Boston College, Lynch School of Education, TIMSS and PIRLS International Study Center, 2008); Michael O. Martin and others, *TIMSS 2007 International Science Report* (Boston College, Lynch School of Education, TIMSS and PIRLS International Study Center, 2008).

17. Alan Richards and John Waterbury, *A Political Economy of the Middle East* (Boulder, Colo.: Westview Press, 2007).

18. Maggie Kamel, "Situational Analysis of Youth Employment in Egypt" (Cairo: Center for Project Evaluation and Macroeconomic Analysis, Ministry of International Cooperation, 2006).

19. World Bank, *Unlocking the Employment Potential in the Middle East and North Africa.*

20. David G. Blanchflower and Richard B. Freeman, "Introduction" and "The Declining Economic Status of Young Workers in OECD Countries," in *Youth Employment and Joblessness in Advanced Countries,* edited by David G. Blanchflower and Richard B. Freeman (University of Chicago Press, 2000); David T. Ellwood, "Teenage Unemployment: Permanent Scars or Temporary Blemishes?" in *The Youth Labour Market Problem: Its Nature, Causes, and Consequences,* edited by Richard B. Freeman and David A. Wise (University of Chicago Press/NBER, 1982); Paul Ryan, "The School-to-Work Transition: A Cross-National Perspective," *Journal of Economic Literature* 39, no. 1 (2001): 34–92; Carmen Pages and Claudio Montenegro, "Job Security and the Age-Composition of Employment: Evidence from Chile," *Estudios de Economia* 34, no. 2 (2007): 109–39.

21. Ragui Assaad and May Gadallah, "Pathways from School to Work for Egyptian Youth," Middle East Youth Initiative Working Paper (Wolfensohn Center for Development at the Brookings Institution and the Dubai School of Government, forthcoming 2009).

22. Lant Pritchett, "Where Has All the Education Gone?" Policy Research Paper 1581 (Washington: World Bank, 1996). See also Jeffrey Nugent and Mohamed Saleh, "Inter-Generational Transmission of and Returns to Human Capital and Changes Therein over Time: Empirical Evidence from Egypt," ERF 15th Annual Conference (Cairo: Economic Research Forum, 2008), and Nader Kabbani, "Labor Force Participation, Employment and Returns to Education in Syria," Nader Kabbani (presenter) and Henrik Huitfeldt, 8th International Conference on the Economics and Finance of the Middle East and North Africa, Byblos, Lebanon, May 22–24, 2006.

23. World Bank, *Gender and Development in the Middle East and North Africa: Women in the Public Sphere* (Washington: World Bank, 2004).

24. Cynthia Lloyd, ed., *Growing Up Global: The Changing Transitions to Adulthood in Developing Countries* (Washington: National Academies Press, 2005). In contrast, 77 percent of East Asian men and 69 percent of Latin American men in this age cohort are married.

25. Diane Singerman, "The Economic Imperatives of Marriage: Emerging Practices and Identities among Youth in the Middle East," Middle East Youth Initiative Working Paper 6 (Wolfensohn Center for Development at the Brookings Institution and the Dubai School of Government, 2007).

26. Ibid.

27. World Bank, *The Macroeconomic and Sectoral Performance of Housing Supply Policies in Selected MENA Countries: A Comparative Analysis* (Washington: 2005).

28. Ragui Assaad and Mohamed Ramadan, "Did Housing Policy Reforms Curb the Delay in Marriage among Young Men in Egypt?" Middle East Youth Initiative Policy Outlook 1 (Wolfensohn Center for Development at the Brookings Institution and the Dubai School of Government, 2008).

29. '*Urfi* marriages are common-law marriages that are typically kept secret and not registered with the government. *Misyar* marriages are transient marriages in which the husband visits his wife but is not contractually and legally obligated to support and provide housing for her. *Mut'a* is another form of temporary marriage within Shi'a Islam. For more details, see Singerman, "The Economic Imperatives of Marriage: Emerging Practices and Identities among Youth in the Middle East."

30. Ibid.

31. UNAIDS, *2008 Report on the Global AIDS Epidemic* (Geneva: Joint United Nations Program on HIV/AIDS, 2008).

32. Ragui Assaad and Ghada Barsoum, "Youth Exclusion in Egypt: In Search of 'Second Chances,'" Middle East Youth Initiative Working Paper 2 (Wolfensohn Center for Development at the Brookings Institution and Dubai School of Government, 2007).

33. For a deeper analysis of the role of institutions in youth exclusion, see Navtej Dhillon and Djavad Salehi-Isfahani, "Looking Ahead: Making Markets and Institutions Work for Young People," in this volume.

34. Sackmann and Wingens, "From Transitions to Trajectories"; James E. Rosenbaum and others, "Market and Network Theories of the Transition from High School to Work."

35. Carmen Pages and Claudio Montenegro, "Job Security and the Age-Composition of Employment: Evidence from Chile."

36. World Bank, *Doing Business 2009* (Washington: 2008). *Doing Business* defines the comparable worker as one who is at least 42 years old, has twenty years with the same company, and whose income (including benefits) is equal to the average wage for the country.

37. Assaad and Barsoum, "Youth Exclusion in Egypt: In Search of 'Second Chances.'"

38. Djavad Salehi-Isfahani and Daniel Egel, "Youth Exclusion in Iran: The State of Education, Employment, and Family Formation," Middle East Youth Initiative Working Paper 3 (Wolfensohn Center for Development at the Brookings Institution and the Dubai School of Government, 2007).

39. Djavad Salehi-Isfahani and Navtej Dhillon, "Stalled Youth Transitions in the Middle East: A Framework for Policy Reform," Middle East Youth Initiative Working Paper 8 (Wolfensohn Center for Development at the Brookings Institution and the Dubai School of Government, 2008).

40. Ibid.

41. Ibid.

DJAVAD SALEHI-ISFAHANI *and* DANIEL EGEL

2

Beyond Statism: Toward a New Social Contract for Iranian Youth

"I didn't study for seventeen years to do this. I can't marry on this salary. The government can solve all our problems if they set their minds to it. All they need to do is give us loans for marriage and to buy a house."
—Twenty-five-year-old university graduate selling fruit from a stall[1]

Youth in Iran have become a major political and social force. Accounting for nearly 40 percent of the voting-age population, young people demonstrated their importance most recently in the 2009 presidential election by playing an instrumental role in the campaign of reformist Mir Hossein Moussavi and, in the days and weeks following the election, by demonstrating in the streets of Tehran and other large urban areas to protest the announced victory of the incumbent Mahmoud Ahmadinejad. This trend of youth political activism is not new: young Iranians were reportedly an influential force in the landslide victories of the reformist president Mohammad Khatami in 1997 and 2001 and in the election of his ideologically very different successor, Ahmadinejad, in 2005.[2] Although the discontent of young Iranians has caught the attention of political observers outside Iran and is the subject of several recent books, the social, economic, and institutional environment that is shaping the life choices of this generation is still not thoroughly understood.[3]

Transitions to adulthood in traditional Iranian society were typically smooth and predictable. Young men were expected to adopt the profession of their parents or inherit the family business. Family and community networks worked together to ensure a smooth transition to marriage for young men and women, and these same networks worked to support them as they started families. But with the gradual disappearance of traditional society, the predictability in the transitions to adulthood that the family and local community offered has also disappeared. These changes have been compounded by a demographic boom resulting from high fertility rates in the late 1970s and early 1980s that has increased the proportion of youth in the population from 28 percent in 1996 to 35 percent in 2006. Together these changes have led to the emergence of significant uncertainty in the transitions to adulthood for today's youth.

The main elements of a successful transition to adulthood include acquisition of skills for productive employment, finding a job, and setting up a family. All these elements have come under pressure from the youth bulge at a time when new institutions and mechanisms for successful transitions are not yet in place and those that are in place are highly distorted and therefore operate inefficiently. Adding to the complication, these transitions are closely linked, so that failure to succeed in one increases the probability of failure in other dimensions, along with the risk of social exclusion. In Iran, long spells of unemployment, measured in years rather than months, deny young men and women the ability to marry and set up a home. These conditions of exclusion exist despite a low overall incidence of poverty and relatively high education.

Those growing up in poor families naturally face greater obstacles in all aspects of their transition. They often face very different educational and employment choices—whether to take a job at an early age to support their families or stay in school—and are disadvantaged because, for example, they may be unable to afford the necessary preparation for the crucial university entrance exams. Experiences of young men and women differ not only on the basis of socioeconomic background but also gender. The gender dimension of youth exclusion has obvious relevance for Iran, where Islamic codes of *hejab* and jurisprudence confine and inhibit women in many ways. The separation of men and women in schools, workplaces, and other public spaces, and their asymmetric treatment under the law imply differences in the experience of exclusion. Women who fail to obtain a sufficient education, who cannot find white collar jobs, or who are unable to marry may feel a greater sense of exclusion because of their spatial confinement.

While youth have made significant gains in the past twenty years, mainly in education and in the narrowing of gender differences therein, these gains have not succeeded in making Iranian society more inclusive of the young. To the contrary, their frustration in finding jobs and forming families has increased in the past ten years, and therefore they may feel even more excluded than past generations. Indeed, the much larger size of the current cohort of youth is putting considerable pressure on traditional mechanisms that have previously sorted individuals into schools and jobs and assisted them in marriage and family formation.

Understanding the key institutions that facilitate these youth transitions—schools, the labor market, and social norms regarding marriage—is another important part of the analysis. These institutions have failed to rise to the challenge of Iran's demographic transition. The markets for labor and marriage appear inflexible and unresponsive to the needs of the young. The relatively long stretch of economic growth since 1999, aided by a huge inflow of oil revenues, has moderately reduced unemployment rates for youth but has done little to help them set up families of their own. Various policies targeting youth exclusion have been discussed or adopted in recent years; however, these have been mostly ad hoc and unconnected and have met with varying degrees of success.

The Youth Bulge

Beginning in the 1970s and continuing into the 1980s, Iran experienced a period of extraordinarily high fertility in the midst of declining child mortality rates. Today, the unusually large cohort of youth resulting from this baby boom has led to overcrowding in schools, gender imbalance in the marriage market, and increased pressure on Iran's rigid formal labor market.

The baby boom, and subsequent bust, is illustrated by comparing fertility and child mortality rates in Iran since the 1960s with those of Egypt and Turkey, the two other large countries of the Middle East. All three countries experienced a similar decline in child mortality during the period. But while fertility rates in both Egypt and Turkey decreased throughout the period, the fertility rate in Iran increased during the early 1980s before falling precipitously. Toward the end of the 1990s, following several years of rapid decrease, Iran's fertility rate reached the level of Turkey and was below that of Egypt. Today, fertility rates in Iran are the lowest in the region.[4] The impact of the fertility boom and bust has resulted in an unusually pronounced youth bulge in Iran.

Though overall population growth in Iran has slowed to about 1.3 percent a year, the youth bulge has resulted in rapid growth in the labor force that began in the mid-1990s and will continue through 2015. To demonstrate the effect of this youth bulge, figure 2-1 compares the changing size of the 15 to 29 age group over the 1960–2020 period using Turkey as a baseline.

Figure 2-1. *Following the Youth Bulge in Iran: Youth Aged 15 to 29, 1950–2020*

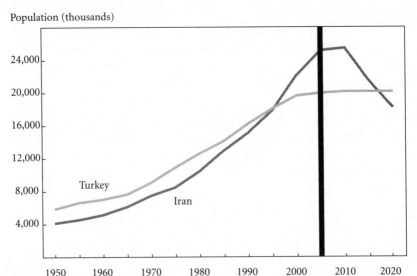

Population (thousands)

Source: UN World Population Prospects, 2008 revisions using medium variant population projections.

(The group aged 15 to 19 represents youth of secondary school or university age, the groups aged 20 to 24 and 25 to 29 are individuals entering the labor market, and the 15 to 29 age category describes the overall youth bulge.) The sharp upward turn in the line representing Iran relative to Turkey, which has the same total population of about 70 million, indicates the effect of the fertility swing in Iran. Ten years ago, Iran had as many people in the 15 to 29 age group as Turkey, but in 2005 Iran had about 5 million more. Roughly speaking, Turkey would be experiencing Iran's youth bulge if it suddenly had to absorb an additional 5 million young people. By 2020 Iran is projected to have fewer people in this age group than Turkey.

Some aspects of the youth bulge have created challenges for young people in Iran: there are obvious disadvantages to belonging to the country's largest youth cohort ever. But the more recent reduction in fertility rates is reminiscent of the demographic transition that took place among the "Asian Tigers" during the mid-1970s and led to the "demographic gift" that is believed to have played an important role in their success.[5]

In the short term the benefits of the demographic transition accrue as a growing labor force drives economic growth. In the long term the decline in fertility leads to increased investment in human capital for generations growing up in smaller families. Indeed, in Iran the ratio of adults aged 20 to 54 to children aged 0 to 14 has increased from 0.78 in 1986 to 2.09 in 2006 and will continue to increase for a few more years.[6] This effect is likely to be even more pronounced in rural, and typically poorer, areas where the fertility decline has been relatively greater; total fertility rates in rural areas fell by six births per woman between 1985 and 2000 compared with four in urban areas. Although the effect of the rise in adult-child ratios on investments in the health and education of current cohorts of young people has not been examined systematically, one can attribute a large part of the improvement in health and education of the post-baby-boom generation to the demographic gift.

On balance, the effects of past demographic behavior upon today's young people need not be negative. The youth bulge presents a number of challenges, but smart policies could help Iran take better advantage of its demographic dividend by creating an environment conducive to higher productivity and economic growth. The returns on Iran's past investments in health and education can be harnessed by providing new schooling and employment opportunities to this generation in transition.

Education

The last twenty years have seen a dramatic rise in educational attainment of Iranian youth, which has been driven by rising enrollment rates. Despite these clear successes in increasing access to education, however, the educational system has been relatively ineffective in giving youth the skills they need to succeed in the labor market. As in many other countries in the Middle East region, the formal labor market in Iran has historically offered disproportionately high rewards to those with university degrees. This has led to the development of an educational system focused on granting degrees and diplomas rather than providing skills and training relevant in the job market. Because of the limited supply of spots in universities, the youth bulge has dramatically increased competition for securing university education. Further, acceptance to a university, which functions as a signaling device to employers of high-achieving individuals, is currently mediated by an exam that measures capacity for memorization rather than critical thinking abilities. Policymakers have begun to introduce alternatives to university track education, such as programs that teach vocational skills and give on-the-job training. However, these programs are still heavily stigmatized as the destination for those rejected by the formal schooling system.

Rising Enrollments and Attainment

Basic and secondary education in Iran has expanded significantly during the last twenty years. Even with rapid growth in the size of the youth population, enrollment rates have increased substantially, with particularly large gains for female students. Average years of education have nearly doubled within a generation; those born in the 1980s attained more than nine years of schooling compared with less than five years for those born twenty-five years earlier.

Educational attainment in Iran is slightly higher among women than men in urban areas, although the reverse gender gap still persists in some regions, particularly rural areas. Despite lower enrollment rates in lower secondary education (ages 11 to 13), female enrollment is higher in upper secondary schools and universities, resulting in a higher ratio of urban women with upper secondary and tertiary degrees compared with their male counterparts. Over 60 percent of urban women aged 18 to 30 are reported to have an upper secondary degree compared with just over 50 percent of urban men.

Despite universal provision of free primary and lower secondary education nationwide, educational attainment is more strongly affected by household income or location than by gender. As the cohort becomes older, this effect becomes more pronounced because wealthier individuals have greater opportunities for attending upper secondary schools or universities. However, a difference of nearly a year of education between the richest and poorest quintile is evident as early as age fourteen. The effect of income is particularly strong for both urban and rural women. By the time they complete their education, young women in the upper income quintile have 50 percent higher average attainment, in terms of years of schooling, than those in the lowest quintile.

Being born into a rural household also has a strong effect on educational attainment, especially for females. Beginning at a young age, rural women from the wealthiest quintile have lower educational attainment than even the poorest of their urban counterparts, reflecting much lower rural enrollment rates. These low enrollment rates probably result from the lower availability of schools and teachers for girls in rural areas—the urban-rural gap is much smaller for men. Schools are segregated by gender, and male teachers typically are not assigned to girls' schools. But gender segregation may have helped increase female schooling, because it enables girls from conservative families to attend school.[7]

An important caveat to these results is that overcrowding of schools may reduce the quality of each year of education. Rising pupil-to-teacher ratios over the past twenty years provide suggestive evidence for this effect: the ratio for secondary schools has risen from about fifteen pupils per teacher in 1982 to nearly thirty by 2002.[8] Indeed, as the size of the group aged 5 to 9 surged from 5.8 million in 1980 to over 9 million in 1990, lack of resources prevented construction of additional schools, and many schools were forced to introduce a two- or sometimes even three-shift school day.[9] At the same time, school administrators moved toward an educational system based on multiple-choice tests that are much cheaper to administer and offer a more objective criterion for evaluation. This new system has been criticized for encouraging rote memorization rather than the development of a range of productive skills, including analytic and writing skills.

As pupil-to-teacher ratios have begun to fall for both primary and secondary students in recent years, the ill effect of overcrowding should gradually lessen.

Inefficient Tracking in Secondary Schooling

The largest attrition from schools occurs after the first year of high school, at about age fifteen. This is also the age when compulsory education ends and the grade in which all students are evaluated and directed to one of three separate high school tracks: *Nazari,* which is the theoretical or academic curriculum; *Fanni-Herfei,* or technical and vocational education (TVE); and *Kardanesh,* which teaches more basic skills through on-the-job training. Students with weaker academic records are typically only eligible for the latter two tracks.

Most students pursue *Nazari* in the hopes of passing the onerous national university entrance exam, the *concour,* and entering university. However, because a major complaint from the private sector in Iran is the lack of practical skills among recent graduates, both the TVE and *Kardanesh* programs may be well suited to the Iranian economy.

This tracking system causes many students to drop out of school. Because upper secondary school is not obligatory, those who need to work, such as students from poor families, are the most likely candidates to leave school at the end of lower secondary school. However, a large number of youth actually leave school after the first year of upper secondary education when they are assigned to tracks. Although there are no available data on the percentages of students assigned to each track, the low number of students enrolled in TVE or *Kardanesh*, as compared to *Nazari*, suggests that those assigned to these less preferred tracks are more likely to drop out. As an example, for the cohort of female students who began their upper secondary education in 2003–04, nearly one-third of the students dropped out between the first and second year of school. The resulting shares of students in TVE and *Kardanesh* are both less than one-quarter the size of students in the *Nazari* track.

The potential exclusionary effect of tracking is likely caused by both the low quality of instruction in the vocational tracks and the lure of a university education. Until recently, only theoretical (*Nazari*) track students were eligible to take the *concour* exam. Because the opportunity for a university education was closed to students in the vocational tracks, it is likely that many students who failed to qualify for the theoretical track dropped out of school completely. To respond to demands made by parents and encourage students to continue with the nontheoretical tracks, the government has recently made it possible for *Kardanesh* graduates to participate in the entrance exams and maintain the option of university education, with some restrictions.

Universities and the Role of National Examinations

The lure of tertiary education in Iran is driven by high private returns to university education, reflected in large wage premiums and increased job security for those with college degrees.[10] In particular, the public sector, which offers both good job security and good pay, is by far the largest employer of university graduates in Iran. A university degree is a minimum requirement for many desired public sector jobs, which means that passing the national entrance examination and securing university enrollment is expected to yield high returns in the labor market.

Over 1 million youth take the *concour* each year, and only 20 percent score high enough to be admitted to either a public or private university. The impact on the one million youth who fail this exam is quite significant. Evidence suggests that they have considerably worse labor market outcomes than people who pass in terms of risk and length of unemployment, indicating that the *concour* may function as a signaling device for employers. Additionally, there is a significant social stigma attached to being among the *concour* rejects (*rofouzeh hayeh concour*) within Iranian society.

This system of selection into universities may also be responsible for lowering the quality of education. The *concour* and most other exams are multiple-choice, and students who take the exams rely heavily on memorization. As a result, teaching methodologies in the school system have gravitated toward rote memorization. Though this system may have a positive effect on motivation, it likely produces future educational benefits only for a very select number of students, such as those enrolled in elite engineering and medical schools.

Disparities created by this system are apparent in the divergence between the performance of a selection of Iranian students in international competitions such as math or science Olympiads versus the Trends in International Mathematics and Science Study (TIMSS), which tests knowledge of math and sciences for a random group of students. While Iran consistently performs well in the math and science Olympiads, it has performed relatively poorly in the TIMSS evaluation of eighth graders, particularly in mathematics. Iran was among ten countries, plus the Canadian province of Quebec, with lower average mathematics scores in 2007 than in 1995. In Iran, steady declines in these scores have occurred since 1999.[11] The results of the eighth-grade science examination are not as bleak. The average score of Iranian eighth graders in 2007 (459) represented an increase from respective scores in 1999 (448) and 2003 (453), placing Iran above most countries in the Middle East, with the exceptions of Bahrain, Israel, and Jordan.[12]

Iran's educational system suffers because it rewards only high academic achievers. To move forward, a serious effort must be made to identify and use the myriad talents possessed by all youth rather than focus on a small group of "geniuses."[13]

Educational Reforms: Look to the Labor Market

Iranian policymakers are well aware of the wide gap between what is learned in the classroom and what skills are needed to be productive on the job. The TVE and *Kardanesh* programs exist to compensate for this skill mismatch. However, they rely on a network of public training centers, which often use old equipment and fail to keep up with rapidly changing technologies and the needs of the market.

The government is considering a major reform of these training centers with financial and technical advice from the World Bank. As a central component of this reform, public training centers may be replaced by centers run by the private sector. Indeed, privatization of these centers may improve both the efficacy and efficiency of training programs because private sector training centers have been shown to outperform government-run ones in a variety of developing countries.[14]

Despite the potential of private sector training centers, reform of the current system is unlikely to be sufficient in convincing students to choose either TVE or *Kardanesh* over the track offering the option of a university education. Rigid labor laws in Iran make layoffs quite costly, and as a result employers hesitate to hire individuals from these programs when the only measure of their ability is multiple-choice exams. Unlike students in Germany, where considerable resources are spent evaluating TVE graduates, TVE and *Kardanesh* students in Iran have little else besides their exam scores to prove their skills and qualifications to prospective employers.

To increase the enrollment and performance of TVE and *Kardanesh* students, the government needs to create incentives for employers to hire graduates of these programs. One potential policy would be to provide exemptions in the labor law for TVE graduates, which would encourage small- and medium-size employers to hire these graduates and thus increase their returns to education. Policymakers should also devise a mechanism for graduates to accurately signal their abilities and address uncertainties about the quality of their education.

Policymakers in Iran have begun to recognize some of the negative effects of the *concour*, and there have been suggestions to reduce its role in selection into universities. In particular, they have discussed and are now moving ahead with adding high school grades to the selection criteria for universities, as Japan and a number of other countries with similar examinations already have done.[15] The 2007 *concour* was the first of these examinations to incorporate these reforms in Iran. Now admission to university will depend in part on students' grades in the third year of secondary school.[16]

Transition from School to Work

After completion of schooling, Iranian youth face several obstacles in their transition to employment. Recent graduates face high unemployment rates and long durations of unemployment. Iran's rigid formal labor market is ill prepared to absorb the growing number of young people looking for suitable employment.

Total unemployment in Iran, at about 10 to 11 percent, is quite similar to that of Egypt or Turkey but quite a bit higher than the very low values (3–4 percent) reported for, say, Mexico. Steady economic growth in Iran has reduced overall unemployment rates by nearly 5 percentage points since 2000, though unemployment still remains quite high among youth. Indeed, the average unemployment rate for those aged 15–29 is more than 20 percent, compared with less than 5 percent for those who are 30 years and older. While rigidity in the Iranian labor market is likely responsible for high youth unemployment, youth unemployment rates of about two or three times the national average are not uncommon in transition economies.[17]

The decline in youth unemployment rates since 2000 has disproportionately benefited the least educated and men. Unemployment rates for men with a secondary education or below have fallen dramatically, and the benefit of having a tertiary education, which once substantially reduced the risk of unemployment, has been reduced significantly. This change may have been caused by the rapid expansion of higher education and the decline in its quality. There is also some indication that female unemployment rates increased between 1997 and 2004, with nearly half of the women in the labor market in 2004 unable to find work. However, because only 20 percent of women report being in the labor market at any time, this apparent increase in unemployment could be driven by compositional changes in the women who report being in the labor market.[18]

The left panel in figure 2-2 reports expected length of unemployment for all graduates at the time of graduation, and the right panel reports the same statistic for those who are unemployed immediately following graduation. The former reflects the risk faced by the average graduate and the latter the risk by the subset who do not find a job immediately after graduation. In each case, the results are disaggregated by type of education. Two striking results emerge from these graphs. First, youth who are unemployed immediately after they graduate (right panel) are expected to experience about three years of unemployment, which is a very long time for a young person to remain unemployed. Second, youth graduating with an upper secondary education face a much longer expected duration of unemployment than other graduates (left panel), although the disadvantage disappears if they happen to find a job immediately after graduation. Thus, the long expected durations for those with upper secondary degrees is driven by the very high rates of unemployment for this group.

Long unemployment spells early in life not only deplete a person's human capital, they can also dash hopes, reduce self-esteem, and even cause depression. One manifestation of this phenomenon in Iran is drug abuse among the young. According to UNICEF, Iran has one of the highest rates of drug abuse in the region.[19] Further, a survey of drug users revealed that the majority were young people.[20]

Figure 2-3 provides another insight into the transition from school to work, where youth who are not in school or working are compared with

Figure 2-2. *Expected Duration of Unemployment, 1997–2003*

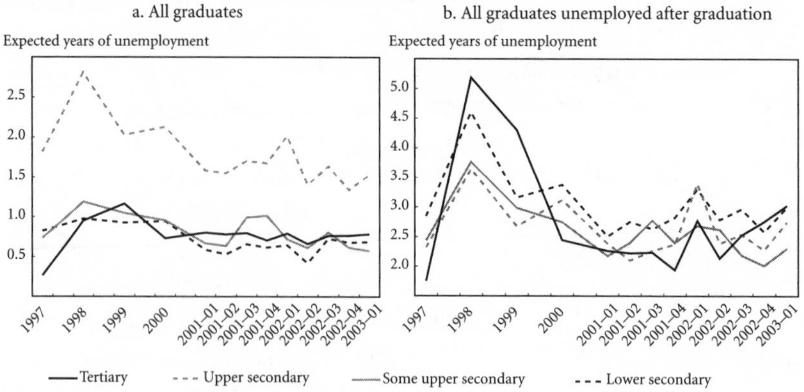

a. All graduates

Expected years of unemployment

b. All graduates unemployed after graduation

Expected years of unemployment

——Tertiary   - - - Upper secondary   ——Some upper secondary   - - - Lower secondary

Source: Author's calculations from data files of the Household Employment and Unemployment Survey, Statistical Center of Iran, 1997–2005.

those who are working. These shares are plotted by age for two years, 1995 and 2005. The gap between the two lines for each year represents the share of youth who have left school but are not gainfully employed (are unemployed or homemakers).

For both rural and urban males, the "Left School" curve has shifted up between 1995 and 2005 for individuals over age 17, indicating the increasing numbers of youth leaving school and the consequent decreasing educational attainment. This shift has not been accompanied by an upward shift in the share of those working, indicating increased unemployment among these youth. The opposite effect occurs for women. Among rural women, there is a downward shift in the "Left School" curve between 1995 and 2005, which is consistent with the expansion of secondary education in rural areas. Similarly, there is a noticeable decrease in the percentage of urban women who leave school between the ages of 19 and 22. Presumably these women who do not leave school attend college. Despite these improvements in the education of women, employment rates have fallen by a larger share than increases in school attendance can explain. This result indicates that an increasing number of women are either unemployed or homemakers, although, as described later, this interpretation is complicated by whether women accurately report their work status.

Differences in the average age of youth at their first job highlight the varying education and employment experiences of men and women in rural

Figure 2-3. *Shares of Youth Not in School vs. Youth Employed, 1995 and 2005*

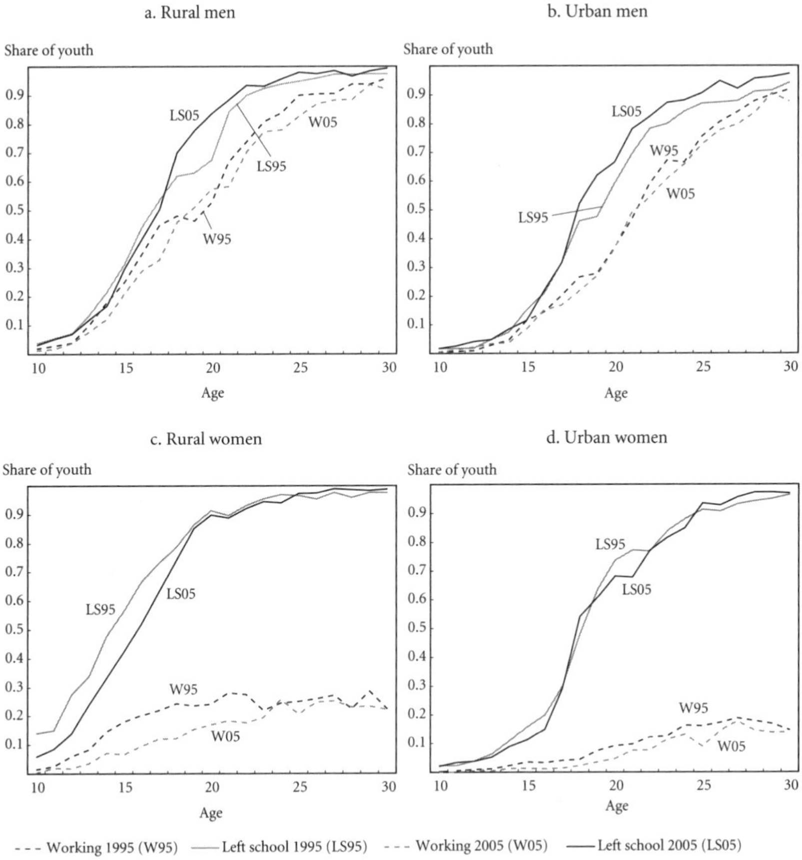

a. Rural men   b. Urban men

c. Rural women   d. Urban women

- - - Working 1995 (W95)   ——— Left school 1995 (LS95)   - - - Working 2005 (W05)   ——— Left school 2005 (LS05)

Source: Authors' calculations based on data from the Household Expenditures and Income Survey (HEIS), Statistical Center of Iran, 1995 and 2005.

and urban areas. Average age at first job is highest and has been the most rapidly increasing among urban women, indicating that they are on average more educated than other groups upon entering the labor market. In comparison, rural women begin work at a very young age, which is one likely explanation for their low educational achievement. Women in rural areas still join the labor force before men, although this gap has decreased substantially over the past decade. This early entry into the labor force reflects family decisions to invest in the human capital of male over female family members.

Rigidity of the Formal Labor Market

Labor market rigidity is a key factor in the social exclusion of youth.[21] In a dynamic and flexible labor market, new vacancies are created by both job creation and turnover. In Iran, creating employment opportunities for new entrants is particularly important because the labor force of about 25 million is expanding at a rate of 3 to 4 percent a year, with nearly 1.2 million youth entering the labor market annually and only 300,000 workers retiring. Iran's labor market is one of the most rigid in the developing world because of the "social contract" developed during the revolution.[22] Similar to those in other countries in the Middle East, this contract is a government commitment to provide public sector jobs, which has been detrimental to the economy's capacity for job creation.[23]

The postrevolution social contract still enjoys wide support among Iranians, even among reformists, despite varied interpretations of how this bargain should be realized. However, since the early 1990s, some reforms to the social contract have been pursued, including policies to reduce the size of the public sector payroll by freezing salaries and restricting hiring. As a result, the share of public sector wage and salary employment fell from 53 percent in 1997 to 45 percent in 2004. However, nearly 80 percent of recent university graduates still find employment in the public sector, although this rate has declined substantially from 93 percent in 1997. Most desirable public sector positions still require a university degree—a requirement that encourages ambitious youth to obtain degrees rather than the skills necessary for these positions. Ahmadinejad's administration, despite its populist nature, has not retracted these reforms, but no attempt has been made to improve the signals youth receive regarding degrees versus skills.

Legal restrictions on the hiring and firing of workers in the private sector also contribute to labor market rigidity in Iran. The Labor Law of 1990 makes it difficult for private employers to lay off workers. According to the law, labor councils composed of three representatives of workers, employers, and the Ministry of Labor have the final authority to rule over grievances filed by dismissed workers. If the council rules in favor of the worker, the employer is fined and has to reinstate the worker. These restrictions lead to low turnover in the formal labor market and limit the ability of the private economy to create new, long-term employment opportunities. At one level, low turnover hurts young job seekers because they cannot compete for jobs held by those already employed. At another level, low turnover leads to distorted incentives for learning and skill acquisition. Because it is costly to lay off employees once they are hired, firms are compelled to select workers based on a priori verifiable skills and degrees rather than potential productivity.[24] This also encourages students to invest in degrees rather than a more balanced set of skills that would be useful in the labor market.

Because of the heavy penalties imposed by the law on employers for dismissing workers, many employers now rely primarily on short-term contracts, creating "marginal" and temporary jobs for youth.[25] This reliance on short-term contracts leads to higher turnover for new workers and can have negative effects on firm productivity. Although reliable data on this practice are limited, the proportion of new private sector jobs that are short term is estimated to be as high as 50 percent.

Informal Labor Market

Rigidity in the formal labor market often pushes new entrants into the informal sector. The informal sector is defined as "consisting of unincorporated enterprises, with fewer than five workers in urban areas, engaged in sectors other than the agricultural and technical sectors."[26]

The informal sector in Iran is quite large: 57 percent of total enterprises in the country have only one employee and 95 percent of industrial enterprises have fewer than ten employees.[27] Estimates of the total number of employees in the informal labor market vary widely. Official estimates put its size closer to 50 percent.[28] Using a slightly different definition, the total size of the "underground economy" is estimated at 30 to 35 percent of the total economy.[29]

Existing surveys do not allow a separate identification of youth working in the informal labor market, so it is not possible to estimate the direct implications of these jobs for individuals.[30] Existing literature suggests that there are advantages and disadvantages to an informal labor market of this size. In economies with rigid formal labor markets such as Iran's, one important advantage is that informal sector employment generally expands in economic downturns. At times when formal firms cannot afford to hire new employees at the prevailing wage rate, wages in the informal market are flexible and can adjust downward temporarily, allowing firms in the informal sector to continue hiring new employees.[31] A major disadvantage is that many informal sector employees do not have insurance or social security despite guarantees in the constitution for "universal" coverage.[32]

Female Employment

Despite a significant rise in the share of the female workforce employed in large industries— from 6 percent in the early 1990s to 12 percent in 2001— the majority of women are employed in the informal sector. Many other women who are not "employed" in a standard sense are actively involved in work with nongovernmental organizations, foundations, or as tutors for their children, either to help with schoolwork or to compensate for the lack of sports and other extracurricular education at schools.[33]

Understanding the labor market faced by today's young women requires an analysis of these informal labor markets. Such an analysis is difficult because of lack of data and because many women with jobs in the informal sector are likely to describe themselves as homemakers rather than employed or unemployed.[34] Preliminary evidence for this underreporting of female labor market participation includes the large number of families in Iran that report more than one homemaker. For example, if all unmarried women aged 15 to 24 who are recorded as being homemakers are added to the labor force, female youth unemployment rates would increase from 23 to 59 percent in urban areas and from 54 to 71 percent in rural areas.[35]

In general, although women still have only limited formal employment opportunities, the "culture of work" is changing so that it is becoming increasingly acceptable for female family members to work outside the home. And though formal discrimination against women is still prevalent, as evidenced by the March 2004 order of the interior minister banning women from working as coffee shop waitresses, some employers prefer women as employees because they "remain in one place and work harder."[36]

Labor Market Policies

A variety of job creation schemes have been implemented during the past few years. In 2004 Khatami's government initiated a program allocating 6 trillion rials (about $2.2 billion) for the employment of young college graduates at private firms. This program was hastily and poorly designed and ended shortly after the change of administration. Since it did not include an evaluation component, it is impossible to estimate its effect on employment. A problem with this program was that it gave priority to those with more education (university degrees followed by high school), thus intensifying the distortions of incentives in education created by credentialism.

In June 2006 President Ahmadinejad launched a much larger program to raise 180 trillion rials (about $60 billion) through publicly owned banks (later joined by the Social Security Organization) for projects with "quick returns," aimed at creating jobs for youth and targeted to small and medium enterprises.[37] The program came under criticism because of its sheer size relative to the resources available to banks for evaluating projects and for its lack of good monitoring.[38] The program anticipated nearly 1 million new jobs, but because of lack of attention to impact evaluation in the design stage, it is impossible to assess its impact.[39] In 2009 official figures indicate that banks had allocated 198 trillion rials to the program, which in nominal terms exceeds the initial intended size and in real terms accounts for about half of that amount. From the announcement it was not clear if this amount had been actually disbursed or simply approved. In 2008 inflation reached nearly 30 percent, prompting the Central Bank to restrict the banks' lending programs in general and this program in particular. Recent figures show that in 2008 unemployment actually *increased* by about two percentage points, suggesting that any positive effect from the program may have been small.

Among other active labor market policies was the establishment of a nationwide network of employment centers to increase access to information about employment opportunities and employment promotion and skills development programs. The objective of these centers is to assist in matching firms with employees. The impact of these centers is not yet known.

Reforms in the Labor Law of 1990 have been initiated to reduce its negative effects on small and medium-size employers. In 2003 the government passed legislation exempting firms with fewer than five workers from the law's layoff restrictions. Recently, the government also permitted exemptions for firms with fewer than ten workers, conditional on a three-way agreement between the government, employer, and workers. In this way, the government has maintained the labor law, which is an important part of the social contract, while at the same time providing small employers with much needed flexibility. The effect of these exemptions is large, because roughly 95 percent of wage workers are employed by firms with fewer than ten workers. However, the effects of these changes on job creation are not known.

In February 2007 the Iranian parliament announced that it would support several amendments to increase the flexibility of the 1990 labor law.[40] But opposition to these amendments from groups of lawmakers and workers is significant, and the future success of these reforms is unclear.[41]

Marriage and Family Formation

Family life in Iran has gone through dramatic changes during the last two decades. In addition to falling fertility rates, both men and women are waiting longer to marry. The percentage of unmarried men and women between the ages of 25 and 29 has increased rapidly, rising from 8 percent in 1985 to over 25 percent in 2004 for women and from less than 20 percent to nearly 40 percent for men during the same period.

The rise in the age of marriage may be a positive phenomenon. In particular, it may reflect a growing desire of both men and women to invest more in education before forming a family. However, the delay in marriage also signals a new problem in the transition to adulthood. Delayed marriage may reflect inflexibility in the marriage market stemming from the increased costs of marriage, buying a home, and raising a family. The ability of the marriage market to cope with imbalances is particularly important, as can be seen with the current youth bulge in which there are currently more women of marriageable age than men.

The Marriage Market

Marriage in Iran is recognized as a contract between the couple and also between their families. Today's rising age of marriage combined with recent imbalances in the ratio of marriage-age men to women will likely compel changes in the standard terms of the marriage contract. Because currently there are more women than men of marriageable age, it is easier for men to "marry up," taking wives who are more educated than they are or from higher social classes. The traditional five-year age gap between the age of a man and his wife that is driving this imbalance is already declining. Other adjustments, such as larger dowries or smaller *mahrieh* (insurance for the wife in case of divorce), may also occur, but so far there is no evidence of such changes.

Traditionally, Iranian women marry men about five years older than themselves. In the 1970s the male-to-female ratio was quite low, as shown in figure 2-4, with only seven men aged 25 to 29 for every ten women aged 20 to 24. And while the ratio of men to women approached parity in 1995, an imbalance of similar magnitude has returned to the marriage market as the women of the youth bulge reach their early to mid-twenties and outnumber eligible men. However, this imbalance is expected to reverse in the coming years, and by 2020 there will be nearly fourteen eligible men for every ten eligible women.

Figure 2-4. *The Marriage Imbalance: Ratio of Men Aged 25 to 29 to Women Aged 20 to 24, 1950–2050*

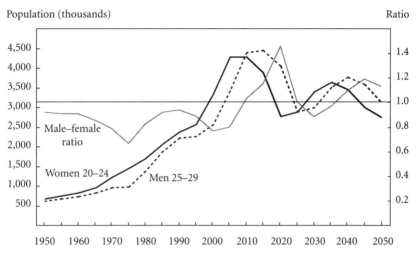

Source: United Nations Population Projections, 2004 revision.

The extent to which such shifts in the gender ratio disrupt social life depends on how quickly the marriage market and its institutions can adjust. The most obvious form of adjustment is a change in the age gap between spouses. There is evidence that the age gap is narrowing as a result of the recent increase in the number of women over men. Further flexibility in the marriage market is noticeable in that the number of men with a primary education who marry more educated women has increased dramatically. This trend partially reflects the increasing educational attainment of women as well as the preference of women to marry men who have left school and already have stable employment.[42]

Marriage and Housing

Between 1999 and 2007, housing prices increased 28 percent faster than overall consumer price inflation. The high cost of housing is a likely impediment to the ability of men to marry and of couples to start families. The proportion of men aged 20 to 29 who live with their parents increased from about 50 percent in 1984 to about 75 percent in 2005. For women, this proportion increased from 20 percent to about 48 percent. This phenomenon is more pronounced for those with upper secondary and university education; today, nearly two-thirds of these men live at home. This phenomenon has put pressure not only on youth themselves but also on their families who thus share in the cost of youth unemployment.

The likelihood of living at home is inversely related to education. This suggests that, at least for men, the inability to live independently is a function of current employment status rather than lifetime earning potential. As noted earlier, unemployment rates are lower for the less educated. Further, because the current gender ratio favors men, inability to pay rent or buy a home is the most likely explanation for why men with reasonable earning potential cannot afford to marry or live independently. Lack of sophisticated financial institutions in Iran, the mortgage market in particular, prevents young men from purchasing a home by borrowing against future earnings. Financial markets in Iran have developed very slowly because until recently all banks were government owned and had little incentive to expand lending in new areas. Only a few private banks operate currently, but at least one—Bank Parsian—has announced plans to launch a mortgage-lending program.

There are obvious links between the labor, marriage, and housing markets. To marry, young men need to have a job or a house. To borrow money for a house, they need a job. Clearly, even in a well-developed financial market, unemployed young men would find it very difficult to borrow for marriage and housing. But for those who find jobs, the ability to use future earnings toward buying a home might help them get married and settle. In a society with a developed mortgage market, the prospect of owning a home adds to the reward of finding a job for many young men.

Marriage Market Flexibility: Dowry and Mahrieh

An important source of marriage market flexibility is the change in the value of dowries provided by brides' families to the newlyweds. With a declining male-to-female ratio in recent years, one would expect dowries to have risen. However, estimates suggest that the share of the dowry in total expenditures fell between 1995 and 2003.[43] That means that other factors may be stronger determinants of the size of dowries than a decline in the number of eligible males. The size of the dowry is affected by multiple factors, including the relative income potentials of the bride and groom and the expected duration of the marriage. Because dowries are very difficult to recover upon divorce, the recent increase in the divorce rate may have contributed to lower dowries.

Low-income groups seem to contribute a smaller proportion of total expenditures to dowries than higher-income groups, but the size of these contributions is still large for those in the lowest quintile. The average family in this quintile would spend about $400 on a dowry, equivalent to nearly three months' wages. Also, it is likely that the estimates for low-income groups are biased downward because expenditures on durables such as furniture, which make up a significant part of the dowry for low-income families, are not included.[44]

While the dowry reflects the cost of marriage for the family of the bride, the groom and his family must cover the costs of the wedding ceremony and *mahrieh*. Although estimates of expenditures on wedding ceremonies are not available, the groom's family is typically expected to spend an amount equivalent to the dowry provided by the bride's family. The *mahrieh* is a prenuptial commitment by the groom to pay, upon request, a fixed sum or a specific asset value. As such, it does not constitute an immediate cost for the groom. However, when the marriage contract is signed and the groom agrees to a specified *mahrieh*, he must have these assets at his disposal. The rising education and employment potential of women in recent years is purported to have increased the size of the *mahrieh*, making it a significant impediment to marriage and family formation.[45]

Marriage Delay and Policy Responses

The increasing age of marriage has been identified as a significant challenge by a number of political and religious leaders. These leaders often identify rigid social customs that require families to incur significant expense as the major reason for delayed marriage. One effort to help young couples manage these costs and reduce the age of marriage is a recent program promoted by President Ahmadinejad that provides loans to low-income couples. This *Mehr-e Reza* Fund was initially endowed with about $300 million. It is designed to help targeted young couples overcome costs and other challenges associated with marriage, housing, and employment. Permanent offices of the fund in 336 cities allocate loans as large as 10 million rials ($3,000) per couple. Borrowers are charged a 4 percent interest rate and are expected to repay the loan in thirty-six installments.[46] In 2009 the government allocated 10 trillion rials (about PPP$2 billion) to the fund.[47] While the efficacy of this program is still unknown, anecdotal evidence suggests that it has not been very successful in part because couples often have to wait for an extended period of time before receiving marriage loans.[48]

A variety of other policies have been proposed to address the problem of delayed marriage. Mass weddings have been offered as a way to lower the high cost of weddings.[49] Other policies, such as a cap on dowries and a controversial proposal to limit women's access to universities, have been rejected. Similarly, the government rejected a proposal by former interior minister Mostafa Pour-Mohammadi to encourage temporary marriages for those who cannot afford the high costs of a regular marriage.[50]

One important point often missed in discussions of marriage costs is that the expenses may serve as screening devices or performance bonds. Tough conditions for getting married can serve as rules that protect the two parties, given information asymmetries that are more prevalent in modern urban settings than in traditional rural societies where marriages are often within the family or community. For example, the rise in the *mahrieh* may be a response to lack of security for women under the *sharia,* which gives men the sole right to divorce. If the *mahrieh* were made illegal, women would lose an important instrument to discourage men from unilateral divorce as well as a guaranteed source of income in case of separation or divorce. In a similar vein, the amounts that a prospective groom is willing to pay both for the wedding ceremony and the *mahrieh* may be viewed as an indicator of his quality as a provider and as a disincentive to divorce. Subsidies for marriage, such as mass government ceremonies or interest-free marriage loans, may produce adverse unintended consequences, such as weakened signals of a young man's ability to provide for his family.

Conclusion

Today's youth in Iran face a variety of difficult transitions. Traditional Iranian society, though much poorer, celebrated youth and encouraged the young generation to take over farms, professions, and businesses from the older generation while they set up their families. Modern Iranian society instead offers competitive schools, inflexible labor markets, and a rigid marriage market that, together, contribute to stalled transitions filled with anxiety, unhappiness, and often depression.

The challenges faced by Iran's young generation are in part the result of the baby boom of the 1970s and 1980s, and Iran's education system, labor market, and marriage market have failed to make the adjustment needed to ease the impact of this youth bulge. While demographic transitions often bring with them larger cohorts of youth who have to compete for jobs and resources, they can also confer economic benefits such as a faster-growing labor force and greater potential for human capital accumulation. To take advantage of these benefits, social institutions must be adaptable to changing demographic realities. Iran's relevant institutions—schools, the formal labor market, and marriage—are not sufficiently flexible to take advantage of the country's "demographic gift."

There is much to praise about Iran's system of free universal education, one that promotes students based on merit and objective criteria. It has had a positive impact on enrollments and attainment across regions and income groups. But it is flawed in that it is too competitive and thus excludes a large proportion of the less successful student population. Further, because the education system relies on multiple-choice exams, ignores the arts, and does not encourage students to develop writing skills, learning in schools is reduced to rote memorization, and high school graduates typically are unprepared for the labor market. The formal labor market is similarly more concerned with diplomas and years of experience, which are considered objective measures of productivity, than with subjective employer evaluations. It thus exacerbates the flawed logic of the education system by hiring its winners and rejecting its losers. Together the schools and the formal labor market form a system of exclusion that leaves out the vast majority of educated youth.

The failure of this system manifests itself in several ways. The most obvious is the high rate and long duration of unemployment for the young. Even youth with tertiary education suffer unemployment rates in excess of 20 percent and waste several years before they find their first job. Without a job, many stay unmarried and have to live with their parents for much longer than they would wish. The increasing age of first marriage, which is a sign of falling fertility and rising investment in human capital in some countries, is partly a sign of poorly functioning social and economic institutions in Iran.

Long unemployment spells early in one's working life deplete human capital, adversely affecting the self-esteem and confidence of first-time job seekers and increasing the dependency of the young on their parents. To escape this predicament, the more talented choose to leave the country. Iran's brain drain has received wide attention inside the country and abroad.[51] In addition to those who leave, many more dream of leaving and thus fail to make a good effort at building their lives inside Iran.

The government is currently considering some policy options that address the needs of youth. There is an attempt to move the education system away from reliance on a single test and in the direction of collecting and using more information about student abilities. There is also a move to allow employers to exercise greater independence in judging an individual's productivity. These reforms could affect students' incentives to learn a wider variety of skills than schools currently promote and firms reward. Policies to improve the working of the marriage market are naturally harder to find and implement and are not focused on fundamental reform. One example of public action that could operate at a more fundamental level is to support and promote financial institutions that could help educated youth borrow against their future incomes to finance the costs of marriage and housing and thus move onto the next stage in their lives as adults and full citizens. A better-developed mortgage market could help with marriage and family formation, but little has been done to promote such a market.

Notes

1. Angus McDowall, "Iran Pours Oil Fund Billions into Wooing Disaffected Youth," *The Independent*, September 1, 2005 (www.independent.co.uk/news/world/middle-east/iran-pours-oil-fund-billions-into-wooing-disaffected-youth-504996.html).

2. Muhammad Javad Rooh, cited by Kaveh Basmenji, *Tehran Blues: Youth Culture in Iran* (London: Saqi Books, 2005).

3. Roxanne Varzi, *Warring Souls: Youth, Media, and Martyrdom in Post-Revolution Iran* (Duke University Press, 2006); Shahram Khosravi, "The Third Generation: The Islamic Order of Things and Cultural Defiance among the Young of Tehran" (Stockholm University, Department of Social Anthropology, 2003); Basmenji, *Tehran Blues*.

4. Farzaneh Roudi-Fahimi, "Women's Reproductive Health in the Middle East and North Africa," Technical Report (New York: Population Reference Bureau, 2003). For a more extensive discussion of fertility trends in Iran, see Mohammad Jalal Abbasi-Shavazi and Peter McDonald, "Fertility Decline in the Islamic Republic of Iran, 1972–2000," *Asian Population Studies* 2 (2006): 217–37.

5. Robin Barlow, "Population Growth and Economic Growth: Some More Correlations," *Population and Development Review* 20 (1994): 419–55; David E. Bloom and Jeffrey G. Williamson, "Demographic Transitions and Economic Miracles in Emerging Asia," *World Bank Economic Review* 12 (1998): 419–55.

6. Djavad Salehi-Isfahani, "Human Resources in Iran: Potentials and Challenges," *Iranian Studies* 38 (2005): 117–147.

7. Golnar Mehran, "The Paradox of Tradition and Modernity in Female Education in the Islamic Republic of Iran," *Comparative Education Review* 47, no. 3 (2003): 269–86.

8. UNICEF, "Education Statistics: Iran," technical report (Geneva: Division of Policy and Planning, Strategic Information Section, 2007).

9. The effect of rising class size can be subject to variation. See Angrist and Lavy, who use Israeli data to show that reducing class size has a positive effect for fourth and fifth graders but not third graders. Joshua D. Angrist and Victor Lavy, "Using Mai-

monides' Rule to Estimate the Effect of Class Size on Scholastic Achievement," *Quarterly Journal of Economics* 114 (1999): 533–75.

10. Preliminary calculations from household survey data on Iran using a Mincer-like approach show that returns to basic education are very low, that upper secondary graduates earn a 70 percent premium over illiterates, and that the premium for university graduates is 140 percent.

11. Ina V.S. Mullis and others, *TIMSS 2007 International Mathematics Report* (Boston College, Lynch School of Education, TIMSS & PIRLS International Study Center, 2008) (http://timss.bc.edu/TIMSS2007/intl_reports.html). In the 2007 TIMSS test in mathematics, Iranian eighth graders ranked in the bottom third of participating countries. With an average score of 403, achievement in mathematics falls well short of the TIMSS scale average benchmark of 500.

12. Michael O. Martin and others, *TIMSS 2007 International Science Report* (Boston College, Lynch School of Education, TIMSS & PIRLS International Study Center, 2008) (http://timss.bc.edu/TIMSS2007/intl_reports.html). Iran also showed improvements in fourth graders' test scores in science from the 1995 to 2007 period.

13. Ali Hassouri, quoted in Djavad Salehi-Isfahani, "Population, Human Capital, and Economic Growth in Iran," in *Human Capital and Population in the Middle East*, edited by Ismail Sirageldin (London: I. B. Tauris, 2002).

14. Gordon Betcherman, Karina Olivas, and Amit Dar, "Impacts of Active Labor Market Programs: New Evidence from Evaluations with Particular Attention to Developing and Transition Countries," Social Protection Discussion Paper Series 0402 (Washington: World Bank, 2004).

15. Salehi-Isfahani, "Population, Human Capital, and Economic Growth in Iran."

16. "1.3m to Compete in Concours," *Iran Daily*, February 6, 2007 (www.iran-daily.com/1385/2775/html/panorama.htm#s207222).

17. A similar ratio is found in Egypt, Mexico, South Korea, and Turkey.

18. See the "Female Employment" section below for further discussion on the difficulties of measuring female unemployment.

19. UNICEF, "At a Glance: Iran, Islamic Republic of" (www.unicef.org/infobycountry/iran.html).

20. Houman Naranjiha, "A Rapid Assessment of Drug Use and Addiction in Iran" (Tehran: University of Social Welfare and Rehabilitation, 2005, in Persian).

21. A. B. Atkinson, "Social Exclusion, Poverty, and Unemployment," in *Exclusion, Employment, and Opportunity*, edited by A. B. Atkinson and John Hills (London School of Economics, 1998).

22. Salehi-Isfahani, "Human Resources in Iran"; Djavad Salehi-Isfahani, "Microeconomics of Growth in MENA: The Role of Households," in *Explaining Growth in the Middle East*, edited by J. Nugent and M. H. Pesaran (Amsterdam: Elsevier, 2006).

23. For more details, see Tarik Yousef, "Employment, Development and the Social Contract in the Middle East and North Africa," technical report (Washington: World Bank, 2004).

24. Djavad Salehi-Isfahani and Russell D. Murphy, "Labor Market Flexibility and Investment in Human Capital," working paper (Virginia Tech, Department of Economics, 2004).

25. Atkinson, "Social Exclusion, Poverty, and Unemployment."

26. F. Bagheri and others, "How to Measure the Informal Sector in Iran," technical report (Tehran: Statistical Research Center of Iran, 2002).

27. E. Etminan and K. Chaker-ol-Hosseini, "Social Protection for Informal Workers: Iranian Experience," paper presented at the Fifth International Research Conference on Social Security (Warsaw, March 5–7, 2007).

28. Official estimates from the International Labor Organization (ILO) using official national data (www.ilo.org/public/english/bureau/stat/download/comp2a.pdf). Etminan and Chaker-ol-Hosseini estimate larger sizes for the informal labor market, "Social Protection for Informal Workers."

29. Jahangir Amuzegar, "Iran's Underground Economy," *Middle East Economic Survey* 36 (2003). Roughly speaking, Amuzegar's definition of the "underground economy" includes all nontaxed parts of the economy.

30. The Statistical Research Center of Iran has proposed including a question about the size of the firm in which an individual works as a way of identifying those in the informal sector.

31. For a discussion of the informal labor market in the countries of Latin America, see Guillermo E. Perry and others, *Informality: Exit and Exclusion* (Washington: World Bank, 2007).

32. Etminan and Chaker-ol-Hosseini, "Social Protection for Informal Workers."

33. Elaheh Rostami-Povey, "Women and Work in Iran," *State of Nature* 1 (2005) (www.stateofnature.org/contentsOne.html).

34. Diane Singerman, "The Family and Community as Politics: The Popular Sector in Cairo," in *Development, Change and Gender in Cairo: A View from the Household*, edited by Diane Singerman and Homa Hoodfar (Indiana University Press, 1996); Diane Singerman, "Engaging Informality: Women, Work, and Politics in Cairo," in *Middle Eastern Women and the Invisible Economy*, edited by Richard A. Lobban Jr. (University of Florida Press, 1998).

35. Further analysis of our data might allow us to identify whether these homemakers are more likely to be informally employed or unemployed. In particular, regional variation in economic performance and the corresponding changes in the size of the male and female labor force may reveal if informal workers or the unemployed are being undercounted.

36. Rostami-Povey, "Women and Work in Iran."

37. Measured in purchasing power parity.

38. One such report, quoted in the parliament by a prominent deputy, Ahmad Tavakoli, found that 46 percent of the loans did not even exist. See the 2008 report in BBC Persian Service, "Iran's Largest Employment Program under Question"

(www.bbc.co.uk/persian/business/story/2008/05/080525_ba-ka-profit.shtml) (in Persian).

39. Mohammad Ali Darvish, "Supporting Small Ventures," *Iran Daily*, October 9, 2007 (www.iran-daily.com/1386/2961/html/economy.htm#s263757).

40. "Majlis Supports Labor Law Amendments," *Iran Daily*, February 20, 2007 (http://iran-daily.com/1385/2787/html/economy.htm#s210945).

41. "Labor Law Reform Inevitable," *Iran Daily*, February 3, 2007 (http://iran-daily.com/1385/2772/html/economy.htm#s206880).

42. See Diane Singerman, "Networks, Jobs, and Everyday Life in Cairo," in *Everyday Life in the Muslim Middle East,* edited by Donna Lee Bowen and Evelyn A. Early (Indiana University Press, 2002). As suggested by Singerman, these differences in educational attainment may have a significant impact on household bargaining. Future work exploring the impact of the educational differential on intrahousehold allocation could prove quite interesting.

43. Household Expenditure and Income Surveys data provided by the Statistical Center of Iran separately report dowry expenditures only for 1995–2003. Estimates are generated by regressing the share of a dowry on the log of real household expenditures and urban and province dummies (with interactions) using the 6,000 households that reported nonzero expenditures for a dowry. The coefficients from these regressions are then used to predict the share for the entire population (for which quintiles could be more clearly defined). These figures do not say that the average household spends this much on a dowry each year. Rather, we would expect it to spend this much on a single wedding.

44. The questionnaire notes that part of dowry expenditures may be recorded under durables. But because we cannot disaggregate expenditures for durables for the family from those for the dowry, we do not include these in our estimates.

45. Nader Habibi, "An Economic Analysis of the Prenuptial Agreement (*mahrieh*) in Contemporary Iran," *Economic Development and Cultural Change* 45 (1997). Although the evidence on rising *mahrieh* is largely anecdotal, it has been discussed in the press. See, for example, McDowall, "Iran Pours Oil Fund Billions into Wooing Disaffected Youth."

46. "Ten Trillion Rials for Mehr-e Reza Fund Program Approved by the Government," *IRNA News*, June 25, 2009 (http://209.1.163.225/View/FullStory/?NewsId=563843).

47. "Mehr-e Reza Fund Granting Marriage Loans," *Iran Daily*, July 18, 2006 (www.iran-daily.com/1385/2613/html/panorama.htm#s159471).

48. Maziar Bahari, "How Popular Is He Really?" *Newsweek*, September 11, 2006 (http://www.newsweek.com/id/45532)

49. McDowall "Iran Pours Oil Fund Billions into Wooing Disaffected Youth."

50. This proposal was criticized by a variety of different groups; see "Gov't Denies Promoting Temporary Marriage," *Iran Daily*, June 8, 2007 (http://iran-daily.com/1386/2862/html/national.htm).

51. Frances Harrison, "Huge Cost of Iranian Brain Drain," *BBC News*, January 8, 2007 (http://news.bbc.co.uk/1/hi/world/middle_east/6240287.stm). See also William J. Carrington and Enrica Detragiache, "How Extensive Is the Brain Drain?" *Finance & Development* 36, no. 2 (1999) (www.imf.org/external/pubs/ft/fandd/1999/06/carringt.htm).

RAGUI ASSAAD *and* GHADA BARSOUM

3

Rising Expectations and Diminishing Opportunities for Egypt's Young

Egypt, like most countries in the Middle East, is experiencing a "youth bulge"—a period in which the proportion of youth in the population increases significantly compared with other age groups. Currently, around 28 percent of the Egyptian population is between the ages of 15 and 29.[1] In the coming decade, this young generation will be the biggest group in Egypt's long history to make its way to adulthood, representing both an opportunity and a challenge. As the country's youth population reaches working age, its ratio to the older and younger nonworking populations will rise, constituting a "demographic gift" that will lower the country's economic dependency rate. At the same time, however, this youth bulge places enormous pressures on the educational system and labor and housing markets.

The transition to adulthood is a crucial stage in a young person's life—the time during which one makes important decisions about education, employment, and family formation. To a large extent, the quality of an individual's adult life depends on the outcomes of the decisions made during this critical period. While some young Egyptians successfully transition to quality education, decent jobs, financial stability, and personal independence with the ability to form families of their own, most experience substandard education, endure periods of unemployment, end up with dead-end, low-paying jobs, and defer forming families because of the high financial costs of marriage and housing.

Promoting successful transitions requires the recognition that the exclusion of young Egyptians is a multidimensional process. Their transitions to education, work, family formation, and active citizenship are interdependent. Poor learning leads to poor job prospects. Forming families and achieving personal independence are closely tied to productive employment and adequate earnings. Civic participation is essential for young people to successfully transition to meaningful adult roles and full inclusion in society. Yet, facing exclusion on so many other fronts, many young Egyptians refrain from such activities, because they do not believe that their participation is encouraged or valued by society.

Each of these transitions is shaped by the emergent economic and social conditions across Egypt. Recently, Egypt has experienced an economic revival, with average annual GDP growth reaching around 5 percent from 2004 to 2007. Labor market conditions have improved markedly since 1998, with greater access to employment and higher earnings.[2] Labor force participation and employment rates have increased while unemployment has decreased.

However, these trends have not resulted in a noticeable reduction of poverty because of the rapid growth of low productivity, nonwage employment, and the powerful impact of the 2003 devaluation of the Egyptian pound on prices of food and other necessities that the poor depend on disproportionately. Poverty constitutes the root of exclusion for many young Egyptians. The children of the poor are those most likely to drop out of or fail to enroll in school. When they do enroll in the education system, they are the population that is most vulnerable to its poor quality. Because education is closely connected to the labor market, they end up in low-paying, low-skilled jobs. Furthermore, economic mobility, especially for this poor population, is limited; young workers are reported to have the lowest earnings in the Egyptian labor market and have experienced the slowest increase in real earnings. Despite increasing access to education, the promise of a better life remains elusive for most young Egyptians.

Finally, gender has much to do with being excluded. Female school enrollment rates have increased a great deal in the past few decades, but a significant minority of girls remains deprived of schooling, particularly in rural Upper Egypt. Moreover, while female enrollment through secondary school exceeds 40 percent, women's labor force participation rates remain low, and those entering the labor market continue to face high levels of unemployment.[3]

Education: Challenges in Access and Quality

Access to quality education can lead to a smooth and successful transition to the labor market with lifelong benefits. Limited access to education and training, or access to poor-quality education, perpetuates a vicious cycle of limited job prospects and low-tier employment opportunities. Those students who benefit the least from their schooling also tend to perform poorly in the job market, thereby setting off a chain reaction of cumulative exclusion.

Accessibility and quality are two fundamental measures of the success of an education system and its role in determining levels of social inequality and social and economic exclusion. School enrollment in Egypt has increased significantly, but early school dropout and nonenrollment continue to be problems among select groups and in certain parts of the country. This process is gender- and class-based and reflects important regional disparities, with females in Upper Egypt being the most disadvantaged.[4]

Quality of education is central to understanding exclusion in the educational system. Poor acquisition of basic literacy and mathematics skills and the need for private tutoring continue to plague the educational system. Similarly, many schools in poor and rural communities are deprived of basic resources such as usable seats and desks and functioning sanitary facilities. While better-off families are able to compensate for these deficiencies by sending their children to private schools and hiring tutors, the poor are trapped by the deficiencies of the system, thus perpetuating their exclusion.

Access to Education: Enrollment and Dropping Out

Access to the Egyptian education system has expanded dramatically in recent years: more children get to school, and they stay in school for longer periods. Enrollment rates increased across the board from 1988 to 2006: in primary education from approximately 84 percent to nearly 97 percent; in secondary education from 48 percent to 62 percent; and in higher education from 20 percent to 24 percent.[5]

Despite rapid growth in school enrollment at all education levels and near-universal enrollment in primary schooling, there are still those who are excluded from receiving basic education. Mandatory basic education in Egypt covers the primary education stage (six years) and the preparatory stage (three years). Afterward, students can choose between vocational (technical) or general secondary education, with the former offering them limited opportunities to enroll in the higher education system. However, mandatory education in its current form is a relatively recent development: it was limited to the primary stage until 1991. Furthermore, the law mandating schooling through the preparatory stage is still not strictly enforced.

While universal enrollment in primary education is the norm in metropolitan areas, there are serious regional disparities. A significant proportion of boys and girls in four Upper Egyptian governorates are deprived of schooling: total gross enrollment in primary education is 81 percent in Menia and Qena, 79 percent in Suhag, and 78 percent in Assiut. The figures for girls are even more alarming, with nearly one-quarter of girls in the four governorates excluded from education.[6]

Quitting school early is another detrimental factor contributing to the exclusion of young Egyptian men and women. Gross enrollment ratios in preparatory education show that Upper Egyptian governorates continue to rank lowest in preparatory school enrollment. Attrition among girls is also highest in the four governorates. For example, in Menia, 72 percent of girls enroll in primary schooling, but only 57 percent continue on to preparatory education and complete the mandatory education phase.[7]

The regional disparities in primary school enrollment correspond with the prevalence of poverty across governorates in Egypt.[8] Governorates with the highest proportion of school dropout rates are the poorest in Egypt. This highlights the strong connection between poverty by region and poor education outcomes.

In addition, access to schooling has an important correlation with gender. Girls in rural Upper Egypt make up the largest group of those left behind in education. They face major mobility constraints for cultural reasons related to norms of gender propriety.[9] Limited accessibility to nearby schools in rural areas, combined with girls' household responsibilities and household poverty in general, push girls out of the educational system. Elbadawy and others show that girls are 2.3 times more likely than boys to have never been to school.[10] Yet other evidence shows that the primary gender gap in education exists in initial school enrollment only: once in school, the probability of dropping out is the same for girls and boys.[11]

The Effects of Low-Quality Public Education

In a global economy, quality education is essential for development and growth. However, the 2005 Egypt Human Development Report concludes that the quality of education is a major challenge in Egypt. While the report stresses the need to go beyond the acquisition of basic learning and address issues of "excellence," it emphasizes that schools in Egypt encounter difficulties in simply providing basic skills.[12] Similarly, a strategic direction paper produced by the Ministry of Education in 2005 highlights "equality in quality education provision" as a major goal for education reforms.[13]

For more than a decade, the education system in Egypt has been showing serious signs of declining quality. These have included low pass rates, poor acquisition of basic literacy and arithmetic, and the phenomenal spread of private tutoring to compensate. Furthermore, large classes exacerbate the experience of poor schooling for many students. Although class size is officially limited to thirty-six, only 20 percent of schools comply with this rule, with one-third of schools having class sizes of forty-five or more. To tackle this issue, an estimated 30 percent of schools implement double shifts, a practice that shortens the school day for students, further limiting their learning experience. Moreover, a majority of schools suffer from shortages of teachers—a problem that is more pronounced in rural areas in both Lower and Upper Egypt.[14]

Compared with other countries, Egypt scores poorly in basic skills. In the 2007 Trends in International Mathematics and Science Study (TIMSS) examinations, Egyptian eighth graders obtained an average score of 391 in math and 408 in science, placing Egypt among the bottom quarter of participating countries in both subjects. Only 5 percent of Egyptian eighth graders taking the test achieved or surpassed the high benchmark score of 550 in math, and only 7 percent were high performers in science. Moreover, around 45 percent of Egyptian eighth graders failed to achieve even the low benchmark score of 400 in both mathematics and science. This benchmark indicates possession of "some basic" or "some elementary" knowledge of math and science.[15]

Teaching methods in Egyptian schools commonly employ rote learning, even at the university level.[16] Such an approach limits students' acquisition of critical thinking skills such as problem solving and the ability to apply knowledge to real problems.[17] This in turn limits opportunities for graduates to compete in a global economy and is reflected through complaints by employers about the inability to find skilled laborers in a market that has a surplus of workers.

Households try to compensate for the limitations of public education through private tutoring, with approximately 40 percent of students receiving private tutoring.[18] The prevalence is highest among secondary school students, at 60 percent. No gender bias is involved in family decisions to provide private tutoring. To a certain extent, access to private tutoring is a privilege and reflects regional disparities. For example, private tutoring is more prevalent in urban areas (44 percent) than in rural areas (35 percent) and is highest in Greater Cairo.[19]

Finally, Egyptian youth face limited access to information technology, both at school and at home, and thus these globally valuable tools play almost no role in enhancing their education. Recent data show that 73 percent of those in school have no access to computers. Similarly, a recent survey of youth in six governorates found that only 10 percent of those interviewed had access to computer technology.[20] Interviews illustrate that more young people have access to the Internet through cyber cafes in Cairo and other urban centers, but technology use among young people is primarily limited to chatting, downloading songs, and viewing religious sites.[21] Overall, young Egyptians are not acquiring substantive knowledge through the use of information technology, nor are they using it to advance their employment prospects.

Skills Mismatch: Preparing Today's Workforce for Yesterday's Labor Market

Despite poor returns in the labor market, a significant proportion of secondary school students continue to turn toward technical education. Research has documented that these vocational schools provide insufficient and often irrelevant training.[22] Limited public spending, lack of qualified teachers, outdated curricula, and little interaction between firms and those developing curricula all lead to poor skill acquisition and a mismatch between what these schools provide and the needs of the labor market.

During the past two decades, technical schools have consistently enrolled a higher proportion of students than general secondary schools. Antoninis argues that the expansion of technical education is a result of misguided political decisions initiated by Gamal Abdel Nasser's government and perpetuated during the 1980s with the support of donor agencies.[23] He further notes that despite the demise of Nasserite industrialization, policy guidelines until the mid-1990s continued to aim for enrolling 70 percent of all students in technical secondary schools. By 2007–08 the share of students in technical secondary education had dropped to 58 percent.[24]

The Egyptian government's long-standing policy of guaranteeing government employment to secondary, postsecondary, and university graduates has contributed to the skill mismatch problem by giving households distorted signals from the labor market.[25] These signals have encouraged households to invest heavily in forms of education, such as technical secondary and technical postsecondary institute education, that qualify youth for government jobs but that have very low returns in the private sector. Faced with strong demand for such education from the public, the government supplies it at the expense of being able to guarantee quality basic education to all of those who are eligible for it. The government also uses technical schooling as a way of limiting university enrollment because technical schooling acts as a separate schooling track. This combination of educational and hiring policies, when applied over a long period, results in the distortion of household decisions and the misallocation of human resources to unproductive activities, leading to the observed low productivity of those resources in the economy.[26]

Youth and the Workplace

UN estimates and projections of the age structure in Egypt show that the share of youth in the general population peaked at 29 percent in 2005 and is expected to gradually decline (figure 3-1). This youth bulge translates into the largest group of youth ever to enter the Egyptian labor market, both in absolute and relative terms. The number of new entrants to the workforce has more than doubled over the last three decades, rising from about 400,000 a year in the late 1970s to about 850,000 in the early 2000s. During this period the total population increased by about 70 percent.[27] Currently, about one in two people of working age (47 percent) is from the youth age group, underscoring the young age of the labor force and the fierce competition among young people for a limited number of good jobs.

The result of these intense labor supply pressures is a process of exclusion in which a growing number of youth are relegated to marginal sources of livelihood or to the ranks of the unemployed. Recent labor force projections show that despite the slowing growth of the youth population, increasing female participation rates, driven by rising educational attainment, will continue to exert significant pressure on the labor market until about 2010, when the growth of the labor force is expected to moderate.[28]

New entrants to the labor market make up the largest group among the unemployed. At the same time, a large proportion of youth who do work are trapped in bad jobs that are low paying and provide limited or no stability, benefits, social insurance, or potential for career development. As a result, many young people cannot afford the costs of marriage and family formation and thus find it difficult to complete their transition to adulthood. Moreover, the gender gap in unemployment is one of the highest in the region: young women are almost four times as likely to be unemployed as young men.

First Jobs in a Changing Economy

During the past three decades, significant growth in educational attainment has dramatically shifted the composition of new entrants to the labor mar-

Figure 3-1. *Age Structure of the Egyptian Population, 1950–2050, Estimates and Medium Variant Projections*

Percent of total population

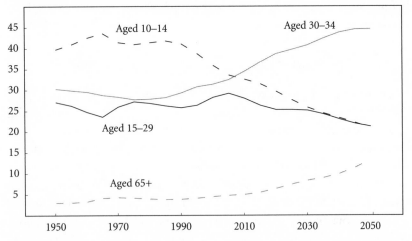

Source: Population Division of the Department of Economic and Social Affairs of the United Nations Secretariat, *World Population Prospects: The 2004 Revision.*

ket. In 1980 about 40 percent of those entering the market had not achieved a primary level of education. By 2005, 70 percent had received a secondary education or more.[29] But this dramatic change has not been accompanied by a commensurate shift in the quality of jobs for new entrants. In the late 1970s about one-third of jobs for the newly employed were in the public sector and about 5 percent were in the private sector, with the rest distributed between informal wage and nonwage employment. By 2005 the proportion of formal jobs for new entrants had dropped to 28 percent (18 percent public and 10 percent private), and the share of informal employment soared to 72 percent (figure 3-2).

Egyptian youth face a virtual devaluation of their educational credentials in comparison with previous generations. After more than three decades of guaranteed public employment for secondary, postsecondary, and university graduates, the education system has become more focused on granting degrees and diplomas rather than on training students for productive employment in a market economy. As a result, significant increases in the quantity of education achieved over the past three decades have translated into very little in terms of increased productivity. Returns, in the form of higher wages, have dropped significantly as youth find themselves facing an increasingly priva-

Figure 3-2. *Distribution of New Entrants in Egypt by Type of First Job and Year of Entry, Four-Year Moving Average, 1975–2005*

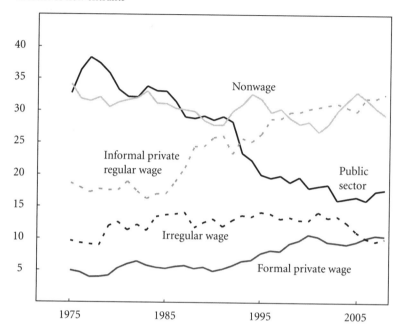

Percent of new entrants

Source: Authors' calculations.

tized labor market that does not provide premiums for degrees and diplomas if such credentials do not result in increased productivity.[30]

Young Egyptians, especially women, face serious difficulties and challenges in finding career jobs after leaving school. Across the Middle East, the slow pace of educational systems in adapting to increasingly market-oriented and open economies has resulted in significant mismatches between skills demanded in the job market and those acquired by new entrants.[31] This mismatch leads to protracted transitions from school to work.

A recent study by the International Labor Organization in Egypt shows that only 17 percent of respondents between the ages of 15 and 29 had completed the transition from school to a career job, which is defined as a regular job that the worker has no immediate plans to change. One-quarter of respondents were still in transition—that is, either unemployed or working but not yet in a career job. The rest had not begun their transition because they were still in school or not planning to seek work.[32]

Young women experience much longer transitions from school to work than their male counterparts. In 2006, 50 percent of male graduates had found their first job within two years of leaving school, down from three years in 1998. Seventy-five percent had found jobs within five years of leaving school in 2006, whereas in 1998 it would have taken nearly eight years for that percentage of young men to find jobs. Although this represents an improvement, the prospects for young men remain troubling. Female rates of transition from school to work are much lower; even after fifteen years, fewer than a quarter of women have found jobs.[33]

Besides fierce competition from their peers and a severe shortage of opportunities, young job seekers lack access to information about available job opportunities, the skills that are in demand, and training opportunities. Programs that seek to address this issue in Egypt reach only a fraction of young job seekers. Those who come from low-income households are particularly disadvantaged because they have limited guidance from members of their families and few social networks upon which to rely.[34]

Unemployment

Unemployment largely affects youth entering the job market. More than 80 percent of the total number of unemployed are in the 15 to 29 age group, and 47 percent are between the ages of 20 and 24.[35] Recent data show that youth unemployment stood at 16.9 percent in 2006, down from 25.6 percent in 1998. While declining, the youth unemployment rate is still much higher than the overall unemployment rate, which decreased from 11.7 percent in 1998 to 8.3 percent in 2006. A total of 1.6 million youth in Egypt are unemployed, divided almost equally between urban and rural areas.

Unemployment in Egypt is primarily a problem of educated youth. Young people with a secondary education or above account for 95 percent of youth unemployment, up from 87 percent in 1998. Unemployment rates at the end of the 1990s were highest for those with a technical secondary education, followed by technical postsecondary institute graduates and university graduates. Figure 3-3 shows the relative unemployment rates at different education levels, by gender. By 2006 the pattern had changed, with university graduates experiencing the highest unemployment rates among young men and technical postsecondary institute graduates experiencing the highest rates among young women. In fact, university graduates are the only educational group whose unemployment rates have increased since 1998.

Figure 3-3. *Unemployment Rates by Educational Attainment and Sex, Ages 15 to 29, 1998 and 2006*

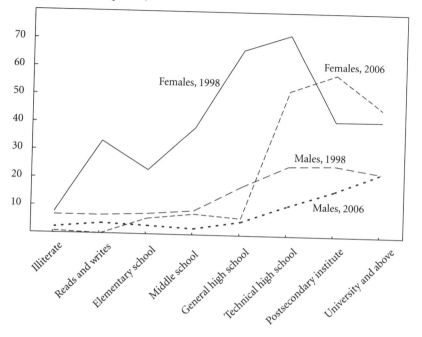

Source: Authors' calculations using standard unemployment and market labor force definitions.

The gender gap in unemployment in Egypt is among the highest in the region. Overall, women are four times as likely to be unemployed as men, and *young* women are 3.8 times as likely to be unemployed as *young* men. The very high unemployment rates for educated women are illustrated in figure 3-3. Unemployment rates for young women with technical secondary degrees have declined since 1998, while those for women with postsecondary technical institute degrees and university degrees have increased. The dramatic contraction in government hiring from 1998 to 2006 has led to fewer applications for government jobs among female technical secondary graduates. Because private sector wages are below the reservation wage for many young women, they grew discouraged and dropped out of the labor market altogether. Labor force participation for educated women in general also declined as a result of reduced employment rates in government during this period.[36]

The Search for Quality Jobs

The good news about declining unemployment among Egyptian youth is marred by growth in what the World Bank terms "bad jobs," or low-paying jobs that provide little in terms of social insurance, stability, and potential for advancement. Because employment is so important for securing livelihoods, social integration, and individual self-esteem, obtaining decent work is fundamental to improving quality of life.

A majority of young Egyptians are starting their careers in low-quality jobs. Only 33 percent of employed youth who receive wages have a legal contract with their employers; 30 percent have social insurance coverage; 21 percent have medical insurance, and 15 percent are members of a labor syndicate or a union. Moreover, just a fraction of youth receive a basic package of nonwage benefits such as paid vacations (23 percent) and sick leave (22 percent). In terms of earnings, 69 percent of working youth can be classified as low earners, based on the low earning threshold of the national poverty line.[37] Thus, the majority of youth who are able to obtain paid employment in fact work in poor-quality jobs that do not allow them to start families and complete their transition to adulthood and independence.

Barriers to Women's Employment

When it comes to women's access to employment, two major characteristics define their work trajectory. First, many are economically inactive, and their rates of inactivity are rising. This trend is especially pronounced among educated women. The proportion of female postsecondary and university graduates entering the labor market decreased dramatically from 1998 to 2006. A large proportion of young women never enter the labor market.[38] In contrast, employment is almost universal among men by age 29.[39] The decline in the number of young women in the job market probably can be attributed to the dearth of employment opportunities in the government, where most of these young women would have taken jobs in the past.

Second, a significant proportion of those who are economically active are unpaid family workers. As shown in table 3-1, only 22 percent of young women aged 15 to 29 were economically active in 2006 compared with 63 percent of males. While the share of those currently studying is about the same for young men and young women, the share of those who are inactive and not in school varies widely by gender.

Among employed females, nearly 37 percent are unpaid family workers, compared with 25 percent for males. The second highest form of employ-

Table 3-1. *Gender Disparity in Labor Market Participation for Youth Aged 15 to 29, 2006*
Percent

Employment status	Total population		Employed	
	Male	Female	Male	Female
Government employee	4.3	3.2	7.6	22.8
State-owned enterprise worker	1.7	0.3	3.0	1.9
Formal private wage worker	6.9	1.4	12.1	9.9
Informal private regular wage worker	18.1	2.7	31.8	19.3
Irregular wage worker	8.0	0.4	14.0	2.8
Unpaid family worker	14.1	5.2	24.8	36.6
Self-employed	3.9	0.9	6.8	6.7
Total employed	57.0	14.1	100.0	100.0
Unemployed	6.1	8.2		
Economically active (employed and unemployed)	63.1	22.3		
Student	27.6	24.0		
Inactive	8.6	53.5		
Disabled	0.7	0.2		
Total	100.0	100.0		

Source: Economic Research Forum, "Egyptian Labor Market Panel Survey, 2006" (www.erf.org.eg).

ment is as government workers, a status that young employed women are three times as likely to achieve as young men. Given the slow rate of growth in government employment, this underscores the fragility of future employment opportunities for young women.

If it is true that young women are withdrawing from the labor force because of the decline in government employment opportunities, the question is then: why are they unable to find appropriate jobs in the private sector?

On the supply side, evidence shows that more women are seeking to participate in paid work, but women continue to face barriers in the labor market. Many Egyptian women, including mothers, want to work if given the opportunity.[40] Their desire to work, however, is contingent on their ability to combine child care and work and whether a job is sufficiently rewarding to cover the many expenses incurred by being a working mother. Among the challenges that women face is employer discrimination, particularly against married women. Employers widely believe that the productivity of women declines after marriage and childbearing and that their absenteeism is higher than that of men's, especially when they have children.[41] Women, therefore, are preferred only in occupations that are not intensive and where turnover is high.

The cultural norms of the workplace present another obstacle to women's labor force participation. Women carry the brunt of a growing informality in the private sector. Working conditions in some parts of the private sector have been described as "unsuitable and hard," ultimately discouraging women from pursuing jobs in the private sector.[42] Small companies (those with fewer than ten workers) account for up to half of total employment opportunities in Egypt but do not give women the same sense of security as larger, more populated workplaces.[43] The fear of sexual harassment in smaller work settings has been cited as one of the major reasons why many female graduates decide to "respect themselves and stay at home," instead of exposing themselves to precarious working conditions.[44]

Another reason for the limited participation of women in the workforce is their restricted geographical mobility. Working women commute significantly less than men at a time when private sector employment requires workers to commute more.[45] Furthermore, job opportunities in the private sector are highly segmented across gender lines. Nine job types encompass 95 percent of all female nongovernmental paid work. Clerical work, teaching, and domestic service are the three major occupational fields for women.[46] The overcrowding of women in a limited number of occupations places downward pressure on their wages. Women in the private sector are paid significantly less than men. One study shows that female wage inequalities increased between 1988 and 1998, marking another barrier to women's work since their earnings are often well below the cost of their time, especially after marriage.[47]

The Transition to Marriage, Housing, and Family Formation

Two issues related to the timing of marriage and family formation are central to youth exclusion in Egypt. First is the persistence of underage marriage. Data show that almost 9 percent of women are married by the age of 15 and nearly 30 percent are married by 18.[48] Early marriage for young women in rural Egypt is closely related to limited or a lack of education, limited potentials for labor market participation, and early childbearing, which poses severe health risks to women in the form of maternal mortality and morbidity. However, the problem of early marriage seems to be declining: the percentage of women married by the age of 15 has dropped from 13 percent among women currently aged 45 to 49 to 3 percent among women currently aged 20 to 24.

Second, there is a trend toward delaying marriage, both for men and women, and, therefore, the existence of an increasing number of single people, particularly among men. Delayed marriage is primarily an urban phenomenon. Research attributes this phenomenon to the increased cost of marriage that, in turn, is connected to the increase in access to education.[49] Delayed marriage is a form of exclusion because these young people postpone forming families and leading independent adult lives; it is also connected to the emergence of nontraditional forms of marriage. These are often described as a way for young people to cope with the high costs of marriage, but they can also undermine women's legal rights as wives.

According to the most recent data, more than 9 percent of women are not married by the age of 34. The situation is much more pronounced for men: nearly 57 percent of men in urban areas are not married by the age of 29, and 22 percent are still unmarried by 34.

Marriage marks an important transition to adulthood in the Middle East. It is the stage at which young men and women are considered adults, since the unmarried generally continue to live with their parents. Delayed marriage, as rightfully described by Singerman, is a form of delayed adulthood or "wait adulthood."[50] In a society that frowns upon premarital sexual relations and ostracizes children born out of wedlock, delayed marriage is a serious form of youth exclusion.

A decline in economic opportunities available to young men is contributing to the delay in marriage.[51] Additionally, couples are more likely to aspire to live in independent households separate from their parents after marriage and to purchase more durable goods than couples in the past, making marriage in Egypt very costly.[52] Marriage costs are estimated at four and a half times the per capita gross national product and eleven times annual household expenditures.[53] In establishing a new household for a newlywed couple, the bride, groom, and their families invest significant resources, representing the largest intergenerational transfer of wealth for Egyptians. This transfer is often larger than that following the death of a parent.[54] Celebrations of marriage serve as a public display of the upward mobility of both the couple and their families, and saving for marriage is a major component of the budgets of working youth, particularly for women.[55]

The rising costs of housing also directly relate to the delay in marriage. In a survey about marriage trends in the Middle East, 59 percent of parents identified the cost of housing for a married couple as the main problem facing Egyptian youth.[56] In rural areas where delayed marriage is less prevalent, newly married couples tend to live with the man's family, thereby eliminating, or substantively decreasing, housing costs.

Finally, nontraditional forms of marriage often are described as a way for young people to cope with the high costs of marriage. Evidence-based research on the prevalence of 'urfi, or informal, marriage in Egypt is limited, but newspaper articles and television programs often mention its occurrence. The practice draws on the minimum Islamic requirements of the presence of only two witnesses for a marriage to be legitimate. This type of marriage is usually secret and carried out without informing parents. Consequently, women's legal rights as wives are undermined within this arrangement. Another form of wedlock is what has been termed *summer marriages*, whereby Arab tourists marry young Egyptian girls over the summer in return for a significant price. Most of these unions end in divorce at summer's end. Aside from the potential danger of sexually transmitted diseases, children born of these marriages have not been entitled to Egyptian citizenship or to the associated benefits of free government education and health care until recently.[57]

Exercising Citizenship

Active civic participation by youth has positive developmental outcomes and is integral to youth inclusion. It facilitates collective action, which can yield more effective and better-targeted youth services. It can also reduce corruption by allowing for channels of accountability.[58] Conversely, a lack of opportunities for civic participation by youth can lead to risky behavior and negative social roles, including criminal activity and religious militancy.

Outlets for civic participation by youth are very scarce in Egypt. One striking example is on-campus student activities. Interviews with several activists in universities reveal that outlets for activism are permitted only at private, elite universities because these campuses are considered less prone to violence and less susceptible to the influence of fundamentalist religious groups.[59]

For the majority of university campuses, security mechanisms designed to curtail activism of fundamentalist religious groups are applied to all student groups. For example, campus security officials impose strict censorship rules on the contents of student newsletters to avoid unrest. As a result, it can take up to six months for a youth group on campus to distribute a newsletter. A campus play must be approved by the dean and can be canceled without prior notice. Female students constitute a small minority of activist youth for reasons related to the proper role of women and to the overall limitations of these outlets for participation.

Consequently, many youth become cynical and unwilling to participate in what they perceive to be a closed system. Social disparities, widening gaps between rich and poor, a sense of limited future prospects given high unemployment rates among graduates, and the difficulties in forming families create a general sense that the system is corrupt and caters only to the privileged elite. For many youth, the main contact with the state is through the police, who are widely considered to be hostile and needlessly violent.

A recent United Nations Development Program (UNDP) survey reveals a prevailing apathy and lack of initiative among Egyptian youth, which is closely tied to their limited outlets for civic participation.[60] Young people report having "little faith that their own voices (and) efforts might be appreciated, heard or considered," and 67 percent admit to never being involved in any extracurricular school activities. Only 13 percent of respondents engage in some kind of volunteer work. While they report having a reasonable amount of leisure time, watching television is the most frequently performed activity, followed by listening to music and spending time with friends and family. The survey also reveals low levels of tolerance and acceptance of the "other," particularly those of a lower socioeconomic background and of different belief systems.

With the failure of secular channels to integrate youth as active civic participants, some have argued that Islamist movements provide an "alternative social, cultural, and moral community" for alienated groups, including youth.[61] Religious organizations can also provide space for youth volunteerism. Islamist social organizations also provide youth-specific services to young people from lower socioeconomic backgrounds. These include libraries, sports facilities, language and computer classes, video and television sessions, lectures, tours, and holidays. For many youth who participate in these activities, the religious social organization is the only avenue open to them for expanding their constrained environments. "Islamic weddings" are also examples of how these organizations cater to the needs of youth.[62]

The religious alternative also provides space for another socially alienated group: women. Bayat documents that weekly gatherings (*halaqat*) in urban neighborhoods assemble women from diverse socioeconomic backgrounds not only to learn about Islamic precepts but also to gain a sense of belonging to a moral community and to share experiences.[63]

Policies Promoting Youth Inclusion

There is much evidence that employment creation, particularly for youth, is at the top of the government's policy agenda. The "Putting Our Youth to Work" (*Shababna Ya'mal*) program, recently launched by the National Democratic Party, aims to create 4.5 million jobs in industry, agriculture, and tourism between 2005 and 2011. In 2003 Egypt became a lead country in the Youth Employment Network (YEN), which was instituted by the United Nations to develop and implement strategies that address youth employment.[64] The Egyptian national action plan is being formulated according to YEN's top four priorities: employability, equal opportunities for men and women, entrepreneurship, and employment generation.

Successful policies and interventions that address youth should be multisectoral and have a broad—not piecemeal—approach.[65] A number of indirect policies have an impact on youth by enhancing the economic environment and fostering job creation. Macroeconomic policies that seek to improve the investment climate, expand the private sector, and help trade to flourish by attracting foreign direct investment can have an indirect impact on youth through job creation. These include investment incentives to labor-intensive projects, trade liberalization, tariff reductions, international trade agreements, investment laws, and fiscal and monetary policies. The full impact of these policies has yet to be seen, but evidence of growth in private sector employment, particularly in textiles and clothing, can be attributed to some of these macroeconomic policies.[66] Active labor market and employment generation policies, education reforms, and housing sector policies can all have a direct impact on youth.

Labor Market Policies

The major structural change in labor market policy in recent years was the passage of a new labor law (Law No. 12 of 2003). Under the old labor law contracts of indefinite duration essentially meant lifetime job security unless a worker committed a "grave error" that would result in cause for dismissal. Under the new law employers have more flexibility in hiring and firing. Contracts for a defined period are permitted, can be renewed, and are not necessarily transformed into indefinite contracts. Moreover, the conditions under which employers can terminate an indefinite contract have been loosened significantly. Given the widespread evasion of labor regulations and the prevalence of informal employment relations under previous labor laws, however, the 2003 law will most likely lead to more formalized employment rather than new job creation.

Active labor market policies include employment services and job search assistance; training programs for the unemployed and youth; and job creation through wage and employment subsidies, public works, self-employment, and microfinance services. Examples of policies and programs at the ministerial and local government level include employment generation through the Public Works Program of the Social Fund for Development; the National Program for Integrated Rural Development through the Ministry of Local Development; small and microenterprise development programs through the Social Fund for Development; the Technical and Vocational Training Program (TVET) administered through the Ministry of Trade and Industry, with funding from the European Union; and employment services provided through the Ministry of Manpower and Migration.[67]

Most active labor market programs are provided primarily through governmental or quasi-governmental bodies. These suffer from a heavy reliance on international donor support, limited efficiency and impact evaluation, and skewed targeting; many programs are insufficiently institutionalized or integrated into a policy framework. Despite the success of some programs run by nongovernmental organizations, these programs remain small in scale and depend heavily on grants, limiting their sustainability over the long term. In addition, there have been no systematic evaluations of most of the programs and policies addressing youth employment in Egypt. Studies with pre- and postintervention designs involving control and intervention groups are very rare. This lack of evaluation creates a huge knowledge gap that hinders learning from experience and the creation of new projects. Finally, it has been argued that these programs have failed to meet their target.[68] For example, the impact of the public works program is limited to alleviating poverty during its implementation, with no sustainable job creation outcomes. Similarly, the majority of jobs created by the rural development program, *Shorouk*, were temporary.

Small and microenterprise programs primarily provide credit. Research shows no evidence that these programs have led to a significant growth of new jobs in Egypt. Credit programs in Egypt operate within two major models: business enhancement and economic survival (also known as poverty alleviation).

The business enhancement and growth model seeks to create employment by providing credit to existing businesses that are relatively capital intensive. Credit is provided chiefly by the Social Fund for Development through its Enterprise Development Program, the National Bank for Development, and business associations established as part of a U.S. Agency for International Development (USAID) initiative that started in 1988. Many credit programs lack follow-up and evaluation and are not successful because they require a certain level of formality, making them inaccessible to the large number of firms in the informal economy.[69] Thus, despite the plethora of microfinance programs, there remains an unmet need because of the restrictive requirements of many of the programs that provide credit.[70]

The economic survival model primarily deals with providing credit to home-based, small-scale economic activities and is the only credit mechanism available to those in the informal economy. Programs under this model provide credit primarily to women within a more development-oriented agenda through nongovernmental organizations and with substantial donor support. These programs have no clear focus on youth because the majority of their recipients are less-educated, older women. Finally, one significant gap in these microfinance programs is the lack of lending mechanisms for poorer men.[71]

Many government vocational training programs are initiated without proper outreach and therefore have limited coverage. The majority also are short term and therefore do not allow for apprenticeship and comprehensive and thorough training. The Technical and Vocational Training program involves twenty-two agencies and ministries.[72] TVET has been criticized for its poorly equipped and outdated facilities, unqualified teachers, and obsolete curricula; recently, a national strategy was finalized to redesign and upgrade its operation.[73]

A number of nongovernmental organizations operate vocational training programs. These include the Center for Development Services and the Coptic Evangelical Organization for Social Services. These nongovernmental organizations provide financial support for training through existing workshops, both in the informal and the formal sector.[74] Some evaluations show a high rate of employment (from 60 to 70 percent) for participants who have completed the training, but the vocational training programs operate on a very small scale, with limited outreach and questionable sustainability.

A more promising vocational training model is the Mubarak-Kohl Initiative, which started in 1994 with support from the German government and was scheduled to run until the end of 2008. The program targeted students who had completed their basic education. Students attended school two days a week and underwent practical training for the rest of the week.

Upon successful completion of their studies, students received a Ministry of Education diploma and a certificate from a relevant private-sector business association. Implementation depended on the active involvement and participation of the business community, where businesses contributed training opportunities and paid a stipend to apprentices during their training period. An evaluation of the first phase of the program showed that program graduates were in demand in the labor market. However, the evaluation also showed that 60 percent of the graduates decided to pursue higher education after receiving their diplomas instead of working as technicians. This was an atypical pattern, which signifies that the program is reaching only above-average students. This program faced major obstacles including the limited participation of the business community and financial sustainability issues.

Programs that provide labor market information and employment services are limited in Egypt. Youth lack information about where to find jobs, where to receive training, and what types of training are needed in the labor market; no programs specifically address these needs. Barsoum illustrates the case of female graduates seeking clerical jobs who fail to choose appropriate computer training courses and end up taking irrelevant classes.[75] The Canadian International Development Agency is implementing a program designed to provide counseling services, job-matching services for employers and employees, and job-related databases for job seekers, employers, trainers, and government agencies. A similar program is being implemented by nongovernmental organizations with support from USAID to establish employment and career development service offices at Cairo University and Ain Shams University for students and recent graduates.

Education Reform

A recent strategy paper by the Ministry of Education highlights two central areas for education reform. The first area is equality of quality education, which primarily addresses issues of class size, teacher qualifications, curriculum development, and teaching methods. The strategy paper notes that "a system that serves a small minority with a 'high standard,' but serves a large majority poorly, cannot be considered equitable, and such a system would produce lowered rates of return to education investment."[76] The second area for reform is efficiency of education expenditures, a concern that relates to issues of access to schooling, school construction, and targeting and implementation. This objective also addresses textbook costs, which accounted for 6 percent of overall pre-university expenditures during the 2003–04 school year.[77]

A number of additional education reform initiatives and programs are being implemented. In general, these programs and reforms rely heavily on donor support and have not yet been evaluated. A UNICEF initiative is designed to establish girl-friendly community schools. The program was offered initially to the National Council for Children and Motherhood and has been adopted by the Ministry of Education. The Egypt Education Reform Program is a bilateral agreement between the Ministry of Education and USAID. It seeks to replicate in seven governorates a pilot program first introduced in Alexandria to decentralize education, increase community participation through boards of trustees, and improve teacher training. The World Bank Skill Development Project was created to help employers in small and medium-size firms identify their human resource and skill training needs. Linking trainers and employers and stimulating private sector demand for training are among the project's objectives.

Housing Reform

A recent World Bank report argues that the urban housing crisis in Egypt is the result of distortions in the housing market caused by an "accumulation of ill-conceived and inadequate policies that led over time to creating a mismatch between supply and demand and to severely curtailing private sector investment in housing supply."[78] These policies include major government involvement in construction activities and a history of rent control legislation and rigid tenant protection practices that inhibited private sector investment in housing. As a result, it is recommended that the government devise affordable housing policies and strategies to address the distortions that prevent the housing market from functioning efficiently.

Recent housing policy reforms have been two-pronged. The first approach is the new housing law (Law No. 4 of 1996), which seeks to remove rent control legislation. The objective of the law is to encourage private owners of vacant units and investors to return to the rental market on a free market basis without government restrictions on rates or duration of leases. The new law provides a solution for large numbers of newly formed families and middle- and upper-middle-income groups. Recent research suggests that by making rental housing units more accessible to young Egyptian men, the law has also allowed some young men to get married at an earlier age, helping reverse the trend of delayed marriage. However, private owners remain wary of the courts' ability to enforce tenant eviction, limiting the potential impact of the new law. [79]

The government's second approach to housing policy has been to increase the public supply of affordable housing. Recent efforts to expand affordable housing have been criticized for high costs and inefficiencies, however. Moreover, problems related to nepotism and inequitable distribution of affordable housing units have plagued the program.

Recommended reforms include transforming the government's role from directly supplying housing to supporting and enabling the private sector to deliver housing. Further, the government should move to address problems associated with the land and property registration system in urban areas, which hamper access to mortgage and housing finance. Although the government developed a regulatory framework for housing mortgage finance in 2001, it has had little impact because of the limited registration of properties in urban areas.

Conclusion: Tapping the Potential of a Generation

Inclusion of young Egyptians hinges on success in four critical transitions: education, employment, family formation, and civic participation. Failures in one transition can easily spill over into another. Poor learning leads to poor job prospects—the uneducated tend to become unpaid family workers, while those with an education above the intermediate level are more likely to be salaried workers. Yet, even obtaining a university degree does little to guarantee access to the competitive job market or a stable livelihood. As young people seek to achieve personal independence, their opportunities to marry, acquire housing, and form families are closely linked to productive employment and adequate earnings. The unemployed and those trapped in low-paying jobs face overwhelming challenges in forming families because of the high costs of marriage. Finally, channels for effective civic participation are absent for young people in Egypt and in the Middle East more generally. When these avenues are open, youth can exercise important skills and become exposed to the merits of collective action. When these channels are cut off, young people will be more prone to cynicism, apathy, and risky behavior.

Direct policies to promote youth inclusion are primarily focused on three dimensions: employment, education, and housing. To date, many policies aimed at promoting youth inclusion are implemented without any rigorous impact assessment. Often, policy interventions rely on close donor support, which hampers their long-term sustainability. Those provided through government or quasi-government bodies suffer from limited efficiency and skewed targeting, preventing these isolated efforts from addressing the root problems comprehensively. Well-designed policies can be successful only if key stakeholders and allies—such as youth, parents, educators, and employers—are engaged from the beginning of the process. In this way, Egypt can capitalize on the opportunities for growth and development created by its youth bulge and this historic demographic transition.

Notes

1. Central Agency for Public Mobilization and Statistics, Arab Republic of Egypt, *Statistical Yearbook* (Cairo: 2007).

2. Ragui Assaad and Rania Roushdy, "Poverty and the Labor Market in Egypt: A Review of Developments in the 1998–2006 Period," background paper prepared for the Egypt Poverty Assessment Update (Washington: World Bank, 2006).

3. Central Agency for Public Mobilization and Statistics, Arab Republic of Egypt, *Statistical Yearbook* (Cairo: 2004).

4. Egypt has two major geographic regions: Upper Egypt and Lower Egypt. Geographically, Upper Egypt is a narrow strip of land that extends from the cataract boundaries of Aswan to the area south of Cairo. For the purpose of this analysis, Upper Egypt does not include Cairo: Greater Cairo is counted as a separate region. Lower Egypt is the northernmost section of the country, stretching from just south of Cairo to the Nile Delta in Alexandria on the Mediterranean. For the purpose of this analysis, Lower Egypt does not include Alexandria: it and the Suez Canal cities are counted as a separate region.

5. Calculations by the authors, comparing Egypt Labor Market Panel Survey of 2006 (ELMPS 06) data to Labor Force Sample Survey (LFSS 1988) data.

6. Mae Chu Chang and others, *Arab Republic of Egypt Educational Sector Review: Progress and Priorities for the Future* (Washington: World Bank, 2002).

7. Based on Ministry of Education data.

8. United Nations Development Program (UNDP) and Institute of National Planning (Egypt), *Egypt Human Development Report 2005, Choosing Our Future: Towards a New Social Contract* (New York: 2005).

9. Martha Brady and others, "Providing New Opportunities to Adolescent Girls in Socially Conservative Settings: The Ishraq Program in Rural Upper Egypt" (New York: Population Council, 2007). See www.popcouncil.org/pdfs/IshraqFullReport.pdf.

10. Asmaa Elbadawy and others, "Private and Group Tutoring in Egypt: Where Is the Gender Inequality?" Working Paper 0429 (Cairo: Economic Research Forum, 2007).

11. Cynthia Lloyd and others, "Determinants of Educational Attainment among Adolescents in Egypt: Does School Quality Make a Difference?" (New York: Population Council, 2001).

12. UNDP and Institute of National Planning, *Egypt Human Development Report 2005.*

13. Ministry of Education, Arab Republic of Egypt, "Improving Quality, Equality, and Efficiency in the Education Sector: Fostering a Competent Generation of Youth: A Strategic Decisions Paper" (Cairo: October 5, 2005).

14. Sahar El-Tawila and others, *The School Environment in Egypt, A Situation Analysis of Public Preparatory Schools* (Cairo: Population Council, 2000).

15. Ina V. S. Mullis and others, *TIMSS 2007 International Mathematics Report* (Boston College, Lynch School of Education, TIMSS & PIRLS International Study Center, 2008); Michael O. Martin and others, *TIMSS 2007 International Science Report.* (Boston College, Lynch School of Education, TIMSS & PIRLS International Study Center, 2008).

16. Mae Chu Chang and others (2002), cited in Mattias Lindgren, *Does Schooling Make Sense? A Household Perspective on the Returns to Schooling for Self-employed, Farmers and Employees in Egypt* (Stockholm: Almqvist & Wiksell International, 2005).

17. Ibid.

18. Elbadawy and others, "Private and Group Tutoring in Egypt."

19. Ibid.

20. Magda Abdel Kader, Abdul-ghani Mohamed, and Leila Nuwar, "Awda'a itijaa-hat al-shebaab fi misr (Situation and Attitudes of Youth in Egypt)" (Cairo: Cairo Demographic Center, 2006).

21. Interview by Ghada Barsoum (January 2006).

22. Manos Antoninis, "The Vocational School Fallacy Revisited: Technical Secondary Schools in Egypt," European University Institute Working Papers, Robert Schumann Centre for Advanced Studies Mediterranean Programme Series 22 (Florence: 2001), www.iue.it/RSCAS/WP-Texts/01_22.pdf; Fatma El-Hamidi, "General or Vocational? Evidence on School Choice, Returns, and 'Sheep Skin' Effects from Egypt 1998," *Journal of Policy Reform* 9, no. 2 (2006): 157–76.

23. Antoninis, "The Vocational School Fallacy Revisited."

24. Ministry of Education, Arab Republic of Egypt, *Annual Statistical Yearbook.* (Cairo: 2008). See http://services.moe.gov.eg/egov_statbook.html.

25. Ragui Assaad, "Institutions, Household Decisions, and Economic Growth in Egypt," in *Explaining Growth in the Middle East,* edited by J. Nugent and H. Pesaran (Amsterdam: Elsevier, 2006).

26. Ibid.

27. Ragui Assaad, "Unemployment and Youth Insertion in the Labor Market in Egypt," in *The Egyptian Economy: Current Challenges and Future Prospects,* edited by Hanaa Kheir-El-Din (American University in Cairo Press, 2008).

28. Ibid.

29. Ibid.

30. Ragui Assaad, "Employment and Unemployment Dynamics," paper presented at the Egypt Labor Market Panel Survey 2006: ERF Dissemination Conference (Cairo, October 30, 2006).

31. Ragui Assaad and Farzaneh Roudi-Fahimi, "Youth in the Middle East and North Africa: Demographic Opportunity or Challenge?" (New York: Population Reference Bureau, 2007).

32. International Labor Organization (ILO), "School-to-Work Transition, Evidence from Egypt" (Cairo: 2006).

33. Mona Amer, "The Egyptian Youth Labor Market School-to-Work Transition 1998–2006," paper presented at the Egypt Labor Market Panel Survey 2006: ERF Dissemination Conference (Cairo, October 30, 2006); Assaad, "Employment and Unemployment Dynamics."

34. Ghada Barsoum, "The Employment Crisis of Female Graduates in Egypt: An Ethnographic Account," Cairo Papers in Social Science 25 (Cairo: American University in Cairo Press, 2004).

35. Amer, "The Egyptian Youth Labor Market School-to-Work Transition."

36. Assaad, "Unemployment and Youth Insertion in the Labor Market in Egypt."

37. Assaad and Roushdy, "Poverty and the Labor Market in Egypt."

38. Amer, "The Egyptian Youth Labor Market School-to-Work Transition."

39. Ibid.

40. Ghada Barsoum, "The Balance Act of Mothering and Working in the Private Sector in Egypt: An Ethnographic Account," paper presented at the Economic Research Forum Research Workshop on Gender, Work and Family in the Middle East and North Africa (Tunisia, June 8–10, 2004).

41. V. M. Moghadam, Women, Work, and Economic Reform in the Middle East and North Africa (Boulder, Colo.: Lynne Rienner, 1998).

42. Sajeda Amin and Nagah Al-Bassusi, "Education, Wage Work, and Marriage: Perspectives of Egyptian Working Women," Journal of Marriage and Family 66, no. 5 (2002): 1287–1300.

43. ILO, "The Labor Market Context" (Cairo: 1997); Barsoum, "The Employment Crisis of Female Graduates in Egypt."

44. Barsoum, "The Employment Crisis of Female Graduates in Egypt."

45. Ragui Assaad and Melanie Arntz, "Constrained Geographical Mobility and Gendered Labor Market Outcomes under Structural Adjustment: Evidence from Egypt," World Development 33, no. 3 (2005): 431–54.

46. Ibid.

47. Mona Amer, "Youth Labor Market Trajectories: A Comparison of the 1980s and the 1990s," in The Egyptian Labor Market in an Era of Reform, edited by Ragui Assaad (American University in Cairo Press, 2002).

48. Ministry of Health and Population, Egypt Demographic and Health Survey (EDHS) 2005 (Cairo: Ministry of Health and Population, National Population Council, El-Zanaty and Associates, and ORC Macro, 2006).

49. Diane Singerman and Barbara Ibrahim, "The Cost of Marriage in Egypt: A Hidden Variable in the New Arab Demography," in The New Arab Family, Cairo Papers in Social Science 24(1/2), edited by Nicholas Hopkins (American University in Cairo Press, 2001).

50. Diane Singerman, "The Economic Imperatives of Marriage: Emerging Practices and Identities among Youth in the Middle East," Middle East Youth Initiative Working Paper 6 (Wolfensohn Center for Development at Brookings and the Dubai School of Government, 2007). See www.shababinclusion.org/content/document/detail/559/.

51. Singerman and Ibrahim, "The Cost of Marriage in Egypt."

52. Diane Singerman and Homa Hoodfar, *Development, Change, and Gender in Cairo: A View of the Household* (Indiana University Press, 1996); Homa Hoodfar, *Between Marriage and the Market: Intimate Politics of Survival in Cairo* (University of California Press, 1997).

53. Singerman, "The Economic Imperatives of Marriage."

54. Singerman and Ibrahim, "The Cost of Marriage in Egypt."

55. Abdel Kader, Mohamed, and Nuwar, "Situation and Attitudes of Youth in Egypt."

56. Singerman and Ibrahim, "The Cost of Marriage in Egypt."

57. Bonnie Shepard and Jocelyn DeJong, *Breaking the Silence and Saving Lives: Young People's Sexual and Reproductive Health in the Arab States and Iran* (Boston: International Health and Human Rights Program, 2005).

58. World Bank, *World Development Report 2007: Development and the Next Generation* (Washington: 2006).

59. Interviews by Ghada Barsoum (January 2006).

60. UNDP, "Youth Aspiration Survey: Egyptian Youth: Aspirations, Ambitions, Opportunities and Possibilities," unpublished report (Cairo: 2007).

61. Asef Bayat, "Revolution without Movement, Movement without Revolution: Comparing Islamic Activism in Iran and Egypt," *Comparative Studies in Society and History* 40 (1998): 136–69.

62. Ibid.

63. Ibid.

64. Maggie Kamel, "Situational Analysis of Youth Employment in Egypt" (Cairo: Center for Project Evaluation and Macroeconomic Analysis, Ministry of International Cooperation, 2006).

65. World Bank, *World Development Report 2007.*

66. Assaad, "Unemployment and Youth Insertion in the Labor Market in Egypt."

67. The Social Fund for Development is an independent, semi-autonomous government agency.

68. Nihal El-Megharbel, "The Impact of Recent Macro and Labor Market Policies on Job Creation in Egypt," in *The Egyptian Economy: Current Challenges and Future Prospects*, edited by Hanaa Kheir-El-Din (American University in Cairo Press, 2008).

69. Ibid.

70. Ghada Barsoum, "Who Gets Credit?: The Gendered Division of Microfinance Programs in Egypt," *Canadian Journal of Development Studies* 27, no. 1 (2006): 51–64.

71. Ibid.

72. El-Megharbel, "The Impact of Recent Macro and Labor Market Policies on Job Creation in Egypt."

73. Ibid.

74. Kamel, "Situational Analysis of Youth Employment in Egypt."

75. Barsoum, "The Employment Crisis of Female Graduates in Egypt."

76. Ministry of Education, "Improving Quality, Equality, and Efficiency in the Education Sector."

77. World Bank, "Making Egyptian Education Spending More Effective," Egypt Public Expenditure Review (Washington: Social and Economic Development Group, Middle East and North Africa Region, 2005).

78. World Bank, "Analysis of Housing Supply Mechanisms" (Washington: 2006).

79. Ragui Assaad and Mohamed Ramadan, "Did Housing Policy Reforms Curb the Delay in Marriage among Young Men in Egypt?" Middle East Youth Initiative Policy Outlook 1 (Wolfensohn Center for Development at the Brookings Institution and the Dubai School of Government, 2008). See www.shababinclusion.org/content/document/detail/1226/.

EDWARD SAYRE *and* SAMIA AL-BOTMEH

4

In Search of a Future:
The Struggle of Young Palestinians

Youth in the West Bank and Gaza Strip experience many of the same challenges faced by youth throughout the region, but from their earliest years they are also confronted with a unique political situation. The conflict between Palestinians and Israel influences every aspect of the lives of young people in the West Bank and Gaza. It defines how, when, and where they go to school; their ability to find work and secure jobs that match their skills; and expectations for, and the form of, political participation in which they are involved.[1] Finally, the political situation has even affected fertility rates, implying that the conflict intervenes in the formation of families.[2]

The political situation creates a number of social problems for youth. Normal daily activities of youth are regularly interrupted, and schooling can be interrupted for weeks on end by Israeli-imposed mobility restrictions. Safety concerns often make families wary of allowing children outside. With open battles in the streets of Palestinian cities, young people have few opportunities for outdoor exercise and socializing. Not surprisingly, the most common leisure activity for Palestinian youth is watching television.[3] However, despite the strain on educational resources imposed by the conflict and a rapidly growing youth population, the proportion of young men and women who are staying in school continues to grow each year. More students are staying in school for longer at each level of schooling, and four times as many Palestinians attend college and university than did just a decade ago.

Another aspect of growing up in the West Bank and Gaza is the threat of physical violence. According to a survey conducted in 2003, fully 13 percent of young males and 11 percent of young females had experienced some type of violence during the survey's reference month.[4] While most youth suffer violence at the hands of a relative, especially a sibling or parent, there is a another source of violence for young Palestinians. More than 9 percent of the survey respondents who suffered violence had been subjected to violence by Israeli forces in the previous month. For young men aged 20 to 24, more than a third of those reporting violence against them suffered violence at the hands of Israelis.

Once Palestinian youth have entered the job market, they find that it is intensely constrained by the political climate. Whereas one-third of all Palestinian jobs used to be in Israel, the Israeli labor market is now closed to most Palestinian youth. A generation ago, the Israeli labor market employed 130,000 Palestinians. Today, despite a doubling of the Palestinian labor force, fewer than 50,000 Palestinians work in Israel. Two generations ago, many young Palestinians would have left the West Bank and Gaza to work in the Persian Gulf. However, changes in hiring practices eliminated most of that job market by the mid-1980s.[5] At the same time, industrial zones in Gaza have been closed. Land seizures for the expansion of Israeli settlements in the West Bank have limited economic activity. Political violence has stymied efforts to expand the tourism industry that could produce new jobs. Instead, the only sector in the West Bank and Gaza Strip that continues to grow is the public sector. Funded by outside aid, the Palestinian Authority (PA) has created a rentier state that does not depend upon local production to fund the machinery of government. This has led to a situation where the government is seen as a key provider of employment for youth. The higher salaries earned in the public sector also put upward pressure on reservation wages for recent graduates, leading to longer periods spent waiting for their first job after graduating.

Demography of the West Bank and Gaza Strip

The Palestinian population is characterized by several demographic trends. Most dramatically, Gaza (and the West Bank, to a lesser extent) has undergone a rapidly growing population, especially compared with neighboring Arab countries. This rapid population growth will lead to unique challenges given the relative poverty of Gaza and the continuing pressures of conflict. The population of the West Bank and Gaza has mushroomed from approximately 2.9 million to 3.8 million during the last ten years, representing a dramatic 30 percent increase.[6] In Gaza, the population increased nearly 40

Figure 4-1. *Percent of Population Aged 15 to 29 by Year and Region*[a]

Percent of total population

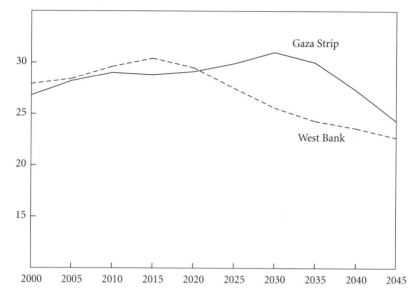

Source: U.S. Census International Database.
a. Numbers before 2007 are actual, while those after 2007 are projections.

percent from 1997 to 2007. Population growth in the West Bank was relatively slower: from 1.9 million in 1997 to 2.3 million in 2007.

Youth are an important and growing part of the Palestinian population. In the West Bank, more than seven in ten residents are under the age of 29. In Gaza, the number is even greater, with three-fourths of Gazans under the age of 29 and nearly half (45 percent) under the age of 15.

The percentage of youth in Palestinian society will continue to grow for another generation (figure 4-1). Specifically, in Gaza the share of the population aged 15 to 29 is expected to remain fairly steady at its current level of 28 to 30 percent of the total population until the year 2035. In the West Bank, the proportion of the population between 15 and 29 is expected to remain between 28 and 30 percent until 2020. Beginning in 2020, decreasing fertility rates in the West Bank will begin to yield smaller and smaller cohorts, until youth make up less than 25 percent of the total West Bank population in 2035.

High fertility in the 1980s and 1990s along with return migration stemming from positive political developments in the 1990s have added significantly to the size of the Palestinian population. Fertility rates in Egypt, Jordan, and Syria have dropped substantially since the mid-1980s, but they have been slower to fall among Palestinian women. The average fertility rate from 1990 to 1994 in the West Bank was 5.8 children per woman. In the Gaza Strip the rate was much higher, at about 7.8 children per woman.[7] These rates are high compared with total fertility rates that fell below 4.0 in Egypt during the 1990s and are currently at 3.5 for both Jordan and Syria.[8] In both the West Bank and Gaza, residents of refugee camps have fertility rates that are very close to the average for the region. The most recent figures estimate that the overall fertility rate for Palestinian women has fallen to 5.6 children per woman.

The continued growth of the Palestinian population will put pressure on the educational system and the labor market for several decades. Currently, each new cohort of Palestinian children entering school for the first year is of record size. This puts pressure on the PA government to find the necessary resources, including classrooms and teachers, to accommodate these students. Continuing fiscal pressures mean that the current budget for education will not be sufficient to accommodate the nearly 40,000 additional students that enter the Palestinian educational system each year.

Education

The status of education in the West Bank and Gaza is mixed. The rapidly growing population is becoming increasingly more educated. Primary school enrollment is nearly universal, and enrollment in secondary and tertiary education is growing. Furthermore, girls and young women are becoming increasingly educated, and their enrollment rates now exceed those for boys at all educational levels in both the West Bank and Gaza. Serious concerns still remain about the overall quality of education for Palestinians, however. While quantifiable measures of educational quality (including class size, student-to-teacher ratios, and total educational resources expended) continue to improve, there are widespread complaints by students about the quality of textbooks and the relevance of the curriculum. Furthermore, the political situation negatively affects young Palestinians' educational experiences by inhibiting the ability of teachers and students to reach schools.

Enrollment Rates

The Palestinian education system at the primary and secondary levels is similar in many ways to those in other Arab countries. However, it also has some distinct features that arise from the political environment and the unique history of occupation and foreign intervention. Palestinian government schools provide education to the majority of children. The private school system is a collection of independent schools, each usually associated with a specific Christian church. These private schools have enrollments that are roughly one-tenth the size of government school enrollment.

A third school system is run by the United Nations Relief Works Agency (UNRWA) and operates solely for the benefit of registered Palestinian refugee families in the West Bank, Gaza, Jordan, Lebanon, and Syria. UNRWA operates 180 schools in Gaza alone and a total of 644 in all five service areas.[9] This education is provided free of charge for all elementary school children and for early stages of secondary school. UNRWA schools have provided rapidly expanding educational opportunities for Palestinians. The growth of the UNRWA school system in the 1950s has led to an increasingly educated middle class of Palestinians and is credited as one of the reasons why Palestinian society has become among the best educated in the Arab world.[10]

With rising enrollment rates in both primary and secondary education, the average level of schooling of young Palestinians has increased. In the mid-1990s young men and women in the West Bank had approximately 9.5 years of schooling (figure 4-2).[11] Both young men and women in Gaza show higher levels of schooling than young West Bank Palestinians. By 2002 the average level of schooling for all youth in both territories had risen to over 10 years. By 2006 the overall level had risen to 10.7 years, with the exception of West Bank men who had less than 10.5 years of schooling. Importantly, women have now surpassed (in the West Bank) or equaled (in Gaza) men in educational attainment.

When looking at enrollment rates by education level and gender, the tremendous gains in education as well as the areas for further improvements become more apparent. At the primary level of education, male enrollment increased from 88 percent to 93 percent between 1995 and 2000 in the West Bank and from 99 percent to 100 percent in Gaza. During the same time period, female primary enrollment increased from 87 percent to 95 percent in the West Bank and from 98 percent to 101 percent in Gaza. At the secondary level of education, male enrollment increased from 46 percent to 48 percent in the West Bank and from 55 percent to 65 percent in Gaza. During the same time period, female secondary enrollment increased from 41 percent to 56 percent in the West Bank and from 47 percent to 66 percent in Gaza.

Figure 4-2. *Average Schooling for Palestinians, 1996–2006*

Average years of schooling of 15- to 64-year-olds

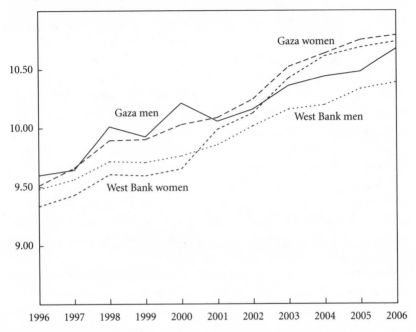

Educational Quality

Standard measures of educational quality indicate clear progress in the Palestinian educational system over the past fifteen years, despite the difficulties facing students posed by the political conflict. Measures such as student-to-teacher ratios, educational expenditures, and dropout rates show that educational inputs and outputs continue to improve in the face of considerable challenges from the increasing numbers of students. For example, the number of students per teacher declined in public, private, and UNRWA schools from 1995 to 2007.

Additionally, the primary school dropout rate for men in the West Bank and Gaza decreased from 2.6 percent in 1994–95 to 1.8 percent 1998–99 and to 0.9 percent in the 2005–06 academic year. The decrease in female dropout rates was even more impressive, falling from 2.4 percent in 1994–95 to 1.4 percent in 1999 and to a miniscule 0.1 percent by 2005–06.

There are two main criticisms concerning the quality of education in the West Bank and Gaza. First, students do not learn what they need to learn to get jobs, become productive citizens, or succeed in college and university. Nearly a quarter of students claim that schools are not appropriately equipped, and nearly a fifth claim that teachers are not sufficiently qualified.[12] Additionally, over half of unsuccessful job seekers claim that there is not sufficient demand for their academic specialty.[13]

Second, curriculum and teaching methods favor rote learning over critical thinking and problem solving.[14] This issue was partially addressed in a recent series of educational reforms undertaken by the Ministry of Education and Higher Education to unify the school systems of the West Bank and Gaza, which had previously used Jordanian and Egyptian curricula, respectively. Additionally, a modified curriculum unveiled in 2000 included support for active pedagogy over rote instruction.[15] Other changes included introducing English and civics in grades one to four; elective subjects, including a third language, in grades five to eight; and additional technical subjects in grade ten. Not surprisingly, some students and teachers have criticized the new curriculum as being too advanced and requiring too much effort on the part of both students and teachers.[16]

Some criticism has been levied at the political nature of the educational system, especially higher education. When asked about their most pressing concerns with education, many students cited the *wasta* system, in which people are selected for a job or admission to a school or program based upon personal or political connections rather than on merit.[17] While the survey is too anecdotal to draw broader conclusions, many of those interviewed generally saw the system of college and university admissions as being unfair.

Higher Education

Once students complete tenth grade, they may enroll in one of three tracks, depending on their grades: sciences, literature and humanities, or vocational education. The highest grades are required for the sciences track, followed by the literary and vocational tracks. Students with the highest grades are automatically enrolled in the sciences track but can choose to switch to the literary or vocational tracks. Students in the literary track can also switch into the vocational track, but students enlisted in vocational education may not switch into the literary or sciences tracks. This tracking system has negative repercussions for vocational education, which is viewed as the most inferior type of education, in which only low-performing students are enrolled.

Graduates of the sciences track who perform well are usually accepted at university and allowed to pursue any subject they wish, whereas graduates of the literary track are restricted in the number of subjects they may pursue at the university level and may not enroll in natural sciences, mathematics, engineering, or medicine. Vocational education graduates normally enroll in vocational colleges and are restricted from a large group of subjects.

Despite these challenges related to the tracking system, more and more young Palestinians are entering higher education. Enrollment in higher education has increased significantly, from approximately 30,000 in 1995 to over 120,000 in 2004.[18] Women now outnumber men in higher education. Counting students enrolled in certificate, graduate, and diploma programs, total enrollment in 2004 stood at 138,000 students in all two-year and four-year tertiary programs. These figures translate into a 48 percent gross tertiary enrollment rate, with a rate of 53 percent for women and 44 percent for men.[19] This growth represents nearly a doubling of the enrollment rate over an eight-year period.

The rise in female enrollment rates (especially at the upper secondary and tertiary levels) is linked to the crucial role of higher education for women's participation in the formal labor market. For some households, higher education provides daughters with a life guarantee in case of future marital breakdown or male joblessness. For others, higher education is a practical investment in the near future, leading to an extra income for the family. Education is also perceived as a benefit in marriage that betters a young woman's chances of finding a suitable spouse and helps her contribute to a better standard of living for her future family.

To meet the growing demand for tertiary education, the number of higher education institutions in the West Bank and Gaza is continuously expanding. Recently several colleges have been established that focus on nursing and technical skills, and the Arab American University in Jenin was opened in 2000. Additionally, Al-Quds Open University was established in 1991 as a distance-learning institution with twenty-four education and study centers spread throughout the West Bank and Gaza. The Open University is now the largest higher education institution in all of the West Bank and Gaza with over 46,000 students.[20]

School-to-Work Transition

When young Palestinians finish school, they face an uncertain job market. Although most recent graduates of vocational schools, colleges, and universities report that they eventually find jobs that match their skills, the search can be lengthy. The median waiting time is almost two years, and nearly a quarter do not have jobs five years after finishing school. While many recent graduates may do unpaid work for a family member while they are waiting for a job, there is a significant gap between the skills gained through higher education and those demanded by employers. Unfortunately, even if graduates have the requisite skills, they often do not have the personal or political connections necessary to get the kind of job they want. Once they find jobs, their wages are lower and their opportunities for advancement are more limited than those of previous generations.

Labor Market Entry

Given the demographic pressures created by high fertility rates and the youth bulge, the labor force is expanding rapidly in the West Bank and Gaza. It grew at an annual rate of 1.9 percent from 1970 to 1980, then increased to 3.2 percent from 1988 to 1993 and further accelerated to 4.1 percent from 1995 to 2000.[21] As large birth cohorts from the 1980s in Gaza began to enter the labor force in 2001, the labor force continued growing at an annual pace of 3.9 percent from 2001 to 2006.[22]

Because they are more likely to still be in school, young people generally have lower labor force participation—meaning that they are either working or actively seeking a job and are not full-time students—than older potential workers, and that is the case for young Palestinians. There is a clear trend of decreasing labor force participation among young men. The labor force participation rate of young West Bank men (aged 15 to 29) exceeded 65 percent between 1995 and 1999, but since then the rate has dropped to just over 55 percent. A similar pattern emerges in Gaza. Between 54 percent and 58 percent of young Gazan men were in the labor force in the 1990s, but since 2000 their participation rate has fallen to less than 45 percent.

Labor force participation rates among women in the two territories are much lower than those of Palestinian men. Slightly under 15 percent of West Bank women and only 8 percent of all Gazan women are included in the labor force. For young women (aged 15 to 29), the rates are even lower, averaging 11 percent for the West Bank and 6 percent for Gaza between 1995 and 2006. These levels are low partially because these young women are still in school or already starting families. Most female college and university graduates that do not seek a job are focusing on their role in the household.

Post-graduation Choices and Youth Unemployment

The choices and activities that graduates of higher education make immediately after completing schooling also determine labor force participation.[23] Over 50 percent of graduates seek work immediately following school but do not get a job within six months. Another 31 percent of graduates either secure jobs while they are in school and start immediately following graduation or find a job within six months. These choices vary by education levels: graduates with bachelor's degrees are most successful in getting jobs quickly, and a full third of these graduates are employed within six months. At the opposite extreme, 22 percent of vocational school graduates do not look for a job after graduation.

Postgraduation plans vary by gender. Twenty percent of women do not seek work after graduating, while only 3 percent of men do not choose to work following school. Nearly three-quarters of the women who do not seek work and are not employed make that decision because they married or specialize in home production (provision of services to the family such as cooking, cleaning, and raising children), or both. Men are more likely to stay in the same job they had during school or to find work almost immediately after graduating.

Similar to other countries in the region, Palestinian youth face substantially higher unemployment rates than older workers. Young men from the West Bank have unemployment rates that are generally 1.5 to 1.75 times as high as the rate for adult men.[24] Young men in the West Bank have an average unemployment rate of 25 percent compared with 16 percent for older men. At an average of 36 percent, the youth unemployment rate in Gaza is generally 1.25 to 2 times the rate of older men, a quarter of whom are unemployed.

There are a few caveats to these numbers. First, the labor force participation rate of young men in Gaza is more than fifteen percentage points lower than the average participation rate. Thus many youth may not be counted as unemployed because they are not in the labor force at all. Second, political shocks cause unemployment rates to fluctuate greatly, so during some periods the unemployment rate for young men in Gaza can reach levels exceeding 50 percent.

Young women are more disadvantaged in the labor market than young men. Young women in the West Bank experience two to three times the risk of unemployment compared with older women in the West Bank, while young Gazan women generally experience two to four times the risk compared with older women.

Exposure to the risk of unemployment varies with age and education. Highly educated Palestinian youth experience higher unemployment rates. In the West Bank, the men with the highest rates of unemployment are those aged 20 to 24 with a university education (table 4-1). This group has nearly three times the unemployment rate as university-educated workers aged 25 to 29. In Gaza, men aged 20 to 24 with a university education have an unemployment rate of nearly 64 percent, compared with an unemployment rate of about 9 percent for workers with the same education aged 30 or older. Young women also suffer from disproportionately high levels of unemployment when they have an associate's level of education (thirteen to fifteen years of schooling). Young women under age 25 with some higher education have nearly four times the unemployment rate of women aged 30 or older with the same schooling. While the unemployment rate is exceedingly high for these educated women in Gaza, these trends are in line with those found in Egypt, where highly educated young women have unemployment rates above 50 percent.[25]

Job Search and Barriers to Employment

This section analyzes the job search process of recent graduates using a recently released data set.[26] In addition to estimating the overall amount of time it takes to find a job, the job search data differ by worker characteristics.[27] Roughly 50 percent of all graduate job seekers find jobs within the first twenty months. However, another 25 percent take more that sixty months to find their first job. Job search patterns vary substantially according to education type and gender. Men are more successful in getting a job quickly after they begin their job search. Nearly 40 percent of all male job seekers are able to find a job within the first year and a half. For women, the percentage is much lower, with just over a quarter of women finding a job in the first eighteen months. Within two years 50 percent of the male job seekers have found employment, while it takes nearly another year for half of the female job seekers to get a job. Likewise, while many young men and women still have not found a job after ninety-eight months of searching, the rate of unsuccessful female job seekers at that point is nearly 20 percent higher than the rate for men.

The job search success rate also differs by education type, but not as dramatically as the gender differences. On average, vocational degree holders find jobs in just twenty-two months while students who finish with at least a bachelor's degree find jobs within twenty-four months. Associate's degree graduates take more than two and a half years, with a mean search time of thirty-two months. However, it is important to note that these figures do not include those who found jobs right away, who continued in their previous work, or who did not seek work.

Recent graduates identify a number of reasons for the delay in finding a job.[28] The most important reason, cited by 63 percent of recent graduates,

Table 4-1. *Unemployment Rates by Age, Gender, and Education in the West Bank and Gaza, 2006*
Percent

	Years of schooling			
Age	0–8	9–12	13–15	16 or more
Men				
West Bank				
15–19	31.0	29.0	29.7	n.a.
20–24	25.5	26.6	23.7	36.4
25–29	24.8	19.7	16.4	13.9
30 or older	19.4	17.7	11.3	4.4
Gaza				
15–19	57.7	55.0	25.0	n.a.
20–24	47.0	48.2	40.2	63.7
25–29	40.2	34.5	27.3	34.1
30 or older	44.1	30.9	19.7	8.9
Women				
West Bank				
15–19	15.2	5.7	n.a.	n.a.
20–24	14.9	23.3	50.0	53.8
25–29	12.0	15.2	35.0	37.1
30 or older	6.7	10.0	12.9	17.2
Gaza				
15–19	n.a.	20.0	n.a.	n.a.
20–24	40.0	35.3	74.5	78.0
25–29	14.3	0.0	46.3	47.5
30 or older	0.7	4.1	19.7	15.3

Source: Authors' calculations using PCBS Labor Force Survey 2006.
n.a.= Not available (the sample size for those cells is so small that estimates cannot be produced).

is a lack of capital to start a business. The second reason for not finding a job, cited by 57 percent of graduates of universities, colleges, and vocational schools, is a lack of job market opportunities for graduates with their particular specialty. Finally, more than half cite a lack of family connections as delaying their job search success. Personal connections are perceived as a primary way of seeking and obtaining employment, with nearly half of all recent job seekers stating that one of the ways that they sought work was through personal connections. Approximately the same proportion registered at the employment office, and nearly one of every three new graduates report doing both of those activities. While young people pursue multiple strategies in their job search, the job market in the West Bank and Gaza is still dominated by the informal connections made through personal or family relations.

The match between human capital from schooling and the skills desired by employers is a key component of the job search process. For those graduates that do secure jobs, a high proportion claim that their jobs suit their educational training. Over three-quarters of holders of bachelor's degrees and nearly two-thirds of associate's degree holders claim that their jobs suit their skills. However, only half of vocational graduates claim that their job matches their skills. Thus, although vocational schools claim to prepare workers for a specific career, this training does not correspond well with skills needed by the job market.

If workers eventually get jobs that match their skills, why do they not get these jobs sooner? Also, if they are not working and not going to school, what do they end up doing with their time? Unfortunately, curent data sets do not allow one to answer these questions fully, but a few points can be highlighted. First, self-employment is very high in the West Bank and Gaza. In 2006, 42 percent of all employed individuals were either employers (4 percent), self-employed with no others employed (26 percent), or unpaid family members (12 percent). Although most of these workers have less education than graduates of higher education, graduates have the same opportunities. Thus, if someone is unable to find a job immediately after graduation, he or she may end up doing various errands and casual work for an extended family member who has a construction or retail business, for example. But graduates may not perceive these temporary jobs as "real" work.

Labor Demand for Palestinians: Migration, Work in Israel, and the Public Sector

Three main components of demand for Palestinian workers affect the economic outcomes of youth today: migration to the Gulf, work in Israel, and work in the public sector.

Historically, there have been four waves of Palestinian migration. During the first three (in 1919, 1948, and 1967), Palestinians fled from their historical homeland of Palestine Mandate, which initially included present-day Israel, the West Bank, Gaza Strip and parts of Jordan and Lebanon. These migrants largely went to the surrounding Arab states, Europe, or the United States. With the rise of oil production in the Gulf states in the 1960s, an economically motivated migration began.[29] These migrants tended to stay for long periods of time and worked in managerial, technical, and professional occupations.[30] In the 1980s the demand for Palestinian workers in the Gulf slowed as Gulf states began to actively recruit Asian workers over Arab workers and as the overall pace of development in the Gulf slowed with the decrease in oil prices.[31] The shift toward Asian workers was partially economic—the Gulf states could pay Asians lower wages than they paid Palestinians. But the shift also had political motivations resulting from concerns about large populations of expatriate Arabs in nations with tiny domestic populations.[32] The trickle of return migration became a flood after 1990, as Palestinians working in Kuwait either fled when Iraq invaded Kuwait or were expelled by the government when the Kuwaitis were returned to power. While most of these returnees initially chose to relocate in Jordan, many of them eventually found their way back to the West Bank or Gaza.

One of the unique characteristics of the Palestinian labor market is the entry of Palestinian workers into the Israeli labor market. Beginning in 1968 there was a controlled flow of Palestinian workers into Israel, facilitated by the Israeli government through its labor bureaus.[33] By 1973 the number of Israeli work permits given to Palestinians grew to over 60,000. Subsequently, there was little control over the flow of Palestinian workers, and the Israeli and Palestinian labor markets for certain types of workers were effectively integrated. However, the types of jobs that Palestinians were allowed to hold in Israel were predominantly lower- and semi-skilled and concentrated in the agricultural and construction sectors.[34]

By the 1980s three main shifts in labor market conditions for Palestinians changed the dynamic of who would work in Israel. The first shift was the decreased demand for Palestinian workers in the Gulf. The second shift was that Palestinian workers were becoming increasingly educated, just as these work opportunities in the Gulf for educated Palestinians disappeared. The final shift was that the Israeli economy began to recover from a period of slow growth in the 1970s, leading to an increase in demand for Palestinian workers, especially in the construction sector.[35] Thus, by the mid-1980s as many as 130,000 Palestinian workers were employed in Israel. This represented a full one-third of all employed workers in the West Bank and Gaza. These jobs generally paid well but still were focused in relatively unskilled sectors. Despite the lower quality of these jobs, the percentage of Palestinians with a college or university degree who were working unskilled agriculture or construction jobs in Israel rose from 1 percent in 1981 to 10 percent in 1987.[36]

After the outbreak of the first intifada in 1987, increasing restrictions were placed on Palestinian workers in Israel. With closures and curfews,

Israeli military officials banned Palestinians from working in Israel for lengthy periods of time. After 1991 restrictions began to ease until the period following the Oslo Accords of 1993. After Gaza and Jericho started their experiment with autonomy in 1994, followed by other cities in the West Bank in late 1995, Israel began to enforce separation between the Palestinian Territories and Israel. These measures included enforcement of the work permit system, an increase in roadblocks and checkpoints, and restrictions on the ability of Palestinian vehicles to enter Israel. Israel often enforced temporary "closures" of the West Bank and Gaza after suicide bombings in Israel.[37]

With the beginning of the al-Aqsa intifada in 2000, these restrictions on movement increased in intensity and frequency. Closures were extended for weeks and then months. Finally in 2003 Israel began to build a separation barrier around the West Bank; the barrier was nearly completed by late 2006. There is currently no unlicensed work by Palestinians in Israel, and all movement in and out of the West Bank is strictly monitored. Since Israel disengaged from Gaza in August 2005, the separation between Gaza and Israel has been nearly complete, with very few Gazans being allowed to work in Israel. Israel also closed its industrial zones on the border with Gaza, which once had employed Palestinians.

Between 1995 and 2006, young men from the West Bank were more likely than workers from Gaza and even more likely than older West Bank workers to be employed in Israel (figure 4-3). Before the al-Aqsa intifada, as many as one-third of employed young West Bank men worked in Israel, compared with between 25 and 30 percent of older West Bank men. Gazan men were less likely to work in Israel than West Bank Palestinians. Older workers had employment rates similar to those from the West Bank, but what is particularly unique is that young Gazan workers were almost completely excluded from working in Israel. At no point do the data show more than 10 percent of employed young Gazan men working in Israel or the settlements. The greater number of Israeli settlements in the West Bank than in Gaza may explain this anomaly. During the al-Aqsa intifada many of the younger West Bank Palestinians worked in the settlements surrounding Jerusalem.[38]

Young women are much less likely to work than men, and those that work are unlikely to work in Israel. Young women from the West Bank are more likely to work in Israel than older women. However, young women's employment in Israel has never exceeded 10 percent of all employed women. Women from Gaza work less in Israel than West Bank women, and by 2006 they ceased working in Israel entirely. Interestingly, Gazan women's work in

Figure 4-3. *Proportion of Palestinian Male Youth and Older Men Working in Israel, 1995–2006*

Work in Israel as a share of total employment

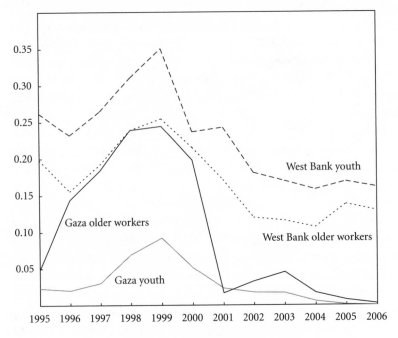

Source: Authors' calculations using PCBS Labor Force Surveys.

Israel disappeared long before disengagement; starting with the al-Aqsa intifada, less than 1 percent of all employed Gazan women worked in Israel.

High Israeli wages, large influxes of aid, and remittances kept Palestinian workers well paid and the Palestinian economy afloat for many years. Additionally, inflated reservation wages contributed to some of the long waits for jobs after graduation. With the closing of the Israeli labor market to Palestinian workers and a slowdown of tax payments remitted from Israel and aid from the West, the last few years have seen a depressing of Palestinian wages for the first time since the economic integration between the Palestinian Territories and Israel.[39] Average wages for Palestinians fell by more than 15 percent in nominal terms (equal to more than 25 percent in real terms) from 1999 to 2005.[40]

Another key feature of the Palestinian labor market is the recent growth of public sector employment. In 1994 the Palestinian Authority took control of government functions in the areas of the West Bank and Gaza that had been granted autonomy. As the PA was created, the size of the public sector continued to expand; new government ministries were established and an extensive security apparatus was built.

By the end of 2004 nearly 40 percent of Palestinians employed in Gaza were working in the public sector. By the end of 2006 the dominance of the public sector in the overall economy of the West Bank and Gaza became even more apparent. In 2006, 56 percent of male and 80 percent of female wage earners in Gaza were working in the public sector, primarily for the PA or UNRWA. In the West Bank, the figures are not nearly as dramatic but are still noteworthy, with one-quarter of employed men who were not self-employed or unpaid family members working for the public sector. As in Gaza, West Bank women were more likely than men to work in the public sector, with nearly half of all female wage workers being employed in this sector.

Family Formation

In the West Bank and Gaza Strip, as in the rest of the world, marriage is an especially important milestone in the lives of youth. Many youth continue to live with their parents and other extended family until they marry and form families of their own. Marriage involves high costs, and because youth tend to be financially dependent on their parents, oftentimes the burden of the cost of marriage is carried by entire families. One reason why the demand for public sector employment is so high (in addition to the stability of these jobs) is that having such a job signals marriage eligibility to potential brides.[41] While the age of marriage has not been delayed in the West Bank and Gaza as it has in other Middle Eastern countries, the pressure to find a good job in order to be able to marry is still a significant factor in the lives of young Palestinians. Several factors that are unique to the economy and society of the West Bank and Gaza help explain why the age of marriage has not risen significantly there as it has in other Middle Eastern countries.

The median age of marriage (counting only those who do get married) measures the degree to which any delay is taking place in the marriage market.[42] If men have to wait longer to marry because of financial and social pressures, then that is another form of exclusion. However, as a society modernizes and becomes more educated, there also will be a natural increase in the median age at marriage as other markers of adulthood, especially education, take precedence. The marriage age for both men and women in the West Bank and Gaza appears to have risen recently. Median age of first marriage for men was 24.1 in 2000 and 24.7 in 2005. For women the age increased from 18.9 in 2000 to 19.4 in 2005.[43] These figures also highlight another important attribute of the marriage arrangement: men generally marry women five years their junior. This rise in the age at first marriage is approximately one year per decade, which is almost identical to the average increase in the level of schooling for men and women.

The mean preferred age at marriage among youth is very similar to the actual age of marriage, and these preferences are almost uniform across a variety of characteristics.[44] For example, females state that their ideal age at marriage is 20. This is just slightly higher than the actual median age of first marriage observed during this time (19.4). Younger boys (aged 10 to 14) say they generally would prefer to marry by 23 or 24, but the older group (those aged 20 to 24) push back the ideal age at marriage to 25.

The high cost of marriage is the most frequently cited reason for postponing marriage among youth.[45] A second and related reason is poor work conditions. In other words, youth perceive the relative scarcity of job opportunities as a direct barrier to starting and supporting a family. Interestingly, this reason is cited by many more Palestinians in the West Bank than in Gaza. Educational pursuits are also cited as primary motivations for delaying marriage. Thus, in the eyes of youth, one needs to complete one's education before marrying, but without the right work conditions and political environment, it is difficult to be able to afford the high cost of marriage.

The tendency of Palestinian men to marry women with less education is partially responsible for a unique feature of Palestinian family formation: because women have become increasingly educated, there are fewer women eligible for marriage. Thus, it has been noted for some time that approximately 25 percent of West Bank women with at least a secondary degree never marry.[46] In the past, the number of Palestinian women with this level of schooling was fairly small, so this phenomenon had a minimal impact on the overall pattern of family formation and fertility.

Another factor contributing to higher numbers of unmarried women is emigration: Palestinian men emigrate in much greater numbers than Palestinian women. Thus, in Gaza there are virtually no unmarried men between the ages of 35 and 60, and there are also very few in the West Bank. On the other hand, between 8 and 17 percent of women, depending upon region, aged 35 to 39 have never married.[47] The women at the greatest risk of never marrying appear to be those with at least a secondary level of schooling and who work outside the home. This raises an important question about the reasons for not marrying. Are working women less attractive partners, or do they have fewer incentives to marry? The available data do not provide a clear answer. It is also possible that fathers are less inclined to marry their daughters off if they are contributing income to the family.

Conclusions and Policy Recommendations

The economic landscape that young Palestinians face today is very different from the one that the previous generations encountered. The possibility of working in Israel has been nearly eliminated, while the importance of working for the public sector has increased. Getting a job in the public sector is desirable for its benefits and job security, but soon the fiscal pressures of a bloated public sector will cause the Palestinian Authority to slow its expansion. More young people will have to depend upon private employers for jobs or start businesses themselves.

The rapid increase in the number of new job seekers will continue to place strains upon the economic and social fabric of the West Bank and Gaza. It is possible that this burgeoning population will become an important asset rather than a liability. Before that is possible, however, many of the current restrictions on the Palestinian economy, especially concerning the freedom for manufacturers to reach their customers abroad, must be loosened. Without some untying of the fetters around the domestic economy, no amount of foreign aid is likely to help. Additionally, reforms of the educational system, financial system, and employment regulations can help increase demand for young Palestinian workers and help them contribute to the growth and development of their economy.

Changes in the economic and political environments are necessary for the survival of the Palestinian economy. For example, as stated by the World Bank, what the Palestinians need more than aid is to have open borders with Israel.[48] Specifically, the Palestinian labor market and Palestinian exporters need to be able to get through checkpoints into Israel quickly and efficiently. Israeli border agents have used the possibility of security threats to keep the main crossing points in Gaza for both people (Erez in the north) and cargo (Karni in the center) closed since 2006. The result is that the unemployment rate in Gaza spiked to 45 percent by the end of 2008.[49]

Thus, there is a clear advantage to opening up access to the Israeli market. However, there is a disadvantage that the World Bank report does not address. Access to the Israeli labor market reduced the returns to skill, not so much by decreasing the wages paid to skilled Palestinian workers compared with other economies in the region but by raising the wages of unskilled work, compared with Jordan and Egypt. The sealing off of the Israeli labor market has contributed to a depression in Palestinian wages in recent years.

World Bank economists Claus Astrup and Sebastien Dessus attempt to answer the following question: Would it be better for the Palestinian economy to have access to the Israeli labor market or not?[50] If low wages in the West Bank and Gaza lead to an expanded manufacturing base in the territories, lower wages could serve as a catalyst to launch export-led growth. Astrup and Dessus found that, in the long run, exporting goods is better than exporting labor. The only problem is that the economy must suffer low wages first, and that may not be politically feasible. Palestinians are beginning to suffer through a period of low wages, implying that a renewed emphasis on exports at this time could be effective in expanding the overall Palestinian economy. These future scenarios of the Palestinian economy are viable only if goods are able to move across borders.

Beyond improvements in the macroeconomy, there are many areas specific to the lives of youth that can increase their labor market performance and help them to be fully integrated economically and socially into Palestinian society. Changes in the educational system can ease the transition from school to work. Greater formalization of the relationship between educational facilities and employers will decrease the importance of personal connections in finding employment. A system of internships and externships and stronger relationships between educational institutions and employers can help make connections between students and potential employers and increase the amount of valuable work experience gained by students.

In addition to better preparing students for wage work in the private sector, policy changes to increase access to credit by youth can help recent graduates to start their own businesses. Only 8 percent of recent graduates went from school directly into working for themselves.[51] Of those, the majority either used their private savings (34 percent), loans from their families (24 percent), or other support from their households (20 percent) as their start-up capital. Only 4 percent of these new graduates received their funding from banks. The Palestinian financial sector is very weak, and reforms in the banking sector could help spur the economy.[52] Although government intervention in the financial sector should not be extensive, the creation of a subsidized loan program for recent graduates would help those that want to start up their own businesses.

The primary labor market regulations for the West Bank and Gaza are found within the Palestinian basic Labor Law of 2000. These regulations mandate a 45-hour workweek and allow 12 hours overtime with an overtime premium of time and a half, two weeks mandatory paid leave, and ten weeks of paid maternity leave. A recent study by the Palestinian Economic Policy Research Institute concluded that the regulations did not have a negative impact on competitiveness of the private sector in the West Bank and Gaza Strip.[53] Instead, the analysis showed that the overall impact was minimal, especially because it unified two disparate labor laws that had been regulating the West Bank and Gaza Strip, and the labor law is still not as intrusive as many of those found in the region. However, recent research by Sayre and Daoud finds that most Palestinian workers in the West Bank and Gaza Strip do not receive the mandatory benefits outlined in the labor law.[54] Thus, the labor law has had little impact—either positive or negative—it is weakly enforced, and employers effectively ignore it.

The labor law should be reformed, but in a way that does not burden employers so that they are willing to abide by it. However, classifying workers as "informal labor" so that they do not need to be given the full benefits of the law will negatively affect reforms to create an effective pension scheme, national health insurance, or any number of policies that may need to be administered through the workplace, leaving a significant number of workers without the mandatory benefits and economic responsibilities that are contained in the legislation. The labor law could be made more palatable for employers. For example, the law has made it more expensive for employers to take on female workers; developing a cost-sharing mechanism between the government and employers for covering maternity leave expenses could encourage employers to take on more young women. As is the case in other countries, this cost should be shared by society at large. Relaxing some of the job security regulations found in the labor law may have a positive impact on employment of Palestinian youth by lowering firing costs and increasing the transition into and out of unemployment.

Formidable challenges face the next generation of young Palestinians. As their numbers swell, it will be increasingly difficult for them to successfully make the transition from school to work to family formation without changes in the fundamental pressures surrounding the Palestinian economy. However, a few policy changes could yield substantial benefits to Palestinian youth. More help with the transition from school to work and additional resources for young entrepreneurs will go a long way in a society as educated and resourceful as that of the West Bank and Gaza.

Notes

1. The Palestinian Central Bureau of Statistics (PCBS) and the Palestinian Authority generally define "youth" as 10- to 24-year-olds, so the youth survey refers to this age group. This chapter defines youth as those aged 15 to 29 unless otherwise noted.

2. Marwan Khawaja, "The Recent Rise in Palestinian Fertility: Permanent or Transient?" *Population Studies* 54, no. 3 (2000): 331–46.

3. PCBS, *Youth Survey, 2003, Main Findings* (Ramallah: 2004).

4. Ibid.

5. Rashid Amjad, *To the Gulf and Back: Studies on the Economic Impact of Asian Labour Migration* (Geneva: International Labor Organization, Asian Regional Program on International Migration, 1989).

6. Figures for total population in the West Bank and Gaza come from the PCBS 1997 and the 2007 Household and Establishments Census. The 2007 data were not fully processed for both the West Bank and Gaza Strip at the time of this writing. Preliminary figures have been released for the Gaza Strip, but final calculations have not been completed because of the current political schism between the West Bank and Gaza and the blockade of the Gaza Strip by Israel.

7. PCBS, *Dissemination and Analysis of Census Findings. In-Depth Analysis Series (07). Characteristics of Youth (10-24) in the Palestinian Territory* (Ramallah: 2005).

8. Djavad Salehi-Isfahani and Daniel Egel, "Youth Exclusion in Iran: The State of Education, Employment and Family Formation," Middle East Youth Initiative Working Paper 3 (Wolfensohn Center for Development at the Brookings Institution and the Dubai School of Government, 2007); see www.shababinclusion.org/content/document/detail/538/. The values for Syria and Jordan come from United Nations Development Program (UNDP), *Human Development Report 2007–2008* (New York: Palgrave Macmillan, 2008); see http://hdrstats.undp.org/indicators/335.html. UNDP lists the current fertility rate for the Palestinian Territories as 5.6 and Egypt's fertility rate as 3.2 children per woman.

9. United Nations Relief Works Agency (UNRWA), "Education" (www.un.org/unrwa/programmes/education/index.html).

10. Amjad, *To the Gulf and Back.*

11. These data are from labor force surveys conducted by the PCBS. These estimates are weighted by the sampling weights based upon the 1995 demographic survey and the 1997 Palestinian census.

12. PCBS, *Youth Survey, 2003, Main Findings.*

13. PCBS, *Conditions of Graduates from High Education and Vocational Training Survey (December, 2005–January, 2006): Main Findings Report* (Ramallah: 2006); see www.pcbs.gov.ps/Portals/_pcbs/labor/Graduates_e.pdf.

14. Nathan J. Brown, *Palestinian Politics after the Oslo Accords: Resuming Arab Palestine* (Berkeley: University of California Press, 2003).

15. Ibid.

16. Susan Nicolai, *Fragmented Foundations: Education and Chronic Crisis in the Occupied Palestinian Territory* (Paris: UNESCO, International Institute for Educational Planning, 2007).

17. Ma'an Development Center, *MENA Voices of Youth: Palestine* (Ramallah: Ma'an Development Center and World Bank, 2007).

18. Palestinian Ministry of Education and Higher Education, *Palestinian Higher Education Statistics* (Ramallah: 2005).

19. The gross tertiary enrollment rates here are calculated as a percentage of all 18- to 23-year-olds.

20. Ministry of Education and Higher Education, *Palestinian Higher Education Statistics.*

21. Leila Farsakh, *Palestinian Labour Migration to Israel: Labour, Land, and Occupation* (London: Taylor & Francis, 2005).

22. PCBS, *Labour Force Survey: 2006 Rounds* (Ramallah: 2007).

23. The data set from the PCBS's *Conditions of Graduates from High Education and Vocational Training Survey* contains a variety of questions that concern the extent of resources available to graduates for making the transition from school to work. This survey is only of graduates of higher education (vocational school, college, or university) and does not capture the transition from secondary school to work.

24. The ratio for young men aged 15 to 24 is closer to 2. Men aged 15 to 19 have the highest rate of unemployment, which decreases as men get closer to the age of 30.

25. Ragui Assaad and Ghada Barsoum, "Youth Exclusion in Egypt: In Search of 'Second Chances,'" Middle East Youth Initiative Working Paper 2 (Wolfensohn Center for Development at the Brookings Institution and the Dubai School of Government, 2007); see www.shababinclusion.org/content/document/detail/540/.

26. Data from the PCBS's *Conditions of Graduates from High Education and Vocational Training Survey.* This analysis includes only those individuals who reported that their main activity after completion of vocational school, college, or university was to seek a job. These data exclude many job seekers, including those entering the labor force directly after secondary school. See Edward Sayre and Samia al-Botmeh, "Youth Exclusion in the West Bank and Gaza: The Impact of Social, Economic and Political Forces," Middle East Youth Initiative Working Paper (Wolfensohn Center for Development at the Brookings Institution and the Dubai School of Government, forthcoming).

27. The Kaplan-Meier survival method was used to estimate the time spent looking for a job over several characteristics. These survival estimates show the probability that an individual has "survived" in the same state for a given amount of time. See Sayre and al-Botmeh, "Youth Exclusion in the West Bank and Gaza" for more details.

28. The PCBS's *Conditions of Graduates from High Education and Vocational Training Survey* collected self-reported reasons why recent graduates experience difficulty finding jobs.

29. Rosemary Sayigh, *Palestinians: From Peasants to Revolutionaries* (London: Zed Press, 1979).

30. Radwan A. Shaban, "Palestinian Labour Mobility," *International Labour Review* 134, no. 5–6 (1993): 655–72.

31. Amjad, *To the Gulf and Back.*

32. Sharon Russell, "Politics and Ideology in Migration Policy Formulation: The Case of Kuwait," *International Migration Review* 23, no. 1 (1989): 24–47.

33. Arie Arnon and others, *The Palestinian Economy: Between Imposed Integration and Voluntary Separation* (London: Brill, 1997); Farsakh, *Palestinian Labour Migration to Israel.*

34. Edward Sayre, "Labor Demand and the Wage Gap in the West Bank and Gaza Strip," *Contemporary Economic Policy* 19, no. 2 (2001): 213–24. Edward Sayre, "Labor Supply, Labor Demand and the Returns to Schooling in the West Bank and Gaza Strip," *Middle East Business and Economic Review* 13, no. 1 (2001): 29–43.

35. Sara Roy, *The Gaza Strip: The Political Economy of De-Development* (Washington: Institute for Palestine Studies, 1995).

36. Sayre, "Labor Demand and the Wage Gap in the West Bank and Gaza Strip."

37. For more details about the Palestinian economy during this time, see Ishac Diwan and Radwan A. Shaban, *Development Under Adversity: The Palestinian Economy in Transition* (Washington: World Bank, 1999).

38. Farsakh, *Palestinian Labour Migration to Israel.*

39. Elizabeth Ruppert Bulmer, "The Impact of Israeli Border Policy on the Palestinian Labor Market," *Economic Development and Cultural Change* 51, no. 3 (2003): 657–76.

40. PCBS, *Labour Force Survey: 2006 Rounds.*

41. Diane Singerman, "The Economic Imperatives of Marriage: Emerging Practices and Identities among Youth in the Middle East," Middle East Youth Initiative Working Paper 6 (Wolfensohn Center for Development at the Brookings Institution and the Dubai School of Government, 2007); see www.shababinclusion.org/content/document/detail/559/.

42. Because this is the median for those men and women who get married, it does not entirely capture the delay that may be happening if there has been an increase in the number who never get married.

43. PCBS, *Demographic and Social Statistics 2007* (Ramallah: 2007).

44. A PCBS survey asked youth aged 10 to 24 their perceptions about marriage and their preferred age at marriage. PCBS, *Youth Survey, 2003, Main Findings.*

45. Ibid.

46. Jon Pedersen, Sara Randall, and Marwan Khwaja, eds., *Growing Fast: The Palestinian Population in the West Bank and Gaza Strip,* FAFO report 353 (Oslo: Fafo Institute for Applied Social Science, 2001).

47. Ibid.

48. World Bank, *Investing in Palestinian Economic Reform and Development* (Washington: 2007); see www.worldbank.org/ps.

49. This unemployment rate represents the situation right before the conflict that began at the end of December 2008 in Gaza. See *PCBS Press Release on Labour Force Survey Results (October- December, 2008),* Round 2/22/2009 (www.pcbs.gov.ps).

50. Claus Astrup and Sebastien Dessus, "Exporting Goods or Exporting Labor?: Long-Term Implications for the Palestinian Economy," *Review of Middle East Economics and Finance* 3, no. 1 (2005): 39–62.

51. PCBS, *Conditions of Graduates from High Education and Vocational Training Survey.*

52. David Cobham and Nu'man Kanafani, *The Economics of Palestine – Economic Policy and Institutional Reform for a Viable Palestinian State* (London: Routledge, 2004).

53. Samia Al-Botmeh and Garry Sotnik, "The Impact of the Palestinian Labour Law on Private Sector Competitiveness" (Ramallah and Jerusalem: Palestine Economic Policy Research Institute (MAS), 2007).

54. Edward Sayre and Yousef Daoud, "Employment Regulations and Unemployment Duration in the West Bank and Gaza Strip" (University of Southern Mississippi, 2008).

JAD CHAABAN

5

The Impact of Instability and Migration on Lebanon's Human Capital

The number of young men and women aged 15 to 29 in Lebanon is currently estimated at almost 1 million people, roughly a quarter of the country's population. The large proportion of young people, resulting from the demographic transition through which Lebanon is passing, is high but is still lower than that found in other Arab countries where the proportion is almost 30 percent. This youth bulge represents a demographic gift because a high number of young people offers a solid human capital base on which economies can grow and prosper—provided that a positive enabling institutional and economic environment is in place.

The demographic impact of rising youth proportions can be evaluated by examining the evolution of the dependency ratio, which measures the ratio of people younger than 15 and older than 65 to the working-age population aged 15 to 64. A larger share of working-age people offers a demographic window of opportunity through the decline in the dependency ratio. This window starts to close when the ratio begins rising again as the population ages and the number of dependents grows. However, the opportunity offered by a large labor force depends on the maximization of employment and economic activity for the workforce.

The dependency ratio in Lebanon started to decline around 1975 and is forecast to start rising again by 2025, much sooner than in other Arab countries. This puts pressure on the Lebanese economy to engage in essential reforms that would allow the country to reap the benefits of the demographic gift.

Lebanon takes pride in its human capital as the only comparative advantage it has over its resource-endowed neighbors. After the end of the civil war in 1990, the country engaged in massive reconstruction and rehabilitation efforts to rebuild the public and private institutions that foster investments in human capital. High social sector spending on education, health, and social affairs, both public and private, reached nearly 21 percent of GDP in 2006. However, these large investments have not resulted in improved outcomes, as reflected in low educational attainment, high levels of unemployment, and alarming emigration rates. The legacy of civil war as well as ongoing political instability and conflict continue to undermine Lebanon's economy, affecting the lives of young people. Their transitions are stalled by the country's macroeconomic and political environment as well as by structural deficiencies in the education and labor markets.

Growing Up with Conflict

There is a stark dichotomy in the role of youth in Lebanese society. On the one hand, Hezbollah, a political and militia resistance group that is on the U.S. list of terrorist organizations, trains boys in their mid-teens to conduct warfare based on the reasoning that "in Islam, a 15-year-old is considered a responsible adult."[1] On the other hand, youth are excluded from the political process that guides their country and lays the groundwork for their future. This is evident in the maintenance of 21 as the legal voting age, whereas large parts of the world consider 18 an appropriate age for active participation in the choice of national leaders.[2] The irony is of course that large segments of Lebanese youth are extremely politicized and made aware of political affairs at a young age.

Certainly, this is the result of decades of civil strife in a country so complex even Lebanese citizens struggle to understand it. Even those who were born after the civil war ended in 1990 have grown up in a society full of divides, political unrest, and even armed conflict. Lebanese society remains plagued by feelings of anger and mistrust of neighbors belonging to other sects, although these feelings tend to remain closely guarded.[3] Indeed, this reality limits the opportunities of youth before they have even become active citizens. The civil war, which began in 1975, not only brought to the surface the deep divides that existed but also deepened them. With a Maronite president, a Sunni prime minister, and a Shiite speaker of parliament, even the reconstruction process became a matter of sectarian interests. Reform of the welfare system fell by the wayside, leaving in place many of the class and sectarian divides that had played a role in the instigation of the war.

Today, young Lebanese who were born after the civil war ended are about to enter the working world. Given the political and economic instability fed by underlying tension and the sporadic eruption of violence, it is tempting to suggest that persistent expectations of further conflict, large or small, have resulted in a level of apathy among youth who see little purpose in engaging with the economy or setting long-term goals. What results is a waiting game where change will not take place unless and until youth are actively encouraged to take part in the reconstruction of their country.

This situation has been further aggravated by the July 2006 war between Israel and Hezbollah. This war not only resulted in human tragedy (1,184 persons killed and 5,500 injured) but also led to the destruction or damage of nearly 300 schools, 80 hospitals and outpatients facilities, and nearly 107,000 housing units in Lebanon.[4] The World Bank estimates the costs of the direct damage from the hostilities at $2.4 billion, while indirect losses accounted for another $700 million to $800 million. The Lebanese economy contracted by almost 6 percent in 2006, and as many as 30,000 workers were estimated to have permanently lost their jobs.[5]

Despite massive reconstruction and recovery efforts since 2006, the Lebanese population, and especially its younger generation, is likely to bear the scars of this war for a long time. Most schools and hospitals were rebuilt, and most of the nearly 1 million people displaced returned to their homes. Yet the war resulted in the migration of an estimated 200,000 persons, mostly skilled workers, and nothing is known yet about how many of them may have returned. To date there are no official data on the incidence of unemployment since the war, especially for the younger generation. Moreover, youth in families that suffered casualties and abrupt displacement may well endure posttraumatic stress disorders, which if untreated could undermine their development and increase their vulnerability.

A prime concern regarding Lebanese youth who feel excluded and alienated from society, especially since the 2006 war, is their vulnerability to recruitment by ethnic, religious, and political extremists who are pursuing their own ends.[6] In a country so clearly divided along sectarian lines, rising political polarization among Lebanese youth should be of concern to policymakers and provide an incentive to engage youth constructively. Indeed, a report from the United Nations Development Program on youth and conflict notes that "exclusion can contribute to the emergence or continuation of violence," which perpetuates the very conditions that Lebanon must overcome to secure a stable and prosperous future for coming generations.[7] As a result, poverty and deprivation become both consequences and potential future causes of political conflict in the country.

Education

With a literacy rate of over 80 percent of the adult population above the age of 15, Lebanon is one of the most literate countries in the Arab world.[8] The first eight years of schooling are mandatory. The education system involves three types of schools: public schools, free private schools, and private schools. The academic performance and success rates of students attending the three types of schools vary greatly, leading some observers to comment on the elitist nature of the Lebanese school system and the low quality of the public schools. Despite their quality, however, most students in the Lebanese school system are enrolled in public schools. Approximately 57 percent of youth pass through the Lebanese public education system, whether through primary and secondary schooling or higher education. Among youth who hold a high school certificate, 71 percent are reported to have achieved their credentials at a public school.[9]

Enrollment at the primary level (ages 6 to 12) is quite high, at 93 percent, and equal among males and females. The success of the Lebanese school system is highlighted by declining dropout rates in primary and secondary education, which decreased significantly during the 1997–2004 period.[10] The primary education dropout rate declined from 16 percent in 1997 to 4 percent in 2004. The secondary education dropout rate declined from almost 71 percent in 1997 to 21 percent in 2004.

While enrollment is high at the primary level, approximately 60 percent of young people aged 12 to 15 are enrolled in intermediate education, while 35 percent of youth are enrolled in secondary education and 18 percent of youth are enrolled in university education.[11] Young women have achieved higher enrollment rates than young men at every level of education.[12]

School enrollment rates vary greatly according to income levels and geographic region. Table 5-1 shows enrollment rates for different levels of welfare, with individuals' yearly expenditures adopted as a proxy for income. While primary school enrollment is nearly universal for all income levels, enrollment increases with individuals' income at the intermediate, secondary, and university levels. For example, 24 percent of high-school-aged youth from the poorest households in Lebanon are enrolled in secondary school, compared with 60 percent of youth from the richest households. University

Table 5-1. *Enrollment Rates by Expenditure Quintiles, 2004*
Percent

Expenditure quintile		Primary	Intermediate	Secondary	University
Poorest	Female	86	63	27	5
	Male	92	47	21	4
	Overall	89	54	24	5
2	Female	94	78	36	12
	Male	94	66	29	9
	Overall	94	73	34	11
3	Female	95	81	48	14
	Male	95	71	33	13
	Overall	94	76	38	14
4	Female	95	86	55	27
	Male	95	75	47	23
	Overall	95	78	51	25
Richest	Female	99	89	66	38
	Male	100	81	55	38
	Overall	99	84	60	38
Overall enrollment		93	60	35	18

Source: Author's computations based on UNDP and the Central Administration for Statistics, *Living Conditions of Households—The National Survey of Households Living Conditions* (2004) (www.cas.gov.lb/Studies_en.asp).

enrollment is only 5 percent among poor youth and nearly 38 percent for the rich. This correlation between income and enrollment indicates that Lebanon's mostly private educational system imposes barriers to entry on Lebanon's poorest families.

Of youth aged 15 to 24 who are active in the labor market, 34 percent do not have high school certificates.[13] This outcome is directly linked with household income levels of youth—three-quarters of youth from lower-income families do not have a diploma. The majority of youth with no high school diploma are reported to reside in the poorer regions of south Lebanon (including the Nabatieh and South governorates) and the Bekaa to the east; more than 54 percent of residents aged 18 to 35 in Nabatieh have not completed high school. In fact, Lebanon's peripheral northern, southern, and eastern regions have always been disadvantaged compared with the capital,

Beirut, and Mount Lebanon. Since Lebanon's creation as an autonomous entity in 1920 by the French mandate, the city of Beirut was promoted as a service and industrial hub for the country, which caused significant internal rural-to-urban migration and a decline in the agricultural sector, the main driver of the peripheral regions' local economies. A series of regional and internal wars and the central government's neglect of the needs of the peripheral regions further contributed to the decline in livelihoods in these areas.

The same income and regional patterns are clearly evident for university graduates. While 29 percent of youth in Beirut are university graduates, less than 9 percent of youth in Nabatieh are holders of a university degree.[14]

Another worrying aspect of Lebanon's educational system is its deteriorating quality. The performance and quality of the education system can be measured by the 2003 and 2007 Trends in International Mathematics and Science Study (TIMSS) scores, which assess student learning in eighth grade in the two fields. In 2003, the first year Lebanon participated in the testing, the national score was 393 in science and 433 in mathematics—both well below the international averages of 474 and 467, respectively. In science, Lebanon was outperformed by all other participating Middle Eastern countries except Saudi Arabia. Furthermore, when adjusted for level of income, Lebanon performed well below expectations.[15] In 2007 the scores averaged 414 in science and 449 in mathematics, the latter being the highest score among Middle Eastern countries that participated in the study. Test scores for Lebanese eighth graders may have improved because students and teachers were more familiar with the format of the exams in 2007 and were better trained to take them. However, Lebanese students still scored well below the international averages in sciences and math.

Problems with educational quality also exist at the university level. With forty-one universities in Lebanon, prospective university students certainly have a range of choices. However, high tuition and fees exclude large portions of the population from these institutions. Lebanese University is the only state-run higher education establishment in the country. However, elitism and economic divides are not the only challenges to Lebanon's youth. The country's universities have long been seen as a channel for acquiring civil service jobs or gaining access to a narrow number of esteemed professions such as medicine, engineering, and law.[16] In the process, technical and vocational education was largely sidelined. The reality is that the structure of the job market is continuously changing, not least with fluctuations in the economy. Still, it appears that higher education in Lebanon is lagging behind in designing academic programs that can effectively meet and match the changing structure of the job market to ensure employment of the country's youth that obtain higher learning.[17]

The inefficiencies of the educational sector in Lebanon can mostly be traced to the inability of public institutions, including the Ministry of Education, to effectively modernize public schools and equip them with the necessary physical resources to achieve better learning environments for pupils. In 2005 the ministry's budget amounted to $568 million, roughly 3 percent of Lebanon's GDP. Only 6 percent of this budget was spent on school buildings and equipment, while 87 percent was spent on salaries for public sector teachers and staff.[18] In addition, there is an oversupply and misallocation of teaching and administrative personnel. During the past three decades, the number of teachers increased by 111 percent while the number of students increased by less than 25 percent. The resources devoted to the surplus of teachers, an annual cost of approximately $160 million in salaries, could be used more effectively to improve program quality and learning outcomes.[19] It is difficult to fire public sector teachers, who rely chiefly on public sector benefits to insure against health and poverty risks and who are part of well-organized and strongly represented unions. Reallocating surplus teachers to underserved areas, accompanied by the right mix of incentives, could be a more beneficial solution. In addition, increasing the budget for education to include more investment in school labs, computers, and other equipment would be a much needed boost to the quality of public education.

Transition to Employment

Upon leaving education, many young Lebanese face a protracted and difficult transition to employment. High rates of unemployment and economic inactivity (neither in school nor in the labor market) represent the most critical component of exclusion for young Lebanese. Gender, income, level of education, and degree of personal connections are all factors that drive the nature of labor market integration and the work conditions faced by youth. Education in Lebanon comes at a high social cost but provides low returns; thus it is not surprising that a large portion of young people consider seeking employment abroad, only adding to the country's loss of human capital.

Unemployment and Inactivity

Having access to decent jobs is a cornerstone of establishing a career, forming a family, and gaining income stability. Lebanon's labor market is characterized by high unemployment rates of as much as 20 percent for the

Table 5-2. *Unemployment Rates by Education Level, Youth and Adults, 2004*
Percent

Age	Female	Male	Overall
Youth 15–29			
Illiterate	11	17	10
Primary	33	18	20
Intermediary	40	18	22
Secondary	9	23	14
Vocational	14	23	20
University	16	18	17
Overall	22	19	20
Adults 30–65			
Illiterate	1	10	11
Primary	24	9	11
Intermediary	28	11	14
Secondary	14	9	11
Vocational	19	13	15
University	12	8	9
Overall	16	9	11

Source: UNDP and the Central Administration for Statistics, *Living Conditions of Households—The National Survey of Household Living Conditions* (2004) (www.cas.gov.lb/Studies_en.asp).

15 to 29 age bracket, compared with 11 percent for adults (table 5-2). Unemployment rates are also higher for females than for males, especially for young females with low educational attainment. The overall unemployment rate is 19 percent for young men and 22 percent for young women.[20] However, the unemployment rate is 33 percent for young women with only primary education and 40 percent for young women with only intermediary education.[21] The lower unemployment rate for older cohorts in Lebanon is a consequence of earlier high migration rates of Lebanese looking for jobs abroad, rather than a reflection of a good domestic labor market.

Between 1997 and 2004 unemployment rates among young women increased by as much as 8 percentage points, from 14 percent to 22 percent, while unemployment rates among young men decreased from 24 percent to 19 percent.[22] During this same time period, the adult unemployment rate increased only slightly, from 9 percent to 11 percent. These changes probably indicate a shift in labor market demand, where more jobs for men were available in construction and related services industries during the reconstruction boom period, while females entering the labor market were not finding enough opportunities. The absence of reliable labor market surveys in the country makes the validation of labor market trends difficult.

Another characteristic of Lebanese youth is their high rate of economic inactivity, defined as people who are neither in school nor in the labor market. Nearly one in five 15- to 29-year-olds is inactive in Lebanon, and a large proportion of these are young women. Thirty-six percent of young women are inactive, compared with 1 percent of young men. This high inactivity rate for females is worrying. Young women seem to be seriously excluded from the labor market, with almost 60 percent of all young Lebanese women either unemployed or inactive, choosing to "stay at home." This figure reflects a major loss to the country's human capital and requires immediate action by policymakers.

These inactive females have an average age of 24 years, 60 percent are married, 90 percent have at most a secondary education, and up to 30 percent are poor.[23] Young women's inactivity in Lebanon is related to poverty and lack of education, where young females are married early and stay at home within an environment of limited engagement in productive activities.

Seeking Employment

Youth with high school diplomas or university education are reported to be more likely to have paid jobs.[24] University graduates in health-related disciplines, education, and management find employment the most quickly after commencing the search for their first job. Similarly, those living in Beirut find jobs more quickly on average than their counterparts in peripheral areas such as the Bekaa. People living in Beirut spend five months looking for their first job compared to ten months for the same demographic seeking their first employment in the Bekaa. While the average time for finding a job is seven months, some report that their first-time search for employment lasted as long as eighteen months.

Personal contacts continue to play a fundamental role in the ability of young Lebanese to find jobs, with 68 percent of all salaried first-time employees having obtained their positions principally as a result of personal or family contacts.[25] Notably, nonspecialized jobs tend to be acquired through an individual's connections rather than through merit.[26]

Attitudes about the qualifications necessary for successful job hunting vary by gender, with 61 percent of all surveyed females but only 25 percent of males citing education and language as a primary requirement for obtaining a job.[27]

Work Conditions

Among youth who have jobs, only half of those with minimal education have permanent jobs, compared with 74 percent of youth with university degrees. Those with university degrees also enjoy the highest salaries. Youth who have not earned a university diploma have an average salary of $308 a month, half as much as the average monthly salary of $657 that university graduates enjoy. Those with further graduate studies are paid on average $832.[28] Salary differences according to gender are prevalent; young women on average earn less than their male counterparts.

Perhaps surprisingly, once young people have found jobs, their positions are relatively secure. According to a recent survey, 82 percent of youth were in their second year in the same job, and 64 percent of these youth stayed in their first jobs for more than five years. Those who did quit their first job did so primarily to take another employment opportunity or for personal reasons. Only 17 percent of those who had left their first job had done so because of company closures, layoffs, or the completion of their contracts.

Two-thirds of young people working in the private sector worked for small enterprises, and, of those, 38 percent were heading their own businesses or were part-owners of a company.[29] In a precarious economy such as Lebanon's, these enterprises are the first to feel the pinch of a credit crunch, leaving these youth with less-than-steady employment.

Seventy-five percent of youth without work claim that there are no available jobs. This claim could result from a number of factors. First, there is simply not a sufficient number of jobs for which Lebanon's youth are qualified in the current job market. This in turn could potentially be traced to incongruity between what is taught in the educational system and what the job market requires. Second, youth without access to *wasta* (connections) are unable to find job opportunities. There is also the possibility that the industries most attractive to graduates are reaching a point of saturation. Young workers with degrees in industry and commerce, one of the most popular focuses among young university students, are those experiencing high unemployment.[30]

Evidence of a gap in the transition from education to employment for Lebanese youth can also be found by measuring the gross private returns to education, or the relative increase in income or salary with one additional year of education. This calculation confirms that a Lebanese education is poorly valued in the domestic labor market.[31] Gross private returns to education are low by international standards: an estimated 9 percent for one additional year of education in Lebanon in contrast with 21 percent world-wide. Social returns are even lower, after accounting for the high level of public and private education expenditures in Lebanon's GDP (almost 8 percent). Adding one additional year of education per student would cost Lebanon (public plus private education expenditures) 26 percent of the average per capita income and 10 percent of per capita GDP.[32] At the same time, one additional year of education adds very little, if any, to the actualized stream of net revenue made in Lebanon for the individual who chooses to spend one more year at school. Given its high cost and low domestic return, educational investment makes sense at its current levels mostly in the context of improving access to better-remunerated jobs abroad.

The failure to close the gap between youth's potential to contribute actively to the country's economy and the ability of the job market to efficiently absorb these individuals exacts a large financial impact on the national economy in forgone earnings.[33] Youth joblessness, which includes the official unemployment rate as well as the inactivity rate of youth who are not in school, costs Lebanon more than 2.7 percent of its GDP annually. That is equivalent to a yearly loss of almost $630 million. The jobless rate also highlights the real impact of the inactivity of the country's young women: the lack of employment of young females costs the Lebanese economy 2 percent of its GDP.[34]

Almost half of all unemployed youth feel they will be unable to find satisfactory wages and working conditions in Lebanon and say they are prepared to find work elsewhere.[35] Young men account for 72 percent of those contemplating this option, while women account for 27 percent. This desire to migrate abroad represents a loss of human capital to Lebanon and is another core cost of youth unemployment.

Lebanese Youth and Family Formation

The conditions surrounding family formation for Lebanese youth have changed significantly over the last few decades. Marriage is being delayed for young men and women. Almost 50 percent of women aged 20 to 24 were single in 1970; by 2004 the rate had increased to 72 percent. The most significant increases were witnessed for the 25- to 29-year-old and 30- to 34-year-old age groups, as the proportion of women remaining single in these age brackets has more than doubled. For the 25-to-29 age group, the proportion of unmarried women increased from approximately 25 percent in 1970 to 50 percent in 2004. For the 30- to 34-year-old age group, the proportion of unmarried women has doubled from 15 percent in 1970 to 30 percent in

2004. The proportion of single Lebanese women across all age groups is the highest in the Arab world.[36]

To date no comprehensive study has focused on the causes and consequences of the changing marriage patterns in Lebanon. However, a number of factors can be identified. The delayed age at first marriage was witnessed chiefly after the civil war and occurred in conjunction with a remarkable increase in the proportion of females never marrying.[37] The delayed age at first marriage resulted mainly from the adverse economic conditions during and immediately after the war as well as from high male mortality, high male migration, and shortages of affordable housing. The economic instability resulting from the civil war has made it difficult for young couples to find suitable employment and housing and thus to afford the high costs of marriage. The rise in the rate of single women is also attributable to the "marriage squeeze," an imbalance between the number of males and females in the prime marriage ages.

Other factors are equally if not more important than the civil war and the resulting instability in shaping marriage patterns. Marriage in Lebanon is still governed by rigid laws and a strong religious culture. There are no civil codes for personal matters, and each religious sect has its own set of personal status laws that encompass such matters as engagement, marriage, dowry, annulment of marriage, divorce, adoption, and inheritance. Marriage between a Lebanese man and woman of different religions cannot be carried out unless one of the spouses, almost always the woman, converts. As a result, the woman may end up being rejected by her native religious community.[38]

Little research has been undertaken on the links between religious constraints and marriage patterns in Lebanon. However, a small study of married couples from Beirut has found evidence of a notable religious endogamy with 88 percent of the marriages occurring within the same religious community.[39] Consanguineous marriages are quite frequent within the religious communities (26 percent of all marriages), the most commonly encountered being marriages of first cousins (63 percent of all consanguineous marriages). Although somewhat old, the study confirms anecdotal evidence that strong communal cleavages still greatly influence the functioning of the Lebanese "marriage market."

The Push and Pull Factors of Youth Migration

The Arab world has experienced international labor migration for a variety of political, religious, and economic reasons since the late nineteenth century.[40] One early surge of migration was largely regional: after World War I, famine drove people across borders within the region. The Arab oil boom of the 1970s also tempted regional migration as people moved to the Gulf countries in search of petrodollars. This regional migration was largely temporary.

Another wave of migration from the Arab world was directed toward the West. This included an outflow of primarily low-skilled labor from former colonies to European countries, as well as the ongoing migration of significantly more educated and skilled labor. By 1976 over one-quarter of engineers and 50 percent of doctors from the Arab world had emigrated, and, more recently, more than 15,000 doctors emigrated between 1998 and 2000.[41] The movement of both unskilled and skilled Arab migrants to Western countries was on the whole more permanent than migrations previously seen within the region.

Lebanon experienced a natural peak in emigration during the civil war period. Between 1975 and 2000, an estimated 600,000 to 900,000 Lebanese left the country. In addition, some 7 percent of the population migrated during this time period but later returned home.[42] Today, 46 percent of the country's population has one or more family members living abroad, having emigrated between 1975 and 2000. In contrast to many developing countries of the world, and notably in the Arab world, where the average annual population growth rate was 2.7 percent between 1975 and 2003, Lebanon's population actually has fallen in the past ten years because of the significant outflow from the country.[43] This population decrease has occurred despite an almost twofold increase in foreigners entering Lebanon for work.[44]

Today, the lack of opportunities and proliferation of conflicts continue to result in significant migration of youth, which perpetuates the vicious cycle of draining human capital from the country. More than one-third of Lebanese youth, both with and without jobs, report that they would like to emigrate or leave the country for a certain period of time. Of those, almost 17 percent want to emigrate permanently.[45]

Unlike migrants during the civil war, today's Lebanese migrants tend to leave the country for determined, but relatively long periods of time to work in foreign enterprises or in foreign offices of Lebanese enterprises. The majority of Lebanese emigrants leave for Arab countries (nearly 44 percent), while just over 18 percent go to Western Europe, and 14 percent to the United States. Approximately 10 percent choose Africa as their destination.[46]

Young Lebanese migrants come from both lower and higher socioeconomic backgrounds and educational levels. Between 1975 and 2001, 25 percent of immigrants were university educated.[47] Based on data in migrant registries, nearly 45 percent of Lebanese emigrants to member countries of the Organization for Economic Cooperation and Development are highly skilled (more than thirteen years of schooling); in contrast, more than 70 percent of registered migrants from North African countries have low skills with less than eight years of schooling.[48]

Although both men and women migrate, the number of male emigrants is significantly larger (approximately 16 percent versus 10 percent). Overall, the majority of migrants are married (around 75 percent), with male migrants more likely to be single than female migrants. Lebanese female migrants are on the whole younger than male migrants.

Youth migration in Lebanon, as in other resource-poor countries in the region, is affected by both "push" and "pull" factors. The push factors include political instability; the high cost of living, especially for young graduates; and a mismatch between education and market needs combined with a tight labor market for skilled graduates. Pull factors include high salaries in Arab petrodollar-rich countries, an established network of Lebanese abroad that facilitates youth transitions out of the country, and opportunities for high-quality graduate studies.

Job opportunities and further education are primary incentives for youth to leave Lebanon permanently or for a longer duration. The more limited survey of Saint Joseph University students found that engineering, medical, and information technology students were the most prevalent among graduates working abroad, indicating insufficient job opportunities in these fields in Lebanon. Male graduates of Saint Joseph University were nearly twice as likely to go abroad for work as female graduates (48 percent compared to 26 percent of female graduates).[49]

Poverty is one of the main push factors for youth seeking to leave Lebanon. Youth living in the suburbs of Nabatieh are most keen to migrate, with some 42 percent of surveyed youth in these areas wishing to leave.[50] This area has one of the highest poverty rates in Lebanon, with almost 50 percent of the residents living below the poverty line.

Current job status is another factor influencing youth attitudes toward migration. Among job categories, youth employed as laborers are most likely to wish to leave Lebanon (46 percent of specialized laborers and 38 percent of nonspecialized laborers). Between 30 and 32 percent of service personnel, medical staff, and social services personnel wish to leave. Among military staff, only 10 percent of the survey sample expresses an interest in leaving.[51] Those in unstable or informal jobs (lacking permanent status) or unemployed are more likely to migrate. Conversely, youth working in the public sector are less inclined to leave the country; 84 percent of the survey sample of youth working in the public sector have no desire to leave the country either permanently or provisionally. It is evident that the public sector with its employment and payment guarantees provides youth with the security and stability they seek.

Unsatisfactory remuneration also plays a part in youth's desire to emigrate. For those earning 500,000 Lebanese pounds or less ($334) a month, 40 percent of those surveyed want to leave. The survey shows that as salaries rise, the desire to leave Lebanon diminishes. Nearly 47 percent of those who are unhappy with their financial situation are prepared to go abroad in search of a better paid job, while only 25 percent of those who are satisfied with their salaries (judging them sufficient and fair) want to pursue other options abroad.[52]

Conclusion: Recapturing the Potential of Lebanese Youth

Lebanon is currently witnessing the highest proportion of young people ever in its population. This youth surge could form the foundation for new economic growth in the country, but this demographic window of opportunity will not last for a long time. Reaping its benefits requires recognition of the various challenges to fully integrating young women and men into society. Living in an adverse political and security environment, Lebanon's youth are excluded from established political processes and many turn toward extremist political and religious groups. Moreover, the quality of education is deteriorating and overpriced, and educational investments generate low returns given domestic work opportunities. As petrodollars have surged in the region, young skilled Lebanese men are more likely to migrate than ever before.

These facts are deeply affecting the way families are being formed in Lebanon, with marriage being delayed and fertility declining sharply, increasing the likelihood that the window of opportunity might close earlier than expected. Unless serious measures are undertaken to place youth at the core of the development debate in Lebanon, the country might see its essential human capital erode significantly over the next decade. Below are a few recommendations for improving the lives of young people in Lebanon in four central dimensions: political inclusion, education, employment, and migration.

Political Inclusion

Lebanon's youth suffer from political exclusion, even though one sees many young Lebanese men and women strongly advocating for local parties or leaders. Lebanon's system of political representation has tailored all forms of civic engagement to serve the country's political elite: a mix of religious and traditional leaders who have established patronage networks.[53] Many young Lebanese are supporters of their sect's or their region's local leaders, but they rarely have a say in the functioning of their leaders' parties. To change this, a first step should be to lower the minimum voting age from the current 21 to 18. In addition, civic engagement courses should be taught at schools and universities, with a focus on delivering a message of empowerment to the younger generation rather than dependency on one's own sect or community.

Education

Lebanon's 2007 Social Action Plan makes special mention of children, women, the elderly, and the disabled as specific groups that will benefit from reforms aimed at reducing poverty, improving social indicators, and achieving the Millennium Development Goals.[54] Youth are neither mentioned nor included. According to the plan, $75 million has been designated to improve conditions for the "neediest population of society." Some of this aid does extend to the education system where the plan aims to reduce the dropout rate in poorer areas by assisting with tuition fees, and providing school meals, books, stationary, and transport to facilitate school attendance. This assistance can be identified as a step toward reducing the exclusion of future youth by ensuring broader access to education, giving otherwise marginalized individuals the opportunity to pursue education at levels equivalent to their wealthier counterparts and thereby affording them more opportunities, including higher wages, associated with more advanced levels of education.

Similarly, the plan intends to streamline the use of the country's education expenditures (currently 4 percent of GDP) to improve education indicators. Notably, the plan targets reductions in the dropout rate in public schools (currently 22 percent) and the repetition rate (48 percent). The plan also outlines ideas for reevaluating the distribution of public schools in the country to minimize the waste of resources.

In addition, the intent to create a safety net for the poor and very poor populations of Lebanon is described in the Social Action Plan, which aims at "reducing regional disparities in accessibility to basic infrastructure, creat[ing] jobs, reduc[ing] unemployment and reduc[ing] internal migration of the rural population to urban regions." One can only assume from the rhetoric used in this document that youth are considered to be part of the overall population, without the need for special consideration.

Modifications in the country's education system could reverberate throughout society. At the heart of the changes that need to be implemented is the notion that quality education must be available to all. It is telling that in its Social Action Plan of 2007, the Lebanese government concedes that the distribution of schools is not based on demographic needs. The result is a waste of resources that could be reallocated to improve schools where dropout and repetition rates are high. These recovered funds could be used to further help children of the most impoverished families to attend school. Of course, another option would be to waive all tuition fees for the poorest families.

Another way to reduce high dropout and repetition rates is to make education more attractive to students. This would require a fundamental reevaluation of the existing curricula and could include more interactive teaching with greater use of technological tools in the classroom.

At higher levels of education, more must be done to encourage and facilitate the attendance of students from poorer regions. Scholarships targeting disadvantaged groups should be encouraged, and state-sponsored student loans should be considered to increase access to higher education for lower-income students.

Furthermore, inconsistencies between the structure of higher education programs and the real needs of the job market need to be resolved. Market studies should be conducted and existing employers consulted, with an eye to designing education programs that meet the needs of the job market. This exercise could result in new technical and vocational education programs at both the secondary and tertiary levels.

Employment

An overhaul of the educational system should serve to make youth more attractive to employers. However, two issues persist: the routes through which youth access their first-time employment; and the situation of youth who remain unemployed.

Although *wasta* is intrinsically embedded in Lebanese culture, alternative routes must be established for youth who may not have the right connections to obtain the employment they desire—even if they are qualified. Considering the cost of private Internet use and the precarious provision of electricity in Lebanon, these alternative networks must expand beyond the Internet. A viable option might be youth employment centers, where youth can go to find jobs and obtain advice on career choices and the best ways to find jobs suited to their particular skills. A secondary benefit of such centers would be the opportunity to actively track unemployment rates among youth.

Greater support must be afforded to youth who struggle with longer periods of unemployment. This support may include financial aid, but it should also offer activities to ensure that youth do not feel isolated or depressed about their inability to find a job. To gain access to decent housing within their income range, youth should have access to mortgages and housing loans.

Promoting youth employment in Lebanon requires active public policies that facilitate the private sector's operations. The costs of doing business in Lebanon remain high, even if one subtracts the indirect costs imposed by the country's high political risk. High telecommunications costs could be reduced, and investments in better telecom technology increased, by promoting competition in this sector. Tax breaks for youth-intensive companies or for firms that provide internships and part-time jobs for students could encourage start-ups and entrepreneurs. Lebanon's public infrastructure remains quite weak, with electricity and water cuts still affecting the operations of many businesses. Public-private partnerships in public works projects that employ Lebanon's youth and at the same time contribute to better infrastructure services could be a way forward.

Migration

A first step in addressing the complex issue of migration in Lebanon is a serious effort to gather more information on this phenomenon. It is unfortunate that a labor-exporting country like Lebanon does not have accurate official information on the extent of emigration and its patterns. A public-private committee or study group should be formed and charged with producing updated analytical information on migration, especially among youth.

A second step would involve tackling the "push" factors that drive Lebanese, especially Lebanese youth, to migrate. The first need here is an economic program to reduce living expenses, especially housing costs, by providing cheaper housing loans for young graduates. Second, there is a need to invest more in skilled public sector jobs, because the country cannot continue to rely on the private sector to provide more job opportunities under an adverse political environment. This does not mean that the government should resort to public hiring across the board, a step that would inflate the public wage bill in an already heavily indebted country. But there is a need to retain skilled Lebanese workers and at the same time upgrade public services, two goals that could be achieved if more, and better paid, job opportunities for talented individuals were created within the civil service. Third, higher education institutions should teach more skills that enable local job creation, making migration an option, rather than a goal, for Lebanon's young labor force.

Notes

1. Bilal al-Naaim, deputy head of Hezbollah's executive bureau, quoted by Integrated Regional Information Networks, "In-Depth: Youth in Crisis: Coming of Age in the 21st Century. Lebanon: Born in the Line of Fire, Shia Youth Politicised Early" (United Nations Office for the Coordination of Humanitarian Affairs, August 27, 2008); see www.irinnews.org/InDepthMain.aspx?InDepthId=28&ReportId=70011 &Country=Yes.

2. On March 19, 2009, the Lebanese Parliament voted to lower the voting age from 21 years to 18 years. The new voting age will apply to the 2010 municipal elections and the 2013 parliamentary elections.

3. Monia Martini, "The Voice of Youth in Post-war Lebanon: Making Peace Building Sustainable," *Tesionline*, June 20, 2008 (www.tesionline.com/intl/indepth.jsp?id= 2400).

4. World Bank, "Lebanon Economic and Social Impact Assessment" (Washington: 2007); see http://intresources.worldbank.org/INTLEBANON/Resources/ESIA-Report-Final-Draft-012007.pdf.

5. Ibid.

6. Office of Conflict Management and Mitigation, *Youth and Conflict: A Toolkit for Intervention* (United States Agency for International Development, 2005), see www.usaid.gov/our_work/cross-cutting_programs/conflict/publications/docs/CMM_Youth_and_Conflict_Toolkit_April_2005.pdf.

7. United Nations Development Program (UNDP), Bureau for Crisis Prevention and Recovery, *Youth and Violent Conflict: Society and Development and Conflict in Crisis* (New York: 2006); see www.undp.org/cpr/whats_new/UNDP_Youth_PN.pdf).

8. UNDP, Regional Bureau for Arab States, *Arab Human Development Report 2005: Towards the Rise of Women in the Arab World* (New York: 2006); see www.pogar.org/publications/other/ahdr/ahdr2005e.pdf.

9. Choghig Kasparian, *L'Entrée des Jeunes Libanais dans la Vie Active et l'Emigration: Enquête Realisée par l'Université Saint-Joseph de Beyrouth*, vol. III (Beirut: Press de l'Université Saint-Joseph, 2003).

10. UNDP and Ministry of Social Affairs, *Mapping of Living Conditions* (Beirut: 1998); see www.undp.org.lb/programme/pro-poor/poverty/povertyinlebanon/

molc/main.html); UNDP and the Central Administration for Statistics, *Living Conditions of Households—The National Survey of Households' Living Conditions* (2004); see www.cas.gov.lb/Studies_en.asp.

11. In Lebanon, primary education is for ages 6 to 12, intermediate for ages 12 to 15, secondary for 15 to 18, and university is taken here for individuals between 18 and 29.

12. Data from the 2004/2005 Multi Purpose Survey (MPS) of household expenditures administered by the Central Administration for Statistics, Beirut.

13. Kasparian, *L'Entrée des Jeunes Libanais dans la Vie Active et l'Emigration.*

14. Ibid.

15. Ina V. S. Mullis and others, *TIMSS 2007 International Mathematics Report* (Boston College, Lynch School of Education, TIMSS & PIRLS International Study Center, 2008); Michael O. Martin and others, *TIMSS 2007 International Science Report* (Boston College, Lynch School of Education, TIMSS & PIRLS International Study Center, 2008).

16. UNDP and Ministry of Social Affairs, *Mapping of Living Conditions.*

17. Kamal Abouchedid and Ramzi Naim Nasser, "Job-seeking Behaviour and Job Outcomes among Lebanese University Graduates in Private and Public Universities," *International Journal for Educational and Vocational Guidance* 6, no. 3 (2006): 167–80.

18. Author's computations based on data from the Lebanese Ministry of Finance.

19. World Bank, "Economic and Social Impact Assessment From Recovery to Sustainable Growth" (Washington: 2007).

20. UNDP and the Central Administration for Statistics, *Living Conditions of Households.*

21. Ibid.

22. UNDP and Ministry of Social Affairs, *Mapping of Living Conditions*; UNDP and the Central Administration for Statistics, *Living Conditions of Households.*

23. UNDP and the Central Administration for Statistics, *Living Conditions of Households.*

24. Kasparian, *L'Entrée des Jeunes Libanais dans la Vie Active et l'Emigration.* The Saint Joseph survey is the only recent survey containing detailed information on the school-to-work transition for Lebanese youth.

25. Ibid.

26. Abouchedid and Nasser, "Job-seeking Behaviour and Job Outcomes among Lebanese University Graduates in Private and Public Universities."

27. Kasparian, *L'Entrée des Jeunes Libanais dans la Vie Active et l'Emigration.*

28. Ibid.

29. Ibid.

30. Ibid.

31. World Bank, "Lebanon Public Expenditure Reform Priorities for Fiscal Adjustment, Growth and Poverty Alleviation" (Washington: 2005).

32. Ibid.

33. Calculating the costs of youth exclusion is based on the following assumptions: youth (aged 15 to 29) earn on average 80 percent of average national wages, females earn on average 25 percent less than males, and the youth unemployment rate is equivalent to adult unemployment (as zero unemployment among youth is unrealistic).

34. Jad Chaaban, "The Costs of Youth Exclusion in the Middle East," Middle East Youth Initiative Working Paper 7 (Wolfensohn Center for Development at the Brookings Institution and the Dubai School of Government, 2008).

35. Kasparian, *L'Entrée des Jeunes Libanais dans la Vie Active et l'Emigration.*

36. Hoda Rashad, Magued Osman, and Farzaneh Roudi-Fahimi, "Marriage in the Arab World," policy brief (Washington: Population Reference Bureau, December 2005) (www.prb.org).

37. Prem C. Saxena, Andrzej Kulczycki, and Rozzet Jurdi, "Nuptiality Transition and Marriage Squeeze in Lebanon: Consequences of Sixteen Years of Civil War," *Journal of Comparative Family Studies* (special issue on Turbulence in the Middle East) 35, no. 2 (2004): 241–59. The civil war lasted from 1975 to 1990.

38. Ironically, Lebanese law recognizes civil marriages performed outside the country. As a result, many Lebanese couples of different religions marry in civil court in neighboring Cyprus or Greece. In the event of a dispute or divorce, the Lebanese courts must apply the law of the country in which the marriage took place.

39. Myriam Khlat and Adele Khudr, "Religious Endogamy and Consanguinity in Marriage Patterns in Beirut, Lebanon," *Social Biology* 33, no. 1–2 (1986): 138–45.

40. Mona Chemali Khalaf, "Women's International Labor Migration in the Arab World: Historical and Socio-Economic Perspectives," paper presented at the Consultative Meeting on "Migration and Mobility and How This Movement Affects Women," United Nations Division for the Advancement of Women, Malmö, December 2–4, 2003; see www.un.org/womenwatch/daw/meetings/consult/CM-Dec03-EP5.pdf.

41. UNDP, Regional Bureau for Arab States, *The Arab Human Development Report 2003: Building a Knowledge Society* (New York: 2003); see www.pogar.org/publications/other/ahdr/ahdr2003e.pdf.

42. Ibid.

43. UNDP and the Central Administration for Statistics, *Living Conditions of Households*; Choghig Kasparian, *Liban: la dimension demographique et economique des migrations,* Mediterranean Migration Report 2006–2007 (San Domenico di Fiesole, Italy: European University Institute, Robert Schuman Centre for Advanced Studies, Euro-Mediterranean Consortium for Applied Research on International Migration, 2007).

44. Kasparian, *Liban: la dimension demographique et economique des migrations.*

45. Kasparian, *L'Entrée des Jeunes Libanais dans la Vie Active et l'Emigration.*

46. Ibid.

47. Ibid.

48. Richard H. Adams, "Migration, Remittances and Development: The Critical Nexus in the Middle East and North Africa," paper prepared for the United Nations Expert Group Meeting on International Migration and Development in the Arab

Region, Beirut, May 15–17, 2006 (www.un.org/esa/population/meetings/ EGM_Ittmig_Arab/P01_Adams.pdf).

49. Kasparian, *Liban: la dimension demographique et economique des migrations.*

50. Kasparian, *L'Entrée des Jeunes Libanais dans la Vie Active et l'Emigration.*

51. Ibid.

52. Ibid.

53. Kamal Dib, *Warlords and Merchants: The Lebanese Business and Political Establishment* (Reading, U.K.: Ithaca Press, 2004).

54. Ministry of Economics and Trade, "Social Action Plan Toward Strengthening Social Safety Nets and Access to Basic Social Services" (Beirut: January 2007); see www.economy.gov.lb/MOET/English/Navigation/News/SocialActionPlan2007.htm.

TAHER KANAAN *and* MAY HANANIA

6

The Disconnect between Education, Job Growth, and Employment in Jordan

The prospects of young Jordanians—perhaps more than any other age group—are being shaped by the interplay between Jordan's exposure to myriad economic and political shocks and the effectiveness with which the country adjusts to these powerful changes. The economic volatility evident in the country has been driven largely by Jordan's dependence on workers' remittances and foreign aid. Furthermore, events such as the 1990–91 Gulf War, the second Palestinian intifada of 2000, the repercussions of the attacks of September 11, 2001, and the U.S.-led invasion of Iraq in 2003 and subsequent occupation have fundamentally changed the economy and demography of Jordan.

In recent years, Jordan has grown more successful in effectively managing external shocks, and through reforms it has created an environment for more sustainable growth. However, these improved economic conditions have not yet worked to the advantage and benefit of young Jordanians. In fact, the recent period of growth seems to have deepened the cleavage between education and employment transitions: education reforms have led to improved school enrollments and quality, but the labor market has moved toward low-skilled jobs shunned by young Jordanians. Jordan's ability to turn around its education system is no longer in doubt. The challenge is whether the economy can fully break away from its rentier characteristics and diversify and deepen its modern service and industrial base, thus creating a labor market that harnesses the talents of an increasingly educated workforce.

Growing Up in a Volatile Rentier State

Over the past three decades, Jordan's main economic challenge has been to reduce its dependence on external drivers of growth. In the years following World War II and independence from Britain, foreign aid was the main driver of economic performance. During the past two decades, remittances of Jordanian workers, especially those working in oil-rich Arab countries, have emerged as a source for sustaining the country's living standards, enabling the economy to achieve high rates of capital formation despite minimal rates of domestic savings.

GDP growth in Jordan has been highly volatile over the past thirty years, rising and falling with oil booms and busts, side effects of regional conflicts, and economic mismanagement (figure 6-1). For most of the 1970s and early 1980s, Jordan experienced high growth and consequent increases in government spending coinciding with the first oil boom. During the 1970s and 1980s, Jordan also suffered from effects of "Dutch disease," as exchange rate appreciation weakened competitiveness of its exports and promoted investment in nontradable goods (construction and services). Between 1983 and 1989, cuts in official assistance from oil-rich countries resulted in weak growth and large debt, which culminated in the economic crisis of 1989, when the exchange rate of the dinar lost about 50 percent of its value. At the same time, government policies did not curb excessive spending, opting to continue business as usual.

Jordan's economy began to recover in the 1990s, helped by the consumption of repatriated Jordanians expelled from Kuwait after the 1990–91 Gulf War. Events after the turn of the century, such as the Iraq war, when Jordan became a supply route for besieged Iraq and home to Iraqi refugees with their enormous savings, triggered a resumption in growth.

During this period of volatile economic performance, Jordan's population rose from 2.0 million in 1976 to 5.7 million in 2007. The average annual population growth rate exceeded 3.5 percent during 1977–95, reflecting markedly high natural growth attributable to increased fertility and improved health. This period also saw an influx of immigrants mainly from the Palestinian Territories and Iraq, including in particular repatriated Jordanians during the first Gulf War. Since 1996 population growth has slowed to an annual average rate of 2.7 percent. Coupled with its volatile economic performance, Jordan's demographic trends have imposed significant pressures on the ability of the economy to provide for human development.

Figure 6-1. *Jordan's GDP Growth Rates per Capita, 1977–2007*

Growth rate per capita (percent)

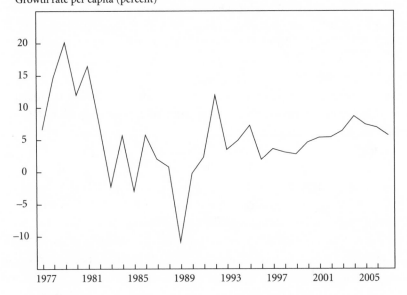

Source: Jordan Department of Statistics website and various issues of the Central Bank of Jordan *Monthly Statistical Bulletin.*

More recently, Jordan's economic performance has improved, showing greater resilience against new external shocks such as the elimination of free oil delivery from Iraq. The surge in economic activity has been broad based and not limited to the robust exports of textiles from Qualified Industrial Zones (QIZs) and exports to Iraq. Manufacturing value added during 2001–04 (excluding the slump year of 2003) contributed more than 35 percent to GDP growth, while the transport and communications sector contributed another 20 percent, and the financial services, retail, and construction sectors around 10 percent each.

Still, the Jordanian economy maintains many attributes of a rentier economy, where significant public revenue accrues from natural resources, such as phosphates and potash, and from external financial assistance and where private household income is largely dependent on family members' remittances from abroad. The transition away from a rentier state to a fully diversified industrial economy is even more urgent given the demographics of the country. Youth aged 15 to 29 are currently the largest demographic category in the country, making up more than 29 percent of

Figure 6-2. *Share of Youth Aged 15 to 29 in Jordan, 1950–2020*

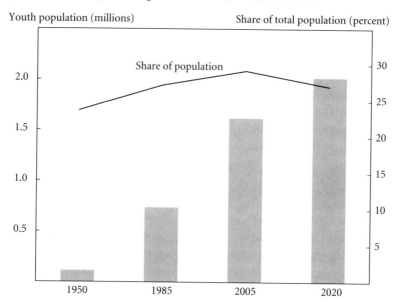

Source: United Nations, "World Urbanization Prospects: The 2005 Revision" (database) (New York: United Nations Department of Economic and Social Affairs, Population Division, 2006).

the population (figure 6-2). A further 38 percent of the population is below the age of 15. The largest five-year age cohort of Jordanians in 2007 was the 10 to 14 age group.[1] This bulge will reach working age over the next decade, leading to increasing labor supply pressure. The government estimates that 50,000 new jobs must be created annually just to maintain the current employment rate. Unless this transition to a more diversified economy is complete, meeting the changing needs of Jordan's youth population will continue to be a challenge for the country, and young people will continue to be marginalized.

Jordan's Education System: A Leading Reformer

Poor in natural resources and lacking a well-developed industrial base, Jordan is dependent on its human capital to drive its economy. As a result, the government has long allocated considerable proportions of its resources to education and has also been a leading reformer of education in the Middle East.

With the onset of educational reform in the early 1990s, educational expenditures averaged 6.5 percent of GDP and 20 percent of the budget during the 1995–2005 period. This is higher than the regional average of 5.3 percent of GDP, and one of the highest rates of public expenditure on schooling in the region after the Palestinian Territories and Tunisia.[2] Wide-ranging government reforms have targeted all sectors of basic education, vocational training, and nonformal education, and have focused on supporting teachers, students, managers, and educational institutions. The reform efforts have been driven by a desire to remodel Jordan's education system for the modern knowledge economy and to equip young Jordanians with the skills that young people need to compete in the global economy. Major reforms have targeted pedagogy methods and curriculum. Jordan has equipped most public schools with computers and Internet connections, making the country one of the first in the Middle East to fully integrate information and communications technology (ICT) as part of school pedagogy.

Two major initiatives, the Education Reform for Knowledge Economy Project (ERfKE) and the Discovery School pilot project within the Jordan Education Initiative best embody Jordan's reformist spirit. The objectives of ERfKE include curriculum reform, teacher training, and introduction and upgrading of school ICT infrastructure. Through the Discovery School pilot project, 100 "Discovery Schools" were selected and provided with basic ICT capacities while their teachers were given needed professional development. Since the project's inception, six e-curriculum tools (mathematics, science, Arabic, ICT, English as a foreign language, and citizenship) have been developed and deployed at the Discovery Schools, reaching 80,000 students and 3,500 teachers. Upon completion of the pilot project, the e-curriculum tools will be introduced in all 3,300 schools in the kingdom.

In addition to curriculum development in core subject areas, Jordan has introduced a new subject—information management— to prepare secondary students for positions in e-commerce, information management, and computer-based accounting. The new curriculum emphasizes both subject-matter skills and other transferable skills that are necessary for success in the private sector, including communication, team work, and analytical and problem-solving skills.

Moving toward Greater Equity and Quality

Jordan's lack of natural resources and its subsequent reliance on human capital to remain competitive has led Jordan's leadership to place signifi-

Figure 6-3. *Gross Enrollment Rates in Primary, Secondary, and Tertiary Education, 1970–2005*

Enrollment rate (percent)

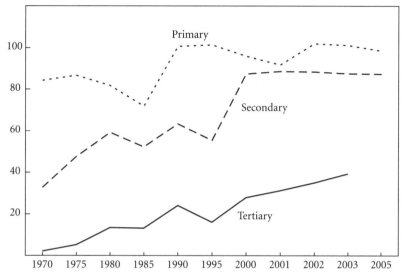

Source: World Bank EdStats Database

cant attention on education services and push for concrete strategies to expand access and improve quality. As a result, Jordan has witnessed a large expansion in its education base, with enrollment rates improving significantly across socioeconomic groups and gender. Urban-rural and gender disparities in education have disappeared, and literacy among youth aged 15 to 29 reached 98.9 percent in 2007.[3] Currently the net enrollment rate is 90 percent for primary education, 80 percent for secondary education, and 40 percent for tertiary education (figure 6-3). In addition, 98.4 percent of children (98.2 percent male and 98.7 percent female) complete a full course of primary school and 87.2 percent (86.7 percent male and 88.2 percent female) complete a course of secondary school. Jordan also has one of the lowest repetition rates in the region (1 percent for primary and secondary education).[4]

Jordan has continued to make strides in improving the quality of education. In the 2007 Trends in International Mathematics and Science Study (TIMSS), Jordan achieved the highest score among any of the participating Middle Eastern countries in the science examination and the second highest score in the mathematics examination for eighth graders.[5] (This excludes

Israel, which outperformed Jordan on the mathematics examination, but not the science examination.) The mean score for Jordanian eighth graders in the mathematics test was 427, and the average scale score for female participants was twenty points higher than that of males. This trend in the performance of young women was even more pronounced in the 2003 mathematics test, when Jordanian females averaged twenty-seven points higher than Jordanian males. Of the forty-six participating countries and four benchmarking entities participating in 2003, only Bahrain had a wider positive gap between female and male students during that year (thirty-three points). (Averaging across all participating countries, girls outscored boys by one point in 2003 and by five points in 2007.)

In the science test, Jordan performed at the highest level of any country in the region with an average score of 482, up from the 1999 (average score: 450) and 2003 (average score: 475) tests. In science 26 percent of Jordanian eighth graders achieved the high international benchmark score of 550, an increase from 21 percent in 2003. Five percent achieved the advanced international benchmark score (625), an increase from 3 percent in the 2003 testing cycle. As a matter of comparison, these percentages put Jordan on par with Scotland. Jordan had greater percentages of students reaching both of these benchmarks than Italy, Turkey, or Ukraine.

These results attest to the relative success Jordan has achieved in expanding access to all levels of education. However, the achievements thus far remain more quantitative than qualitative, particularly with regard to tertiary education. Although the quality of education in Jordan appears to compare well with that of other Arab countries, as shown by its above-average scores on some international tests, the room for improvement is still extensive.

Education Challenges Ahead

A major challenge for the education system is to produce "employable" workers with a spectrum of skills and proficiencies that are sound and flexible enough to close the so-called mismatch between job opportunities generated by economic growth and the abilities of the Jordanian labor force. Improvements in quality of education still have some way to go before they can match the best international standards set by countries such as Korea and Malaysia. Jordan must continue to deepen existing reforms so that education is no longer solely geared to serve the public sector but also is fully adapted to Jordan's private sector economy. To complete this transition, reform must go beyond the "engineering" approach, which views educational development as a technical matter that can be addressed by more funding for schools, teachers, and textbooks.[6] Future reforms must also address the underlying incentives of teachers and students that drive teaching and learning quality.[7]

First, to close the quality gap, a system of accountability should be developed that monitors the performance of teachers and schools and establishes links between their performance and rewards (financial or otherwise). Additional funds should be allocated to improving the educational qualifications, salaries, and social standing of teachers.

Second, the education system must be more accountable for producing results. Parents and students should be equipped with mechanisms to demand better education policies, for example, through the creation of parents' associations. Greater involvement of primary stakeholders in the education system, including the private sector, is needed to maximize returns on investment in education. Reforms in the structure of the education system can also enhance greater public accountability, for example, through decentralization and increased local control over the education system and by making information about resource allocation and education outcomes available to the public.

Third, recent reforms have given much attention to curriculum reform, but future reforms must also focus on continuous learning outside the classroom and on older youth who are beyond the "traditional" schooling age. Education budgets and facilities should be increased to expand extracurricular and participatory activities. Inadequate education budgets together with poorly qualified teaching staff result in a lack of participatory activities and facilities for social and cultural interaction, such as sports and other extracurricular activities, where students can build necessary skills such as creativity and team work.

Fourth, tracking at the secondary education level and its link to university education must be reevaluated to address the social stigma associated with vocational education. Currently, the secondary education level consists of a common core curriculum that ends with the tenth grade. This is followed by an additional two years (up to the twelfth grade) during which the students opt to pursue either the academic (arts and sciences) track or an applied/vocational track. Both the academic and the applied/vocational tracks end with a general secondary education examination, the *Tawjihi*.

The academic track qualifies students for entrance to universities, provided they obtain admission level scores on the *Tawjihi*. Students who opt for the applied/vocational track can also enroll in community colleges to improve their skills and proficiency in their chosen vocation or to get a second chance at admission to university. Alternatively, graduates of the applied/vocational track may choose to upgrade their skills through apprenticeship programs run by the Ministry of Education. This track, rightly or wrongly, is perceived as inferior by most students and parents obsessed with the social esteem of university education. A tentative approach to address this issue is discussed later.

Institutions of higher education include traditional universities and community colleges. Access to higher education is open to graduates with the general secondary education certificate who may choose among eleven public universities, sixteen private universities, and several private and public community colleges. Jordan's community colleges offer specialized two- or three-year programs in a variety of professional fields of study, including education, commerce, computer studies, medicine, pharmacology, hotel management, interior design, social work, nursing, and midwifery. All community college students have to pass a comprehensive government exam (*Al-Shamel*) at the end of their studies. While formal university education focuses on traditional academic fields, community colleges are intended to provide practical skills that are needed in the labor market. However, community colleges are increasingly offering programs in traditional academic fields as a bridge to accommodate students who want to be reconsidered for university admission.

Public university education is highly subsidized by the government, and admission to public universities tends to be more competitive than at the community college level and is generally restricted to those with the highest *Tawjihi* scores. At the moment, admission to all universities in Jordan is based exclusively on how well one does on the *Tawjihi* exam.

While some reforms have been undertaken to change curricula away from rote learning, the *Tawjihi* exam is still not designed to measure critical or independent thinking or to test students' aptitudes for different courses of study within the higher education system. For example, students who earn an "A+" score are directed toward medicine; students who earn an "A-" score are directed toward engineering; and students who earn a "D-" score are directed toward the study of sharia law. Hence, students are directed to courses of study that could possibly run counter to their aptitudes and interests.

Further reforms to the *Tawjihi* testing system and university admissions practices are needed. The benefits of such "differed admission" policies strengthen the case for delinking higher education from secondary and

Tawjihi-level education. Making the *Tawjihi* testing system and university admissions policies more flexible and shifting the criteria for university admission will have a number of positive effects. First, it will relieve the pressure on *Tawjihi* graduates to obtain admission to university in the same year that they graduate. Second, it will secure a second opportunity for those who, because of financial difficulty or other compelling circumstances, joined the labor market right after high school. This will give them a second chance to apply for university admission at a later date when they are more ready or more mature. Third, reforms in university admissions will also save students and parents some of the embarrassment associated with a "poor" *Tawjihi* performance by providing these youth with a second chance to prepare and sit for university admission tests.

Delinking higher education from secondary and *Tawjihi*-level education should be coupled with continued reform in primary and secondary school curricula. These reforms should strengthen the readiness of students to function in the labor market by equipping them with skills appropriate not only for technical vocational jobs but also for clerical and office jobs in manufacturing, construction, and services and for creating and managing their own microbusinesses.

Youth and the Labor Market: Supply Trends

The Jordanian labor market is under severe pressures emanating from the youth bulge, rising female labor force participation from historically low rates, and migration. Job creation is a daunting task for the government, with the official unemployment rate fluctuating around 14 percent in recent years. Moreover, youth unemployment in particular remains quite high at 30 percent, an acute social problem, since nearly 30 percent of the country's population falls within the 15 to 29 age range and nearly 70 percent of the population is under the age of 29.

The labor force has grown at a rate of about 2.2 percent a year since 2000 and stood at 1.4 million in early 2009. That number is expected to reach 1.6 million by 2015, requiring the creation of about 30,000 to 35,000 jobs annually during the next six years (table 6-1). In addition to the 200,000 jobs needed for new labor market entrants, about 172,000 jobs need to be created for the existing unemployed.

The overall participation rate in the labor market decreased slightly from 40.4 percent in 1995 to 39.7 percent in 2006 (table 6-2). The low rates result primarily from a low female labor force participation rate (12.4 percent), as

Table 6-1. *Jordanian Labor Force Size by Gender and Location—Broad Definition*[a]

Labor force	2000 (number)	2006 (number)	Growth rate (percent)	Projections (number)	
				2009	2015
Male					
Urban	707,908	922,883	4.4		
Rural	186,580	115,685	−7.9		
Total	894,488	1,038,568	2.5	1,118,424	1,297,029
Female					
Urban	168,123	194,354	3.5		
Rural	36,590	21,735	−6.7		
Total	204,713	216,089	2.1	230,677	262,851
Total					
Urban	876,031	1,117,237	4.3		
Rural	223,170	137,420	−7.8		
Total	1,099,201	1,254,657	2.2	1,349,101	1,559,880

Source: Ragui Assaad and Mona Amer, *Labor Market Conditions in Jordan, 1995–2006: An Analysis of Microdata Sources*, vol. 1 (Amman: Al-Manar Project, National Center for Human Resource Development, 2007), ch. 1, sec. 4.

a. The broad definition of the labor force includes the employed and those unemployed who are available and searching for work. This definition also includes the discouraged unemployed, the nonemployed who desire and are available for work but who have not actively searched for it.

well as a relatively low male rate by international standards (66.7 percent). These trends are present in both urban and rural areas. Female participation decreased in urban areas but slightly increased in rural areas. Urban participation rates continue to be higher than rural rates for both males and females, but the gap is shrinking.[8]

Recent research on the labor supply trends quantified above shows that labor force growth has decelerated somewhat since 1995 but is poised for another growth spurt as the largest cohort ever of young people makes its way into the labor market over the next decade. Even if recent declines in labor force participation persist at the current pace, the forthcoming increase in the size of the working-age population will more than compensate, leading to an acceleration in the growth of the labor force. If current educational reform efforts are even modestly successful, future cohorts of labor markets entrants are expected to be more educated and thus will aspire to a higher quality of jobs.[9]

Table 6-2. *Labor Force Participation (Ages 15 to 64) by Gender, Location—*
Standard Definition[a]
Percent

Labor Force	1995	2000	2006
Male			
Urban	70.7	69.7	67.1
Rural	65.8	66.5	63.4
Total	69.8	69.0	66.7
Female			
Urban	13.6	13.7	12.6
Rural	9.6	10.5	10.7
Total	12.8	13.0	12.4
Total			
Urban	41.8	41.8	40.1
Rural	34.7	38.8	37.2
Total	40.4	41.1	39.7

Source: Assaad and Amer, *Labor Market Conditions in Jordan, 1995–2006*, ch. 1, table 1.2.
a. The standard definition of the labor force includes the employed and those unemployed who are available and searching for work.

Youth and the Labor Market: Demand Trends

Since the turn of the new millennium, Jordan has experienced remarkable economic growth, which followed a period of stagnation of per capita GDP. The recovery increased real growth of GDP to an average annual rate of 5.5 percent during 2001–03 and to 7.7 percent during 2003–06. However, employment growth lagged behind economic growth, increasing at an annual rate of 2.9 percent in 2001–03 and 6.0 percent in 2004–06 (table 6-3).

The effect of GDP growth on employment was larger in the private sector where employment growth rates reached 4.1 percent in 2001–03 and 6.6 percent in 2004–06. In comparison, employment growth rates in the public sector were much lower, at 0.5 percent in the first period and 4.6 percent in the second period.

A serious concern is that a large proportion of the total increase in employment went to non-Jordanians, especially during the second period of high GDP growth (2004–06). Employment of non-Jordanians increased by 6.4 percent in the first period (2001–03) and by 18.9 percent in the second

Table 6-3. *Effect of Economic Growth on Employment*[a]

Persons employed	Employment average annual increment (thousands)		Employment annual growth rates (percent)	
	2001–03	2004–06	2001–03	2004–06
Jordanians				
Public	1.8	14.4	0.6	4.1
Private	18.6	14.8	3.3	2.4
Total	20.4	29.2	2.3	3.0
Non-Jordanians				
Public	−0.4	2.2	−4.5	33.2
Private	10.5	40.0	6.9	18.5
Total	10.2	42.2	6.4	18.9
Total Population				
Public	1.4	16.6	0.5	4.6
Private	29.1	54.7	4.1	6.6
Total	30.5	71.4	2.9	6.0

Source: Authors' recalculations of tables in Annexes 5 and 7 of Ragui Assaad and Mona Amer, *Labor Market Conditions in Jordan, 1995–2006: An Analysis of Microdata Sources,* vol. 1 (Amman: Al-Manar Project, National Center for Human Resource Development, 2007). The tables are based on Department of Statistics Employment and Unemployment Surveys (EUS) data.

a. GDP grew at an average annual rate of 5.5 percent in 2001–03 and 7.7 percent in 2003–06.

period compared with an increase in employment of Jordanians of only 2.3 percent and 3.0 percent during the same two time periods.

These employment growth rates are associated with an average annual increment of 31,000 jobs a year from 2001 to 2003, and 71,000 jobs a year from 2004 to 2006. In the first period, 95 percent of the total increase (29,000 jobs) occurred in the private sector, and 67 percent of these jobs (20,000 jobs) went to Jordanians. In contrast, during the 2004–06 period, 77 percent of the new jobs were in the private sector (55,000 jobs) and only 41 percent (29,000) went to Jordanians. During the longer 1995–2006 period, the economy created an estimated 55,000 jobs a year, with 53 percent of them going to non-Jordanians.[10]

In 2006 the public sector employed more than one-third of the 1.3 million workforce, wholesale and retail trade employed 17 percent, and the manufacturing sector employed 11.5 percent. Despite the construction boom, construction employed only 6.4 percent of the workforce in 2006. The fastest-growing sectors in terms of employment have been restaurants and hotels, public administration, financial and business services, and wholesale and retail trade. While the agricultural sector has experienced significant growth in recent years, it has not generated new employment opportunities.

The Unemployment Crisis

As noted earlier, real GDP growth in recent years (2001–07) has occurred at an average annual rate of about 6.5 percent, more than 3 percentage points above the rate of population growth. However, some experts have characterized the macroeconomic improvements in Jordan as "jobless growth," or more precisely, growth without a substantial reduction in unemployment. Three trends support this thesis, namely, the limited growth of youth employment, fewer job prospects for young women, and the diminishing status of educated job seekers.

The recent period of economic growth has led to a slight improvement in overall unemployment rates but no major change in the status of young job seekers. Overall unemployment fell from 14.5 percent in 2006 to 13.1 percent in 2007 and to 12.7 percent in 2008. Among males, the unemployment rate declined from 12.4 percent in 2006 to 10.1 percent in 2008, while the unemployment rate for females, which stood at 26.0 percent in 2006, declined to 24.4 percent in 2008.[11]

Jordanian youth are most affected by current unemployment and its persistence. In 2008 unemployment rates were high among those aged 15 to 19 years at 33 percent (table 6-4). However, this group accounted for only 14 percent of the total unemployed. By contrast, youth aged 20 to 29 years constituted a much larger share of the unemployed at 61 percent. The unemployment rate for this group was 21 percent. In comparison unemployment was low among those aged 30 years and over, a group that constituted 25 percent of the unemployed. Hence, the engagement of youth is a priority for economic and social policy in combating unemployment and raising growth rates in future years.[12]

Youth unemployment is particularly severe among highly educated Jordanian youth, reflecting the limited impact of education on employment in Jordan. Unemployment for those with a bachelor's degree or higher is now 18 percent for young men and 49 percent for young women. In comparison, the unemployment rate is 11 percent for those with a secondary education, 15 percent for those with less than a secondary education, and 9 percent for those who are illiterate. In general, a large proportion of first-time job seek-

Table 6-4. *Unemployment Rates and Distribution of the Unemployed, 2008*
Percent

Age range	Unemployment rate			Share of total unemployment		
	Male	Female	Total	Male	Female	Total
15–19	32.0	52.3	32.9	19	3	14
20–29	15.2	39.5	20.7	53	77	61
15–29	17.7	39.8	22.2	72	80	75
30 and older	4.8	9.5	5.6	28	20	25
Total	10.1	24.4	12.7	100	100	100

Source: Al-Manar Project data, based on Jordan Department of Statistics, *Employment and Unemployment Survey*, 2008.

ers encounter difficulties in finding employment, leaving one in every four of these job seekers unemployed (figure 6-4). With regard to the distribution of the unemployed across all levels of educational attainment, in 2005, 39 percent of the unemployed had a tertiary education. In contrast, 14 percent of the unemployed had a secondary school education, and 47 percent of the unemployed had less than a secondary education or were illiterate.

The unemployment situation is particularly grave for young women. The unemployment rate for young females aged 15 to 29 was 39 percent in 2007, compared with 18 percent among young men. Although many young women in Jordan have the same educational opportunities as young men and thus acquire the same level of education, about five young males hold jobs for every young woman who is employed. In 2007 only 11 percent of young women aged 15 to 29 were working for pay, compared with 54 per-cent of males.[13] This outcome is largely linked to the lack of appropriate jobs that are compatible with prevailing social norms that govern the places and types of work that are considered "acceptable" according to sex, age, and social status and thus affect women's access to work. Consequently, over half of females aged 15 and over are housewives and do not participate in the labor force.

The lack of employment opportunities renders young people particu-larly vulnerable to poverty. Young women are more susceptible to unemployment and long-term inactivity, widening the gender gap and depriving society of their capabilities and qualifications. Youth from poorer households, many with minimal education, face the challenge of competing with foreign labor for jobs. In the countryside and remote regions where growth is lower, geographic mismatch in job creation is a challenge because

Figure 6-4. *Unemployment Rates by Level of Education for Youth Aged 15 to 29, 2005*

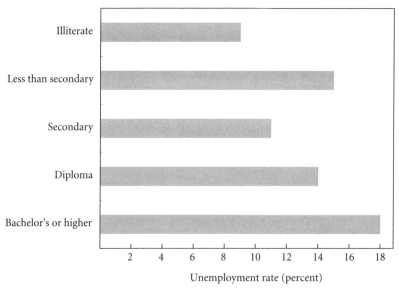

Unemployment rate (percent)

Source: World Bank, "Resolving Jordan's Labor Market Paradox," Report 39201-Jo (Washington: 2008), paragraph 1.17.

labor is less mobile and therefore less able to take advantage of jobs in the capital and main cities.[14]

The exclusion of youth from labor markets is underpinned by a combination of cyclical and structural trends in the labor market. A recent World Bank report on Jordan's labor market attributes the paradox of concurrent growth and high unemployment to mismatches in the Jordanian labor market and high reservation wages among workers within the context of a fairly open labor market where employers can easily meet their employment needs by hiring less costly foreign workers.[15]

Although a large number of jobs have been created in the past few years, especially in the construction sector, most of these new jobs have gone to foreign workers, whereas many Jordanians continue to prefer white-collar employment. Jordanian youth with higher education are increasingly unwilling to accept low-wage employment and prefer to wait for higher-paying jobs in the government or migrate abroad for better opportunities.

In a labor market that has become highly segmented along regional and gender lines, there has been a steady flow of non-Jordanian migrants into the country to fill the gaps in the domestic labor market. Men from more populated or less affluent Arab countries such as Egypt and Sudan take jobs in agribusiness or construction, and women from Southeast Asia take jobs as domestic workers. The absolute number of non-Jordanian workers has more than tripled since 1980 to reach 317,081 in 2006, accounting for 23.6 percent of the labor force. It is estimated that this number would be even higher if undocumented laborers were counted.

Moreover, while large inflows of remittances from Jordanians working outside the country help to support family members, they also contribute to high reservation wages among Jordanian workers at home. Thus, the claimed benefits of out-migration in the form of increased financial remittances can be a "mixed blessing." Expectations for high-quality employment combined with income support from families and from remittances have raised the reservation wages of young workers.

Evidence of this comes from a recent survey, which suggests that more than 50 percent of the unemployed are unwilling to accept available jobs at prevailing wages.[16] This represents one main reason for the poor labor market outcomes in Jordan. The inability of the private sector to create enough high-quality jobs in industry and modern services results from a combination of structural weaknesses in the economy, including business regulations and labor laws that do not encourage the private sector to venture into high-value-added industries. Instead, government policies have allowed incentives for the private sector to expand in industries that create low-skill jobs through tax and investment policy. In these low-skill industries, business firms prefer hiring foreign labor over Jordanian workers for a number of reasons. Foreign workers are willing to work for lower wages, and firms are allowed to hire foreign workers on temporary contracts that do not require employer contributions for social security or severance pay, making the cost of employing foreign labor even less expensive relative to Jordanian workers.

As a large number of foreign workers enter Jordan, growing numbers of young Jordanians are seeking employment opportunities in the Gulf and in Europe and the United States. High youth unemployment rates, rising urbanization, and poor living conditions have contributed to significant emigration, mostly by young males in search of jobs outside the country. While such migration carries some positive economic implications, especially in terms of remittances, it also undermines Jordan's future growth prospects, which require a skilled and educated workforce for a new knowledge-based economy. Emigration of large numbers of any country's labor force, particularly of the more talented and enterprising members, implies a quantitative and qualitative depletion of the country's human capital.

Employment Policy

With an increasingly more educated workforce, the quality of employment will be a growing concern in the future. Achievements on the educational front have thus far not resulted in significantly higher rates of employment or substantial wage increases, partly because of shortcomings in the quality of education and a mismatch between educational outcomes and labor market demands, and partly because of patterns of economic growth in the past decades that have favored the creation of low-wage jobs in certain sectors.[17]

Within this context, Jordan is facing a series of challenges related mainly to the lack of a clear and coherent employment policy framework. This has created a situation in which economic growth has not created quality jobs for Jordanians and has not reduced unemployment and poverty levels. Jordan currently faces three challenges: generating a sufficient number of quality jobs for the burgeoning number of new entrants to the labor market; improving the skills and productivity levels of the labor force to support greater competitiveness of Jordanian enterprises within the global economy; and responding to the needs for increased labor market flexibility, while ensuring that parallel measures for social protection are in place, especially for those workers who cannot adapt to the changing circumstances and skill requirements.

To address the challenge of youth unemployment, labor market policies must adopt separate approaches to address the needs of the involuntarily unemployed and the voluntarily unemployed. To this end, labor market and employment policy should adopt three main priorities.

First, employment policies should assist youth from lower-income households who might be willing to accept lower-paid jobs that currently go to foreign workers through programs such as employment services, training (particularly on-the-job training), and skill development.

Second, employment policy should raise incentives to encourage the voluntarily unemployed to accept existing jobs. This includes offering social protection measures and employment benefits such as maternity leave. It also includes changing civil service hiring practices that encourage young people to wait indefinitely for government jobs and discourage them from accepting alternate employment in the private sector. Not only must government hiring be reduced but hiring procedures that accept general job applications not tied to a specific job or to specific qualifications must be eliminated.

To encourage greater female labor force participation, arrangements that allow women to combine work and family should be supported. These include centralized preschools, kindergartens, and daycare facilities. In addition, flexible work arrangements allowed by the current digital age in combination with innovative business management practices would allow women to engage in a diversity of professions through a home office.

Third, economic policy should promote sectors that will create higher-wage jobs and eliminate distortions in economic policy—including the tax system, investment promotion, trade, migration, and the financial sector—that encourage growth of low-wage jobs.

To this end, Jordan has introduced special youth entrepreneurship training and vocational programs as a way to address the problem of unemployable graduates. These programs have encountered a number of problems, however, including limited private sector involvement, low standards of services, and insufficient information about the needs of the labor market, all of which form barriers for youth trying to enter new economic sectors.

One organization in Jordan, Injaz (Achievement), has provided a pioneering working model for bridging that gap by using an enterprising style of teaching and learning to plant the seeds of change. The main goal of Injaz is to get leaders from the private sector to teach marketable skills to high school and college students. It aims to equip graduates with broad-based skills that can be applied to a wide range of professions. Injaz started in Jordan in 1999 and has spread to twelve Arab countries, reaching more than 300,000 students.

Like most Arab countries, the weakest part in the education-employment nexus in Jordan is vocational training, in part because it is perceived as a lower-status and undesirable parallel system to the main "liberal" track of education. Continuing education and on-the-job training should be key components of any reforms in the vocational training system. The lack of on-the-job training in Jordan and other Arab countries is a significant factor in the low levels of labor productivity in the region.

The Problems of Early and Late Family Formation

Marriage is an important institution in Jordanian society. Married life is perceived as an essential and preferred way of life by all young men irrespective of social or educational level. Two opposing trends characterize family formation transitions in Jordan: early marriage, which is still prevalent though on the decline, and delayed marriage, which is a relatively newer phenomenon.

While the age gap between males and females at first marriage has decreased, Jordanian girls are still more likely than boys to marry as adolescents; 12.7 percent of young women under age 20 and 48.6 percent of young women aged 20 to 24 are married compared with 1.4 percent and 16.1 percent of young men in the same age groups. Despite personal status laws forbidding marriage under the age of 18, in some communities, girls as young as 14 and 15 are withdrawn from school by their parents to get married.[18] Young brides who become young mothers and are confined to their homes quickly lose their education opportunities, thereby further reducing future livelihood choices.[19] Also, young women who marry early begin having children sooner than women who marry later, and they tend to have higher numbers of children, which can have negative effects on maternal health.

A contrary trend is that family formation in Jordan is becoming difficult for many young people, as evidenced by young people involuntarily delaying marriage because of job shortages and insufficient income. Today, the average age of marriage is on the rise in Jordan. In 1979 the mean age at first marriage was 26 for males and 21 for females. Today, it is 29 for males and 26 for females.[20]

There are some positive aspects of delayed marriage, especially for women. Women who marry at a later age are able to obtain more education and enter the labor force. This consequently expands women's opportunities for education and work and also frees them from early childbearing. However, delayed marriage also poses new challenges, particularly for young men, and has profound consequences in a culture where financial independence and marriage are the mark of adulthood and social standing. Moreover, in a culture where sex outside marriage is forbidden, postponing marriage leaves a generation of youth frustrated in this regard.

The costs of marriage in Jordan, like elsewhere in the region, are high and can serve as an obstacle to marriage among many youth. Typically the groom and his family are expected to cover all the expenses of the wedding as well as the costs of setting up a household. In addition, housing costs continue to increase. The inflow of money into Jordan following the U.S. invasion of Iraq has resulted in soaring real estate prices, especially in Amman. Furthermore, while credit and loans allow youth in other parts of the world to leverage future earnings and smooth consumption, poorly functioning credit markets in Jordan make home mortgages and loans more inaccessible. With the growing costs of marriage and household formation, many young men, especially those who are unemployed or who work in low-paying jobs, cannot afford to marry and lead independent lives.[21] Unable to afford the costs of marriage or a house, young Jordanian men are involuntarily delaying marriage, which in the region is a rite to passage for adulthood, independence, and legitimate sexual relationships.

The Future of Youth Policy in Jordan

There are two main approaches to thinking about youth policy in the context of national progress. One approach is to treat youth as a subsector of society that is defined by the special problems that distinguish it from other subsectors of the population. For example, within the broader national problem of unemployment, several specific characteristics of youth unemployment require special attention, such as the challenge of skills mismatch facing first-time job seekers. In this approach, many of these economic and social challenges are seen as temporary, associated with the demographic pressures of the youth bulge.

The other approach is to think of youth challenges not as an adjunct to national economic development but as a core part of it. The challenges that youth face are not solely associated with passing demographic pressures but are also related to institutional and political failures that must be remedied if sustainable and equitable development is to be achieved. This approach paves the way for institutional reforms that empower all citizens to be fully included in society, especially the young who are the future workers and middle class of the nation. A generally accepted prerequisite for such an approach is the full involvement and participation of youth or their representatives in the formation of policy. The other essential prerequisite is a process that encourages tolerance and an appreciation of democratic freedoms of thought and speech. This cannot be isolated from political reform and active participation of youth in elections, political parties, and civil society institutions.

Currently, Jordan's youth policy aims to integrate these two approaches. Early in 2003, Jordanian authorities commenced a significant initiative to draw up a national youth strategy, seeking the involvement of large segments of youth in the process. The National Youth Strategy was launched by King Abdullah II in 2005.[22] Approximately 91,000 young men and women took part in the preparation of that strategy, in cooperation with all concerned government ministries, official institutions, nongovernmental organizations, and relevant international organizations.

The National Youth Strategy aims to achieve youth development and empowerment through three main objectives, incorporating key principles for integrating youth. The first objective involves institutional reform that balances measures to ensure macroeconomic stability and significant economic growth with measures to target social equity and youth empowerment. Meeting the challenge of youth inclusion requires that the institutional environment and macroeconomic policy promote high rates of investment and growth, which can lead to the creation of job opportunities, especially for new entrants in the labor market. This will ensure that the economically active population is engaged in productive employment.

The second objective of the National Youth Strategy is to broaden the opportunities for knowledge acquisition and continuous learning for young men and women of all ages. In particular, this objective involves upgrading education and training systems and creating stronger links between the education system and the requirements of the labor market. For high rates of sustainable investment and growth, the young Jordanian workforce must be educated and trained to demonstrate high levels of skill, productivity, work ethics, and entrepreneurship.

The third objective of the National Youth Strategy is to encourage and institutionalize youth participation in forming public opinion, contributing to public policy choices and decisions, and partaking in civil society activities, all within a democratic and tolerant political and social context. Youth participation can create opportunities for knowledge and skill acquisition through nonformal learning. Participating in clubs and sports associations or volunteering with community organizations can encourage creativity and initiative among youth and can help develop valuable skills such as teamwork and problem-solving skills. The advantage of nonformal learning through civil society activities and in social environments lies mainly in its voluntary and often self-organizing nature, its flexibility, the possibilities of participation, the "right to make mistakes," and the closer link to young people's interests and aspirations.[23]

To conclude, policies and measures that aim at ensuring youth inclusion are key in mitigating the effects of the high costs of human capital depletion and the out-migration of skills. In addition, allowing the voices of youth to help shape the policies that affect them is essential to ensure that those policies and measures are effective. Their effectiveness is further enhanced to the extent that they succeed in reforming the traditional social fabric of Jordanian society and in bringing about institutional change that harnesses the talents and hopes of young people.

Notes

1. United Nations, "World Urbanization Prospects: The 2005 Revision" (database) (New York: United Nations Department of Economic and Social Affairs, Population Division, 2006).

2. World Bank, *The Road Not Traveled: Education Reform in the Middle East and North Africa* (Washington: 2008).

3. Jordan Department of Statistics, *Statistical Yearbook for Jordan* (Amman: 2007).

4. World Bank, *The Road Not Traveled.*

5. Jordan did not participate in the fourth-grade examinations. For the 2007 results in detail, see Ina V.S. Mullis and others, *TIMSS 2007 International Mathematics Report* (Boston College, Lynch School of Education, TIMSS & PIRLS International Study Center, 2008); and Michael O. Martin and others, *TIMSS 2007 International Science Report* (Boston College, Lynch School of Education, TIMSS & PIRLS International Study Center, 2008).

6. Ahmad Galal, "Reform of Education in Arab Countries," lecture sponsored by the Jordan Center for Public Policy Research and Dialogue, Abdul-Hameed Shoman Forum, Amman, March 24, 2007.

7. Djavad Salehi-Isfahani and Navtej Dhillon, "Stalled Youth Transitions in the Middle East: A Framework for Policy Reform," Middle East Youth Initiative Working Paper 8 (Wolfensohn Center for Development at the Brookings Institution and the Dubai School of Government, 2008).

8. Ragui Assaad and Mona Amer, *Labor Market Conditions in Jordan, 1995-2006: An Analysis of Microdata Sources,* vol. 1 (Amman: Al-Manar Project, National Center for Human Resource Development, 2007).

9. Ibid.

10. Ibid.

11. Jordan Department of Statistics, *Employment and Unemployment Survey* (Amman: 2008), www.dos.gov.jo/dos_home_e/emp_round3.htm.

12. Ibid.

13. Jordan Department of Statistics, *Employment and Unemployment Survey: Annual Report* (Amman: 2007).

14. Susan Razzaz and Farrukh Iqbal, "Job Growth without Unemployment Reduction: The Experience of Jordan" (Washington: 2008).

15. World Bank, "Resolving Jordan's Labor Market Paradox," Report 39201-Jo (Washington: 2008).

16. Razzaz and Iqbal, "Job Growth without Unemployment Reduction."

17. Ibid.

18. Ministry of Planning and International Cooperation and the United Nations Development Program, *Jordan Human Development Report 2004: Building Sustainable Livelihoods* (Amman: 2004).

19. Ibid.

20. Jordan Department of Statistics, "Selected Indicators" (Amman: 2007), www.dos.gov.jo/dos_home/jorfig/2007/jor_f_a.htm.

21. Diane Singerman, "The Economic Imperatives of Marriage: Emerging Practices and Identities among Youth in the Middle East," Middle East Youth Initiative Working Paper 6 (Wolfensohn Center for Development at the Brookings Institution and the Dubai School of Government, 2007).

22. "The National Strategy for Youth in Jordan 2005–2009," quoted in Mahmoud Sarhan, *The National Report on Implementation of the World Youth Program* (Amman: Higher Council for Youth, 2008).

23. Commission of the European Communities, *White Paper: A New Impetus for European Youth* (Brussels: 2001).

BRAHIM BOUDARBAT *and* AZIZ AJBILOU

7

Moroccan Youth in an Era of Volatile Growth, Urbanization, and Poverty

Young Moroccans, coming of age at a time when their country is undergoing rapid economic and social change, face challenges unknown to previous generations. Since gaining independence in 1956, and especially during the past quarter century, Morocco has striven to achieve sustainable and diversified economic growth. The country's most persistent domestic challenges include improving living conditions in its urban centers, reducing poverty, and creating enough jobs for the millions of unemployed and underemployed.

Young men and women are at the epicenter of these economic and social challenges. While education policies have ensured that an increasing number of young Moroccans are enrolling in primary and secondary education, this has not translated into a generation that is ready to meet the needs of the labor market. In fact, educated young workers are more likely to experience long spells of unemployment. Deteriorating employment prospects, especially for university graduates and in populous urban areas, reflect the poor match between the education and training system and the requirements of the labor market. Under conditions of high unemployment and poverty, youth are relegated to second-tier jobs in the informal sector, which offer little compensation or career prospects.

Economic hardship for young people spills over into challenges in marriage and family formation. For many young Moroccans, family formation is becoming increasingly difficult, as evidenced by the delays in marriage resulting from limited employment opportunities and incomes that are insufficient to meet the rising costs of living. In addition, increasing num-

Figure 7-1. *Share of Youth Aged 15 to 24 in Morocco's Population, 1971–2014*

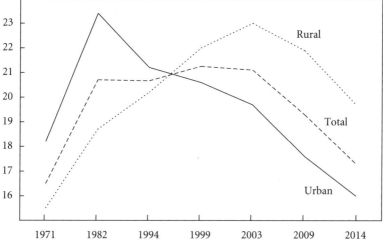

Percent of total population

Source: Authors' calculations.

bers of young Moroccans aspire to live in countries with better economic prospects. As a result, emigration, especially to Europe, has increased by all legal and illegal means. Although migration can provide prospects for a better future, especially for young men who are highly qualified, it deprives Morocco of the population that it most needs to build its economy and whose education has absorbed substantial public funds in a nation with limited resources.

The current age structure of the Moroccan population is characterized by the predominance of youth aged 15 to 24. The share of youth in the population is 20 percent, or about 6.3 million youth, an increase from about 17 percent in 1971 (2.5 million youth). The size of the youth population is expected to reach 6.5 million by 2010. Figure 7-1 illustrates past and future trends in the share of youth aged 15 to 24 in the total population. Even though the share of this cohort is expected to decline to 18 percent by 2014, its relative weight will remain considerable, greatly affecting the future of Morocco.

The youth bulge has been caused by Morocco's entry into a "demographic transition," characterized by an ongoing drop in mortality rates accompanied by an accelerated reduction in fertility. Indeed, the demographics of Morocco have changed significantly during the past five decades. While the overall population more than doubled from 11.6 million in 1960 to 29.9 million in 2004, population growth rates steadily declined from 2.6 percent in the 1970s to 1.4 percent during the 1994–2004 period.

Many problems in Morocco are blamed on this youth bulge. The sizable youth population generates unprecedented demand for education and training, employment, and housing, putting a strain on government resources. However, rather than viewing the youth bulge as a drain on prosperity and stability, policymakers should consider it a "demographic gift" and a window of opportunity. By building the human capital of young workers and providing them with opportunities to use their skills, Morocco can increase incomes per capita, bolster savings, and improve social welfare.

Timing is critical if the benefits of a large working-age population are to be reaped. While the Moroccan population is youthful today, future trends point toward an aging Moroccan society, stemming from the ongoing decline in fertility rates.[1] Morocco's economic and social institutions must respond to the presence and expectations of a large youth cohort. Today, giving young people a stake in society is the most pressing challenge confronting policymakers and other key stakeholders.

The Macroeconomic Context

The arrival of a youth bulge in Morocco coincides with three trends that have set the context for the exclusion of this generation of young Moroccans. The first is poor macroeconomic performance. Unlike many of its neighboring countries, Morocco ushered in a market-based economy and openness to global markets as early as 1956, the time of its independence. More recently, in the 1990s and early 2000s, the Moroccan government initiated economic reforms designed to prepare the economy for the challenges and opportunities of globalization. But despite accelerating liberalization, economic openness and privatization, and the signing of free trade agreements, Morocco's economic performance has been characterized by sluggish long-term GDP growth and wild fluctuations in short-term growth. From 1980 to 2004, GDP progressed at a mean annual growth rate of almost 8 percent in current prices, compared with only 3 percent in constant prices, with large variations across the years.[2] Slow economic growth coupled with a burgeoning youth population has made it difficult for many young people to transition to adulthood successfully.

The second driver of youth exclusion in Morocco is rapid urbanization. The size of the urban population increased from 3.4 million in 1960 to 17.4

million in 2007, representing an average annual growth rate of nearly 4 percent, compared with an average annual growth of 1 percent in the size of the
rural population. Urbanization has direct consequences for youth and their
welfare. It increases pressure on the urban labor market as well as on the
urban housing market. Urban migration is often linked to a deterioration in
migrants' standards of living. Rural migrants settle in substandard living
environments where youth are exposed to poverty and various forms of
risky behavior including delinquency, drugs, and crime. Furthermore,
urbanization disrupts traditional ways of life, which can influence young
people's expectations, values, and visions of work, family, and marriage in
ways that can lead to great frustration and disappointment.

Finally, persistent poverty in Morocco afflicts the young. Nearly 20 percent of all poor people in the country are between the ages of 15 and 24.
Poverty is more widespread among rural youth—22 percent—than among
those in the cities—7 percent. This incidence of youth poverty is explained
by the persistence of unemployment among young labor force participants
and by the great number of dependents in large households. Poverty makes
youth more vulnerable to a cycle of economic and social exclusion.

Educational Reforms

Expanding access to education and increasing enrollment rates have been the
most important goals of Morocco's education policies. Reforms implemented in the mid-1980s targeted elementary (primary) education by
making schooling compulsory until age 15.[3] In 1999 the Special Commission
for Education and Training (COSEF) created by King Hassan II established
the fundamental principles for educational reform. The commission recognized education and training as a national priority for the decade 2000–10
and declared an annual 5 percent increase in public financial resources allocated to education. (In 2003 education spending accounted for 6 percent of
GDP and 28 percent of the government budget.) Additional goals included
achieving universal enrollment of 4- to 16-year-olds by 2006–07, eradicat-
ing illiteracy among the adult population, and, most relevant to the
population aged 15 to 29, improving the quality and content of Morocco's
educational programs to meet the needs of the labor market.

These educational reform efforts have had a positive impact. Access to
education has increased substantially in Morocco during the last fifteen
years, and enrollment rates have increased at the elementary and secondary
levels. Between 1990 and 2004, the gross enrollment rates for elementary

education increased from 64 percent to 119 percent in the first stage (grades one to six) and from 44 percent to 60 percent in the second stage (grades seven to nine). Meanwhile, secondary education enrollment increased from 20 percent to 31 percent.[4]

Retention rates have improved for the first stage of elementary education, increasing by three percentage points between the 1991–92 and the 2002–03 school years. In other words, a greater number of children who begin school stay in school at this level. However, retention rates have decreased by 6 percent at the second stage of elementary education, indicating a growing number of dropouts at that level of schooling. For secondary education, retention rates increased by more than 20 percent during the same period. Furthermore, the gender gap in education is steadily decreasing as more girls are given the opportunity to attend school. The total enrollment rate of girls in elementary school has increased from 26 percent in 1990–91 to 101 percent in 2003–04. Moreover, there has been an increase in the gender parity of primary gross enrollment rates from a ratio of 0.7 in 1990 to 0.9 in 2003 due to increased participation of rural girls.[5]

Although the country has made considerable progress in expanding school enrollment, it still faces the challenge of improving the quality of education. Despite increased spending on schooling, education outcomes remain far from satisfactory. Repetition rates in Morocco are among the worst in the region, at 14 percent for those in primary education. Furthermore, the academic performance of young Moroccan students on international evaluations such as the Trends in International Mathematics and Science Study (TIMSS) tests ranks at the low end of the test score range.

In the 2007 TIMSS examinations of eighth-grade students, Morocco was the only country that did not achieve the minimum acceptable participation rate (measuring both student and school participation). Among those eighth graders that did sit for the exams in Morocco, only 3 percent achieved or surpassed the "high" benchmark score of 550 in science, and only 1 percent passed this benchmark in mathematics. The average scores for Moroccan students were 402 on the science test—outperforming only El Salvador, Botswana, Qatar, and Ghana of the forty-eight other countries participating—and 381 on the mathematics test, also placing it on the low end of achievement.[6] Morocco also did not meet the TIMSS sampling requirements in 2003, but the average scores among participating eighth graders were 396 and 387 for science and mathematics, respectively; thus the country saw no marked improvement in its students' scores over the four-year period.[7]

Even though Morocco spends more on secondary education relative to primary education, the country remains one of a few in the region with secondary enrollment rates below 50 percent. Secondary vocational training facilities also face underenrollment. These low levels of enrollment, combined with low-quality secondary education, contribute to the skills gap that manifests in relatively high unemployment rates for secondary school graduates. Youth with a secondary education diploma or higher constitute only 11 percent of the labor force, but they account for 24 percent of the unemployed. These labor market outcomes for secondary education graduates most likely affect the perception of returns to secondary education and lead many young Moroccans to drop out or never enroll.

In higher education, government restrictions on access to competitive fields such as science and technology have led to low levels of student enrollment in these areas. In contrast, the social sciences and humanities, which have historically led to jobs in the civil service, are not as restricted. The result is that 75 percent of Moroccan students in higher education concentrate in the social sciences and humanities. This enrollment distribution would be consistent with public sector employment that absorbs most university graduates, as was historically the case.[8] However, with a retrenchment in public sector and a development strategy based on private sector growth, particularly in manufacturing and services, this distribution is leading to a growing gap between the skills and training that higher education graduates receive and the demands of a changing labor market. The results are that private returns to education, which averaged almost 16 percent in 1970, have decreased steadily to approximately 12 percent by 1991 and to 8 percent by 1999. Young educated Moroccans are therefore increasingly getting less value out of their education, exacerbating their sense of exclusion.[9]

Transition to Work

Access to employment and decent work in the labor market is a critical determinant of youth welfare, in part because the income young people earn influences their consumption, living standards, and prospects for household formation. However, access to employment and job quality have deteriorated markedly since the early 1980s, exacerbating the economic exclusion of young Moroccans. The economic exclusion of youth can be examined by looking at youth participation in the labor market, youth unemployment rates, and quality of employment.

Table 7-1. *Labor Force Participation Rate of Young People Aged 15 to 24, by Gender and Area*

Percent

Gender	Urban		Rural		Total	
	1999	2007	1999	2007	1999	2007
Males	53.7	45.8	80.5	80.0	67.0	57.4
Females	20.9	15.5	39.4	37.4	29.7	21.9
Both genders	37.0	30.5	60.4	58.7	48.3	39.6

Source: Haut Commissariat au Plan, Rabat.

Youth Participation in the Labor Market

Youth remain underrepresented in the labor force. In 2007 the number of young people aged 15 to 24 participating in the labor market was estimated at around 2.5 million. These youth constitute 22 percent of the labor force, roughly seven points below their 29 percent share of the adult population. Table 7-1 shows that the overall labor force participation rate of youth aged 15 to 24 declined from over 48 percent in 1999 to under 40 percent in 2007. Youth in urban environments account for most of this decline; their labor participation rate has dropped by more than 6 percentage points. Youth in rural areas have also experienced a decline in participation rates, though at lower levels than their urban counterparts.

The reduced supply of labor is largely attributable to young women; their participation rate has declined by nearly 8 percentage points, from almost 30 percent in 1999 to 22 percent in 2007, with urban young women exiting slightly more than rural ones. The participation rate is much higher for young men than for young women—57 percent compared with 22 percent. In urban centers, 46 percent of young men are active as opposed to only 16 percent of young women. In rural areas these rates are 80 and 37 percent, respectively. It is difficult to accurately capture or reflect the situation of rural women in the labor market using traditional statistical methods. Rural women usually work in family-owned enterprises or farms and may easily switch between employment and inactivity with no transitional period of unemployment.[10]

The increase in school retention explains a portion of the decrease in labor force participation; the proportion of youth at school rose from 26 percent in 1999 to 31 percent in 2004, and the percentage of young people in school is over three times as high in the cities as it is in the countryside. Rural youth tend to be less educated and enter the labor market more easily because of the prevalence of family-owned enterprises and farms in the rural economy.

The decision to remain in school longer is related to the situation in the labor market. Bougroum, Ibourk, and Trachen observe that participation in the education system is less likely to be a deliberate choice of youth.[11] Many youths simply stay in school because of the unfavorable situation in the labor market. School has become a refuge of the potentially jobless who have no other alternatives. This behavior, especially as it relates to university studies, is encouraged by policies providing open access to universities and free tuition.

Youth Unemployment

Beginning in the 1970s Morocco's unemployment rate rose steadily for over two decades: from around 9 percent in 1971 to 11 percent in 1982, then to 16 percent in 1994. The situation improved significantly during the 2000s, with unemployment dropping to around 10 percent in 2007. In all cases, urban labor markets have fared the worst. Urban unemployment nearly doubled between 1982 and 2000, rising from 12 to 22 percent. In 2007 this rate dropped to 15 percent; however, it was still nearly four times higher than the rural unemployment rate (4 percent). Further, many of the improvements in unemployment rates during the 2000s mask significant disadvantages among youth, women, and educated workers.

The cohort aged 15 to 24 is most vulnerable to unemployment, especially in urban areas. In 2007, 429,000 youth were unemployed. This number corresponds to an unemployment rate of 17 percent among young people, who are overrepresented in the unemployed population by a wide margin (table 7-2). Youth constituted 39 percent of all of the unemployed, yet they made up only 22 percent of the labor force. This overrepresentation exists in both urban and rural labor markets. In urban areas youth constituted 37 percent of all the unemployed while making up only 18 percent of the labor force. In rural areas youth constituted 50 percent of all unemployed while making up only 27 percent of the labor force.

Unemployment among youth is concentrated in urban areas and among men: in 2007, 76 percent of unemployed youth lived in urban areas and 75 percent of unemployed youth were men. Further, the majority of unemployed youth are first-time job seekers, who account for almost 63 percent of total unemployed youth.

Table 7-2. *Unemployment Rate of Youth Aged 15 to 24, by Gender and Area*
Percent

Gender	Urban		Rural		Total	
	1999	2007	1999	2007	1999	2007
Males	37.8	30.1	10.9	7.7	21.8	17.9
Females	37.9	35.9	3.6	2.3	16.4	15.5
Both genders	37.8	31.6	8.6	6.0	20.1	17.2

Source: Haut Commissariat au Plan, Rabat.

In urban environments the situation for workers improves markedly with age but remains critical even for individuals who are well into their adult lives. The unemployment rate in 2007 was 22 percent among those aged 25 to 34, which is still extremely high, especially considering the large number of educated workers in that group. Within the 35 to 44 age cohort, the unemployment rate was 8 percent. The unemployment rate was 3 percent among urban workers aged 45 and over. These figures suggest that finding a job in Morocco's cities is a long process that consists of a succession of downward revisions of expectations.

In urban areas young women fare worse than young men in terms of employment prospects. Young women run a higher risk than young men of being unemployed in urban environments—36 percent compared with 30 percent. In rural areas, however, the unemployment rate of men is nearly three times that of women. This may not reflect better labor market outcomes for rural women but rather lower active labor market participation resulting from fewer available job opportunities for rural women.

The structural nature of unemployment is apparent in the long spells of joblessness that youth endure. Two of three unemployed young Moroccans are without work for at least a year. Around 70 percent of the unemployed with a degree below the secondary level and 67 percent of the unemployed with diplomas and degrees at the secondary level or higher are unemployed for at least a year.

Unemployment among educated youth has remained persistently high in Morocco. Education should lower the risk of unemployment for youth, foster job market integration, and stimulate economic growth. However, in Morocco, youth with more advanced degrees experience higher levels of unemployment. This is true for youth of both sexes and in both urban and rural areas. In 2007 the national unemployment rate was 9 percent for young workers with no diploma, 27 percent for those with a diploma below the secondary level, and 58 percent for those with a secondary-level degree or higher. Even for the 25- to 34-year-old cohort, the unemployment rate for those with a secondary education diploma or higher remains disproportionately high, at 32 percent.

Initially, the problem of unemployment among degree holders seemed to be a result of the government's contraction as an employer subsequent to implementation of the economic structural adjustment program (SAP) in 1983. At the time, unemployment among educated youth was treated as a business-cycle phenomenon that would rapidly dissipate. However, over twenty years later unemployment has not only persisted but has worsened, mutating into a structural problem and a source of serious social tensions. This situation is explained by a mismatch between the education system and the labor market, sluggish job creation by the economy, and the preference of educated youth for salaried work in the formal sector, in particular the civil service.

This devaluation of education credentials has raised serious questions among Moroccan families about the usefulness of investments in education. The position of the Moroccan government is that low levels of education hamper socioeconomic development. But declining future returns to education can discourage households from investing in higher education. An increasing number of young graduates are forced to take jobs that do not correspond to their qualifications or degrees, calling into question the common belief that a degree is insurance against unemployment and that achieving a high level of educational attainment will improve an individual's life prospects. Exclusion resulting from failure in the labor market affects not only unemployed educated youth but their families as well. Parents invest substantial resources so that their children can succeed in school and thereafter find decent jobs.

For many youth confronted with the specter of unemployment, educational failure, and poverty, prospects for a better life appear stronger on the other side of the Mediterranean. The extent of the emigration phenomenon reveals the malaise and despair among many Moroccan youth who will do anything, including sometimes risk their lives, to cross the Mediterranean. Those who do not succeed in emigrating or who prefer to stay in Morocco generally add to the ranks of unemployed workers or accept work for which they are overqualified.

Quality of Employment

Quality of employment is critical for young people because the skills and on-the-job training they receive during their first jobs determine their future employment prospects and earnings. Yet, young, new entrants to the labor market often depend on work in the informal sector in Morocco, resorting to small-scale trades, which generally are less well paid and unstable. This is especially true of youth in the countryside. The size of the informal sector in nonagricultural employment is 39 percent. Overall, nearly one worker in three is an unpaid family worker, a rate that is much higher in rural areas.

A recent study on the employment of vocational education graduates indicates that self-employment is chosen by a large proportion of graduates, often in the informal sector.[12] Indeed, two of three graduates who are working for themselves set up informal businesses working as handymen or family workers.

Some evidence supports the notion that the Moroccan labor market is growing in informality, given both the size of the informal sector and the decline in wage work. The proportion of wage earners in the labor force fell from 43 percent in 1987 to 37 percent in 2005. Wage work is also becoming more precarious because of underemployment and the rise in temporary positions. The temporary nature of wage employment adds to its unreliability and fosters moonlighting in the informal sector. The Moroccan labor market is experiencing a progressive shift of assets into the tertiary sector—services and commerce—which is increasingly informal, at the expense of the secondary (manufacturing) and, to some extent, primary (agriculture) sectors.

Urban centers are characterized by the proliferation of wage work; however, a significant proportion of young city dwellers, especially men, are employed without pay as family workers and apprentices, relying on their families for lodging. In addition, more men are opting for self-employment, from 15 percent in 1999 to 18 percent in 2004. The situation for youth is more precarious in rural areas, where access to wage work appears to be the exception. In 2004 three out of four men and nine out of ten women in rural areas held nonwage jobs; this form of employment has increased by 4 percent for men and by 3 percent for women since 1999.

A breakdown of the labor force by sector provides insights into how the opportunities available to first-time job seekers have been changing over time. More than half of the workforce is employed in the agriculture sector—a relatively high proportion compared with an average of 35 percent in other lower-middle-income countries.[13] Morocco is witnessing a decline in employment in the industrial and manufacturing sectors along with a reduced rate of creation of new positions in public service. The share of the public sector in total employment, often the preferred sector of employment among degree holders, fell from 11 percent in 1995 to 8 percent in 2005. Conversely, the share of the tertiary sector (services and commerce) rose from 25 to 35 percent during the same period, demonstrating the growing significance of these increasingly informal industries.

As quality of employment has deteriorated, educated young Moroccans continue to queue for public sector employment in the absence of other credible alternatives. Even as the public sector has retrenched, the expectations of young Moroccans have not aligned with the shifting realities of the labor market. In fact, educated youth continue to hold the government responsible for not investing enough in the social sectors and thus failing to create new government jobs.

Employment Policies

Based on the idea that work is fundamental to social integration, the government's policies have focused on job creation and the fight against unemployment, especially among educated workers. Programs and initiatives have proliferated but often lack evaluation to assess success and identify failures or weaknesses. The government agency structures implementing these programs have also undergone changes. Several agencies have been given the responsibility and resources to tackle employment-related challenges, and the government has created new bodies with new mandates. In particular, direct youth employment policies and programs have tended to focus on discouraging public sector employment in favor of wage employment in the private sector, reducing unemployment through job creation and labor law reforms, encouraging self-employment through entrepreneurship and microenterprise, and providing skills training.

Promoting Private Sector Employment

The government repeatedly emphasizes that employment of young Moroccans remains among its top priorities. To discourage graduates' expectations of public sector employment, leaders, including the late King Hassan II, have stressed the limitations of civil service in fulfilling the potential of youth. "The public sector" the king asserted, "offers no opportunity to young workers looking to expand their horizons and wishing to fulfill their capacities. . . . In the public sector, there is no place for adventure or imagination, and in it there is no freedom." While messages such as these serve the strategic goal of steering youth away from dependence on the shrinking public sector, the government also needs to send soft yet credible signals and continue to promote the availability of alternative, quality employment for young people.

One of the aims of the structural adjustment policies implemented in 1983 was to assign a more important role to the private sector in the economy, especially with regard to job creation.[14] Under the plan, the private sector would eventually replace the public sector in the recruitment of educated workers. The Moroccan government considers a strong and competitive economy that creates employment as a natural solution to the problem of unemployed, educated workers; thus sustained growth of the modern private sector is the main objective for current economic policies.

Unemployment and Job Creation Programs

Because worsening unemployment among educated youth and related social tensions continue to plague the Moroccan labor market, the government has formally incorporated these challenges into national strategies. In 1990 the government created the National Council for Youth and the Future to reduce unemployment among graduates.[15] However, the council became inactive after its actions produced little improvement, as confirmed by continued high levels of unemployment among graduates.[16]

The government currently seeks to create jobs for young graduates through a variety of programs and measures; it set a goal of creating 200,000 new jobs by 2008. In addition to the programs outlined in subsequent sections below, special development projects and reforms to the labor code and minimum wage policies have a perhaps indirect effect on the government's youth employment strategy as well. This strategy seems to be working: the unemployment rate decreased four percentage points between 1999 and 2007. The improved labor market benefited the groups traditionally at the highest risk of unemployment, namely, urban workers and workers with degrees at the secondary level or higher. These two groups experienced a decrease of about 7 percentage points in their unemployment rate.

Several national initiatives have been launched that indirectly favor job creation. In 2002 the government created a special development zone with the aim of developing this region, located in the north of the country, as a strategic center for transportation, industry, and trade. Another widescale national project is *Plan Azure*, part of the Emergency Industrialization Plan that aims to attract foreign investment and promote tourism. *Plan Azure* includes the construction and management of a series of recreational resorts that are expected to bring in 10 million tourists annually by 2010, in addition to developments in textiles, agroindustry, offshoring, and a number of other sectors. Finally, an emergency economic program was launched in September 2005.[17]

Reforms to the Moroccan labor code also have implications for youth job creation. The labor code reforms of 2003 have sought to create an environment favorable to investment through a reduction of labor costs and greater flexibility in recruitment and dismissal. Both steps are intended to improve competitiveness and to reduce employment rigidity, which has until now had a negative impact on young entrants into the labor market.

Finally, Morocco's minimum wage policy is regarded as a way to improve standards of living among the working poor. The nominal minimum hourly wage in nonagricultural sectors, normally paid to uneducated workers with no experience, increased twenty-six times between 1948 and 2000. In constant prices, the minimum hourly wage increased on average 2.4 percent per year between 1996 and 2000, compared with a 2 percent increase in the average annual inflation rate during the same period.

The challenge with minimum wage legislation is that not all employers adhere to this legislation, especially those in the informal sector. Moreover, even when enforced, minimum wage policies can end up distorting labor market outcomes in various ways. First, while an enforced minimum wage can offer protection to young workers, it can also undermine prospects for young job seekers by stifling job creation. Furthermore, the benefits of a minimum wage in the Moroccan context accrue more strongly to uneducated and low-skilled workers. Wage employment opportunities and wages have improved for low-skilled youth, and part of this improvement can be attributed to significant increases in the minimum wage over the last two decades. However, in an economy in which the public sector has contracted without the emergence of a large private sector that can offer high-skilled jobs, educated youth appear less likely to benefit from increases in the minimum wage because it raises employer costs associated with hiring young workers.

Promoting Entrepreneurship, Microenterprise, and Self-Employment

Among the main measures to arise out of the national debate on unemployment and skills mismatch was Law 36/87, also called the Young Entrepreneurs Loans Law, which was promulgated in 1987 to encourage young graduates to create their own businesses. Interested graduates are granted loans that can cover up to 90 percent of the total cost of their projects at preferential interest rates. The government encourages young entrepreneurs to take advantage of what is portrayed as a ripe economic environment for the integration of small and very small businesses into the formal economy.

Other, more recent government and nongovernmental programs seek to encourage entrepreneurship and self-employment among youth in Morocco. One such program is *Moukawalati* (My Business), which grants long-term loans to young people at preferential rates to encourage them to create their own businesses. *Moukawalati* sought to create 30,000 firms around the country by 2008, each requiring an investment of up to 250,000 Moroccan dirhams ($30,000) and together potentially generating 90,000 jobs. The budget devoted to this program was 10 billion dirhams ($1.2 billion). This program is intended for people aged 20 to 45 with vocational training, secondary diplomas, or university degrees. *Moukawalati* also tries to facilitate access to bank loans, guaranteeing 85 percent of the value of each loan made by commercial banks to program participants.[18]

Despite these many and varied programs to promote entrepreneurship, the results so far have not been satisfactory. For example, one study shows that the number of university graduates who would consider self-employment as an alternative to unemployment did not increase.[19] Ironically, evidence shows that preference for paid work significantly *increased* after the 1983 SAP, despite the multitude of programs introduced by the government to encourage self-employment. This seems to indicate that youth see nothing positive to gain from self-employment over wage employment, either in terms of wages or other working conditions.

Initiatives encouraging self-employment among Moroccan youth are compromised by several other weaknesses. First, the effectiveness of these programs is questionable, because experience in paid work is required before youth can excel in entrepreneurship. In fact, age is found to correlate positively to entrepreneurship, implying that the older one is, the higher the probability of successful entrepreneurship. Second, the preference for paid employment versus self-employment is shaped by educational level: the higher the educational level, the less likely that an individual will be interested in self-employment and the more likely that the individual will prefer protected (paid) employment. Even those who opt for self-employment are not likely to continue with the track because of the financial risks involved. Indeed, Law 36/87 and the *Moukawalati* initiative failed in achieving their initial goals for the most part because of the reluctance of private banks to grant loans to youth for their projects, which were considered too risky.

Given that a large number of today's unemployed youth have high educational attainment, the strategy to promote self-employment is bound to have limited effectiveness until these more systemic issues are addressed.

Matching Skills and Demand

The government has undertaken several measures to provide more transparent and accessible information to both employers and employees in an effort to better reconcile labor supply with demand. In 2000 the Agence Nationale pour la Promotion de l'Emploi et des Compétences (ANAPEC, National Agency for Promoting Employment and Skills) was created with the mission of collecting job offers from employers and matching them with the labor supply, providing career counseling for job seekers, and assisting young entrepreneurs in fulfilling their economic projects. ANAPEC recently was reorganized to improve its efficiency. In addition, the government also announced the creation of an employment office that would monitor the Moroccan labor market and provide statistics for follow-up, evaluation, and analysis of the impact of public employment programs.

Vocational training (VT) programs in Morocco have sought to improve the employability and skills of young people in various jobs. In 1984 (a year after the implementation of the SAP, which resulted in increased unemployment among graduates following drastic cuts in public sector jobs), major reforms of the Moroccan VT system were initiated to improve links between training and the needs of the labor market.

During the first year of VT reform, the number of trainees increased by 66 percent. A rapid pace of growth was sustained; the number of VT graduates increased by 64 percent between 1988 and 2003, not including graduates of apprenticeship programs. The government set an objective of training 400,000 young people between 2005 and 2007. Unfortunately, such ambitious quantitative policies have too often ended up becoming unfulfilled political pledges with little or no follow-through on the resources and investments needed to reach these goals. And while such policies do spur the demand for and perceived promise of vocational training, in reality the situation of its graduates in the labor market continues to be far from satisfactory.

Paradoxically, and unlike many other Middle Eastern countries, young people and their families perceive and treat vocational training in Morocco as a highly selective and in-demand form of education. This has lead to a proliferation of VT centers, including a surge in private VT centers, which in 2007 accounted for 36 percent of VT graduates. Yet VT graduates face very high unemployment rates, averaging up to 35 percent, and long unemployment durations: 50 percent of graduates are still unemployed one year after graduation and 40 percent are jobless after four years. As in regular education, those with the most advanced vocational training face the highest unemployment rates and longest durations. Furthermore, research indicates that graduates of private centers—which are costly to attend—actually face higher unemployment rates than graduates of public VT centers.

Beyond the formal VT system, the government has sponsored a variety of additional training and technical assistance programs. Following the claim that new graduates lack the professional experience required by private firms, a program called Training for Employment was launched in 1993. This program, which has been updated over time, places recent graduates in eighteen-month training programs in private companies. Companies that receive trainees stand to profit from skilled labor at a lower cost, and they also receive other incentives and exemptions for participating in the program.

Another program called *Idmaj* (inclusion) supports the employability of youth who lack work experience or have problems matching their skills to available jobs. This program targets 100,000 people and matches them with their first paid jobs. Another program called *Taehil* (qualification) is designed for young graduates and seeks to alleviate the discrepancy between education and training and the labor market's needs and aims to benefit 50,000 people. The budget allocated to this program was 500 million dirhams ($60 million) for 2006–08.

While the government's efforts are praiseworthy, it remains to be seen whether these programs and policies will deliver the impact needed without replicating the same inadequacies of the past two decades. Several explanations have emerged for the failure of past programs to create adequate change. First and foremost, there was no long-term strategy to bring the many measures and initiatives into a comprehensive and efficient framework. Second, the absence of follow-ups and evaluation mechanisms meant that there was no assessment of the programs' economic and social impacts. Finally, most of these programs were aimed at income generation with specific "quick-fix" targets. There was no focus on the nature of employment gained, working conditions, or the social impacts on the workers and society.

Transition to Family Formation

In this rapidly changing economic environment, and with increased urbanization and modernization, the dynamics of the traditional Moroccan family are also evolving. Despite changes, the family continues to be a vital safety

Table 7-3. *Evolution of the Mean Age at First Marriage*

Area	Gender	1960	1971	1982	1987	1994	1998	2000	2004
Urban	Men	24.4	26.0	28.5	29.7	31.2	32.6	32.2	32.2
	Women	17.5	20.9	23.8	25.4	26.9	28.3	28.5	27.1
Rural	Men	23.8	24.2	25.6	26.1	28.3	28.8	29.9	29.5
	Women	17.2	18.5	20.8	21.5	24.2	25.5	25.7	25.5
Both areas	Men	24.0	25.0	27.2	27.9	30.0	31.1	31.9	31.2
	Women	17.5	19.3	22.3	23.4	25.8	27.1	27.4	26.3

Source: Authors' calculations.

net for youth. Confronted with a precarious economy and a difficult road to financial independence, marriage, and the status of adulthood, the family remains a refuge for many young people. Thus, today's generation of Moroccan youth is caught between relying on the family for economic support and simultaneously desiring greater autonomy.

Delayed Marriage

Young Moroccans are increasingly delaying marriage. Several decades ago, Moroccan society was characterized by very early marriage. In 1960 the mean age at first marriage was 18 for women and 24 for men. As table 7-3 shows, this situation no longer prevails: as of 2004 the average age at first marriage was 26 for women and 31 for men.

Marriage among those aged 15 to 24 has contracted significantly. For men in the 15 to 19 cohort, the situation has changed little over time, mostly because the legal marrying age is set at 18. Among women in this age cohort, however, the incidence of early marriage, which often interfered with education, is declining: the proportion of single women has increased by 21 percent in thirty years. In the 20 to 24 cohort, marriage has declined precipitously among women; now, seven of ten women in this age group are single, in contrast to two out of ten in 1971. The number of single males in this age group rose from 71 percent in 1971 to 93 percent in 2000.

The marked increase in the average age of marriage results from many interactive variables, including changing lifestyles and increased urbanization. Education also affects age of marriage: there is a significant difference in the mean age at first marriage between those who went to school and those who never did. School attendance, even only at the grade school level, is sufficient to delay marriage by several years among youth. In addition, the schooling of women has improved their status, which has delayed both marriage and childbirth.

The increase in marriage age among cohorts that are already in the labor force or at the end of their studies and entering adult life (25 years and over) reveals that some of the delay in marriage is involuntary, caused by financial difficulties attributable to unemployment, the poor quality of jobs held by youth, the rising cost of living, and difficulties finding housing. According to a recent survey, young people cite inadequate financial means as one of the primary reasons for remaining single: 51 percent of the youth interviewed had no job and 81 percent still lived with their parents or families.[20]

With regard to differences in age at first marriage between the unemployed and employed, Ajbilou observes that the former marry relatively late compared with the latter.[21] Indisputably, economic difficulties are among the most important factors causing young people to delay marriage, considering that several years of working and saving are necessary in order to marry for the first time. In sum, the greater the monetary difficulties, the later the marriage; this is true for both men and women.

Reform of Family Law and Inclusion of Women

Inequality in the treatment of the sexes still exists in Morocco, despite many advances in favor of women in recent years. The representation of women in decisionmaking positions such as government and senior civil service positions and their participation in economic development remain weak.

One policy response to promote the inclusion of women has been through reforms to the family law. The reforms brought about by the *Moudawana* (family code) in 1993 and 2003 rest on the basic principle of seeking justice for women by promoting their status and creating gender equality. The code also allows for the consolidation of child protection laws, the preservation of women's dignity by protecting them against violence, and improvements in the economic status of women. Consequently, the family is placed under the "joint responsibility of both spouses." Both spouses are equally responsible within the household with regard to economic management and their children's education.

By recognizing women as full citizens, in response to Article 6 of the Universal Declaration of Human Rights, the family code assumes gender equality in terms of rights and duties and the abolition of the traditional rule of "the obedience of the wife to her husband." The legal age of marriage for women was raised in 2003 from 15 to 18. The traditional requirement for a male representative to be present for a woman of legal age to marry has been removed. A minor can now choose the parent who would have custody over him or her in the event of a divorce, and the wife has rights equal to those of the husband in asking for a divorce. These reforms signal an unprecedented change. For these reforms to succeed, however, they must be integrated into a national project that engages the government and society as a whole. It may be a long time before women completely close the gap regarding their personal and social status.

Conclusion

In a society transformed by demographic growth, rapid urbanization, limited employment opportunities, and a substantial gap between education and training programs and labor market needs, the challenge of youth inclusion is a pressing concern for local public authorities, international donors, and civil society. Progress toward reducing exclusion and its perverse effects has been modest. Public intervention has been hesitant and piecemeal, and many policies and measures that were implemented did not achieve the expected results. Meanwhile, the state of young people in many cases continues to worsen. Public policies have been based mainly on the theory that economic growth would alleviate poverty and exclusion. This economic reasoning undermines the importance of other factors, such as political, social, cultural, and religious issues, which also generate exclusion. Further, it ignores the fact that economic growth may not be enough to draw marginalized groups—such as young people and women—into full participation.

In examining the portfolio of employment policies and government-sponsored initiatives, one sees that the state's role is often unpredictable and that programs fail to pay adequate attention to the signals and incentives that young people respond to when considering real choices such as embarking on self-employment or waiting for wage work. Moreover, because of budget constraints, many programs for youth are limited in their potential for long-term impact and are unable to reach a broad pool of young people.

International organizations such as the United Nations Development Program and UNICEF and nongovernmental organizations have attempted to make up for the missteps of the public sector. Civil society has become a key actor in Morocco's economic development because of its achievements in poverty reduction and its efforts to combat the exclusion of young people and women. Yet, serious challenges remain.

In the years to come, the demand for new employment positions is expected to be twice the number of jobs that the economy is currently creating. It is also expected that two of every three Moroccans will be living in urban areas by 2015, a situation that has consequences for exclusion, disappointed expectations, and risky behavior. The high illiteracy rate among the adult population, problems with schooling—particularly for girls in rural areas—high school dropout rates, and unemployment of university graduates remain serious challenges to tackle. Finally, young people must affirm their role as critical actors in Morocco's social and economic development and as a priority target of public policies.[22]

Morocco's current generation of youth constitutes a huge human potential that can greatly contribute to the development of the country and its integration into the world economy. For that to happen, the needs of this population in the areas of education and training, health, civic participation, and employment must be addressed through coherent, integrated strategies among all stakeholders, including central and local governments as well as civil society.[23]

Notes

1. The share of the population aged 65 and older is expected to double from 5.5 percent in 2004 to 10.8 percent in 2030; see Haut Commissariat au Plan, "Projections de la population du Maroc par milieu de résidence 2005–2030" (Rabat: Centre d'Études et de Recherches Démographiques, 2007).

2. For instance, GDP growth (in constant prices) was 11.8 percent in 1998 but −2.2 percent in 1999.

3. This encompasses both the first and second stages of elementary education. The first stage of elementary education, grades one through six, includes the 6- to 12-year-old age group. The second stage, corresponding to middle school (grades seven through nine), includes the 13- to 15-year-old age group. Secondary education, which accepts students who have completed both stages of elementary education, lasts for three years and leads to a baccalaureate diploma. The age group for secondary education is 16 to 18 years. All age groups are larger when accounting for grade repetition.

4. The gross enrollment rate is the number of students in a given education level as a percentage of the number of children in the corresponding age group. This quotient can be higher than one when an education level has children who belong to younger or older age groups.

5. World Bank, *The Road Not Traveled: Education Reform in the Middle East and North Africa* (Washington: 2008).

6. Ina V.S. Mullis and others, *TIMSS 2007 International Mathematics Report* (Boston College, Lynch School of Education, TIMSS & PIRLS International Study Center, 2008); Michael O. Martin and others, *TIMSS 2007 International Science Report* (Boston

College, Lynch School of Education, TIMSS & PIRLS International Study Center, 2008).

7. Patrick Gonzales and others, *Highlights from the Trends in International Mathematics and Science Study (TIMSS) 2003*, NCES 2005-005 (Washington: National Center for Education Statistics, 2004).

8. Ibid.

9. Ibid.; World Bank, *The Road Not Traveled.*

10. In 2006 the unemployment rate of women in rural areas was a mere 1.8 percent, but 83 percent of rural women worked in family-owned enterprises without compensation.

11. Mohammed Bougroum, Aomar Ibourk, and Ahmed Trachen, "L'insertion des diplômés au Maroc : Trajectoires professionnelles et déterminants individuels," *Revue région et développement* 15 (2002): 57–77 (www.regionetdeveloppement.u-3mrs.fr/pdf/R15/R15_Bougroum.pdf).

12. Secrétariat d'État Chargé de la Formation Professionnelle, "Formation professionnelle: Bilan au titre de 2003–2004 et plan d'action 2005–2007," administrative document (Rabat: 2005).

13. Pierre-Richard Agénor and Karim El Aynaoui, "Politiques du marché du travail et chômage au Maroc une analyse quantitative," *Revue d'économie du développement* 1 (2005): 5–51.

14. The 1983 Code of Industrial Investments encourages the creation of jobs by providing 5,000 Moroccan dirhams to small and medium-size industrial enterprises for each stable job created during the first four years. However great in theory, this measure never was applied in practice.

15. In French: *Conseil National pour la Jeunesse et l'Avenir* (CNJA).

16. Noureddine El Aoufi and Mohammed Bensaïd, "Chômage et employabilité des jeunes au Maroc," *Cahiers de la stratégie de l'emploi*, Unité politiques de l'emploi, Département de la stratégie en matière d'emploi (Rabat: Bureau International du Travail, International Labor Organization, 2005) (www.ilo.org/public/english/employment/strat/download/esp2005-6.pdf).

17. Ministère des Finances et de la Privatisation, *Projet de loi de finances pour l'année budgétaire 2006* (Rabat: 2005) (www.finances.gov.ma).

18. For more details, visit www.moukawalati.ma/home.cfm.

19. Brahim Boudarbat, "Unemployment, Status in Employment and Wages in Morocco," *Applied Econometrics and International Development* 6, no. 1 (2006): 165–84.

20. Fadwa El Ghazali, "Pourquoi les jeunes ne veulent pas se marier," *l'Économiste*, November 26, 2004.

21. Aziz Ajbilou, "Où va l'âge au premier mariage au Maroc?" *Bulletin du CERED* No.1 (Rabat: Centre d'Études et de Recherches Démographiques, 2003).

22. United Nations Development Program and Comite Directeur du Rapport: 50 Ans de Développement Humain, "50 ans de développement humain et perspectives

2025" (New York: 2006). For a summary of the report in English, see www.rdh50.ma/fr/ index.asp.

23. Haut Commissariat au Plan, "Rapport de la politique de population. La jeunesse marocaine: attitudes, comportements et besoins" (Rabat: Centre d'Études et de Recherches Démographiques, 2004).

NADER KABBANI *and* NOURA KAMEL

8

Tapping into the Economic Potential of Young Syrians during a Time of Transition

As Syria moves toward becoming a net oil importer in the near future, the country is undergoing extensive economic reforms to transition toward a "social market" economy. The government is introducing elements of a new social contract that relies less on state intervention and more on private sector solutions. On the "market" side, the government has removed barriers to private sector entry for most industries; permitted the development of private secondary schools, universities, and banks; and introduced legislation to reform the country's rigid labor laws. The "social" emphasis of the reform effort involves maintaining a central regulatory role for the state and improving social safety nets to support vulnerable groups during the economic transition.

These reforms come at a critical time when Syria is experiencing the effects of a large demographic wave that is moving through the population. In Syria, the 15 to 24 age group peaked at around 23 percent of the population in 2005, up from 19 percent in 1985.[1] The share of youth in the population is expected to fall to 18 percent by about 2020, as the demographic wave moves into the adult years. Syria's youth bulge presents challenges in creating enough jobs and housing units for young people. However, it also creates a window of opportunity because a large working-age population can contribute to greater savings and higher rates of economic growth. If the economy fails to create enough jobs for young people, the demographic dividend could be squandered, undermining prospects for economic growth and development.

While economic reforms hold much promise, the formal and informal institutions in the country have yet to fully adapt to these reforms and extend their benefits to young people. A weak education system perpetuates skill mismatches; public sector employment policies that provide high wages and benefits contribute to queuing for government jobs; rigid labor laws and regulations make businesses reluctant to hire young workers; young people who want to become self-employed or start a business face limited access to credit.

This chapter examines youth economic exclusion in Syria through the lens of the school-to-work transition. It begins with an overview of the education system followed by the school-to-work transition in Syria. This overview lays the groundwork for a discussion on youth unemployment, often used as a key indicator of exclusion. The subsequent sections examine various dimensions of youth exclusion: factors that are suspected to affect young people's transition to work, including labor supply and demand factors; institutional factors (public sector employment policies and access to credit); and social factors. Data limitations restrict our analysis to the 2004–05 period.

Education

Over the past half century, the education system in Syria has been dominated by the public sector. With few exceptions, private schools were allowed only at the primary school level. Free public schooling at all levels of education contributed to remarkable progress in educational attainment over the past five decades. Average years of schooling increased more than fourfold between 1960 and 2000, reaching 6 years among those aged 15 and above.[2] By 2007 Syria had achieved almost universal primary education among both female and male children. While average years of schooling in Syria are now higher than the average for the Middle East (5.4 years), more must be done to close the gap with the world average (6.7 years).

Syria has also achieved major improvements in educational equity. The gender gap has nearly closed at all school levels. At the primary level, the net enrollment rate reached nearly 100 percent among boys and 96 percent among girls in 2007.[3] At the secondary school level, where the enrollment rate for girls was less than half that of boys in 1970, the gender gap was virtually eliminated by 2007. In fact, official figures suggest that in 2005 the number of young women enrolled in secondary schools actually surpassed that of young men for the first time.

Concerted efforts have been made to reach marginalized groups and sparsely populated areas of the country. The education Gini coefficient for Syria exhibits a strong downward trend, falling from 0.71 in 1970 to 0.46 in 2000, reflecting substantial improvements in the equitable distribution of education.[4] Despite these positive developments at the national level, low levels of educational attainment and substantial gender differences persist among some groups and in some geographical locations throughout the country. For example, in some eastern governorates, illiteracy rates among youth still reach 15 to 20 percent. These areas should be a focus of future government intervention and reform efforts.

Three main institutional features confront the Syrian education system: how students are selected into different educational tracks; how the public sector provision of free education copes with increasing demand; and finally, how the quality of education is affected and how it can be improved.

First, until recently, the Syrian school system was divided into primary school (grades one through six), preparatory school (grades seven through nine), and vocational and general secondary school (grades ten through twelve), followed by two-year technical "intermediate" institutes and universities. In 2003 the government combined primary and preparatory schooling into one category called basic education, covering grades one through nine. The government also increased the number of years of compulsory schooling from six to nine years. Students take national exams at the end of basic and secondary schooling. These exams determine whether they continue on to the next level and, if so, whether they are eligible for the general or vocational track.

Students still strongly prefer the general track. Vocational secondary schools and intermediate institutes are infamous for their weak curricula and outdated equipment. Vocational schools are also stigmatized as a path for students with low test scores and are seen as a dead end to further education—with few exceptions, vocational secondary school students are not eligible to continue on to public universities. The fact that unemployment rates are higher among vocational school graduates reinforces these perceptions.[5]

Second, starting in the mid-1980s the progressive public education model came under significant fiscal strain in the face of growing demand for education. The university system, especially, became overburdened and overcrowded, and the government sought to redirect students from the general secondary track to the vocational track by increasing the difficulty levels of the two national exams. Following these changes, the share of students enrolled in vocational schools rose from 19 percent of secondary school enrollment in 1989 to 45 percent by 2000. However, secondary school enrollment rates fell overall as general secondary school enrollment rates declined by 40 percent. In 2001 the Syrian government allowed private secondary schools and universities to open and eased restrictions on entry into public universities. As a result, general secondary school enrollment rates more than doubled between 1998 and 2005, and the vocational share of secondary schooling dropped to 32 percent.

Finally, despite the remarkable gains in educational attainment and improvements in equitable access, the education system is not providing students with the skills they need to succeed in the changing economy. Like schools in many countries in the Middle East, the Syrian school system is focused mainly on imparting knowledge. Students engage in rote memorization with the goal of accumulating the information necessary to pass two national exams in the ninth and twelfth grades. Students are far more focused on acquiring diplomas than on developing key skills demanded by employers.[6]

Occupational mismatch reduces opportunities for young people to participate in the economy in ways commensurate with their capabilities. It often requires young people to accept lower wages and lower quality jobs than their educational achievements would suggest. In addition, limited training opportunities available to Syrian youth, both on and off the job, have led to lower occupational mobility and less ability to adapt to changing demands in the labor market. Findings from the 2005 School-to-Work Transition Survey suggest that lack of educational qualifications and unsuitable education are the most significant obstacles that young people encounter in searching for a job, jointly accounting for 43 percent of total responses.[7] This constraint is followed by lack of experience and by job scarcity, each of which represents only around 16 percent of total responses. The results suggest that young Syrians recognize the lack of suitable education as the primary obstacle to finding work.

The mismatch between the skills of job seekers and the needs of employers is reflected in the exceptionally low returns to education. Huitfeldt and Kabbani found that an additional year of schooling was, on average, associated with a 2 percent increase in wages.[8] This return is low compared with other countries of the world, with average returns of around 10 to 15 percent, as well as with the Middle East region, with averages of around 6 percent.[9] It is also close to the average returns to work experience in Syria, which suggests that the education received in school does not contribute significantly more than experience received on the job. These findings do not necessarily imply that the quality of knowledge imparted by the education system is not good. Rather, it suggests that the knowledge provided does not, on its own, meet the current needs of employers.

Evidence of low labor productivity and low returns to education has encouraged the Syrian government to initiate extensive reforms of the public education system.[10] The Ministry of Education has been revising school curricula at all levels in collaboration with experts from outside the government and, in the case of vocational education curricula, with strong input from the private sector in an effort to make the content more responsive to the needs of the labor market. The ministry has also increased the years required to receive teaching credentials by two years and has retrained over 25,000 teachers under the new system. Higher education is also being reformed. Public universities are revising their curricula to make courses more relevant for the labor market. The Syrian government has also introduced higher institutes of learning in the country with external financial and technical support. One example is the Higher Institute of Business Administration, which was started in 2001 with support from the European Union, including the provision of €14 million for financing the institute.

Reforming the vocational education system remains a priority for the government, but a difficult one. Vocational education and training (VET) institutes report to a large number of different government agencies. Their activities are not adequately coordinated or linked to labor market information systems that can sufficiently identify market needs. In 2005 the European Union funded a €27 million, three-year modernization of vocational education and training (MVET) program in which curricula were revised in collaboration with the private sector. One promising activity was the expansion of an apprenticeship project, started in 2001, that combined three days of school with two days of work each week and that received favorable reviews from participating businesses. However, the MVET program ran into management problems and delays. Given the large number of players involved in VET, any successful future effort will require the development of a comprehensive vocational education reform strategy.

The School-to-Work Transition and Labor Force Outcomes

To depict the transition of youth from school to work, we divide youth into four groups: employed, unemployed (not working, but actively looking for work), in school, and economically inactive (not working, looking for work, or in school). We refer to those who are working or looking for work as being "in the labor force."[11] We use the 2003–04 Household Income and Expenditure Survey (HIES) to show the transitions by age for both young men and women.[12] We also extend the age group covered to 29 years to capture the entire school-to-work transition period.

During the entire school-to-work transition period, young men in Syria are mainly either working, looking for work, or in school (figure 8-1). Inactivity is scarcely visible in the data. At any given age, only 1 to 2 percent of young men are not in the labor force or in school. The share of young men who are working rises sharply with age, increasing from 25 percent at age 15 to 80 percent at age 24. By age 29, 93 percent of young men are employed. The share of young men looking for work initially increases with age, reaching a peak of 16 percent by the age of 21 before declining to under 5 percent by the age of 27. The unemployment rate among young men also peaks at age 21, at 21 percent.

The transition is different for young women. Young women leave school at a slightly earlier age than young men. However, they are far more likely to transition from school to inactivity than to the labor force. Labor market inactivity rates increase from under 20 percent at age 14 to over 70 percent by age 25. By comparison, employment rates increase from 7 percent at age 15 to 19 percent by age 24, remaining at around 20 percent through age 29. Unemployment patterns among women are similar to those of men. The share of young women looking for work initially increases with age, reaching a peak of 9 percent by age 21 before declining to 3 percent by age 27. The unemployment rate among young women also peaks around age 21, at 38 percent.

There are important differences in labor force outcomes with respect to educational attainment, especially for young women. We report both activity rates and labor force participation rates in table 8-1, but focus on the former because much of the variance in participation rates is attributable to school enrollment. While nearly 99 percent of young men are active in the labor force or in school, illiterate young men are an exception. For these young men, the activity rate is only around 80 percent. This lower activity rate reflects the fact that illiterate men are more likely to be engaged in seasonal work in Syria or neighboring Lebanon. Among young women, fewer than half are active in the labor force or in school, but the activity rate rises with educational attainment to over 85 percent among postsecondary school completers. The labor force participation rate among young women is only 20 percent overall, less than one-third the participation rate of young men.

Figure 8-1. *Labor Force Status by Age for Young Syrian Men and Women, 2003–04*

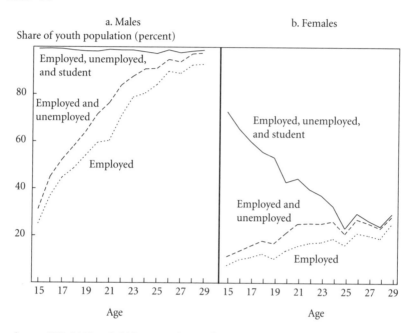

Source: 2003–04 Household Income and Expenditure Survey.

However, it increases to 80 percent among those who have graduated from postsecondary institutes and to 74 percent among university graduates. Educational attainment is thus a main correlate of labor force participation among young women.

Unemployment

To date Syria has had mixed success in tapping into the economic potential of its youth. Unemployment among young people in Syria has declined, from 26 percent in 2002 to 19 percent in 2005. While youth unemployment rates have declined in most countries of the Middle East region, Syria has had the steepest decline among countries with available data. However, while the unemployment rate among Syrian youth is lower than the regional average, estimated at 22 percent in 2007, it remains high when compared with the worldwide average of 12 percent.[13]

Table 8-1. *Activity, Participation, and Unemployment Rates among Syrian Youth Aged 15 to 29, 2003–04*
Percent

	Activity rate (including students)		Labor force participation rate		Unemployment rate	
	Men	Women	Men	Women	Men	Women
Illiterate	79	28	78	28	10	12
Literate	97	31	95	29	9	21
Primary	99	29	87	19	11	31
Preparatory	99	64	41	7	17	49
Secondary	100	73	33	15	22	46
Intermediate institute	100	85	94	80	21	21
University	97	86	79	74	20	17
Total	99	46	70	20	13	29

Source: Authors' calculations using the 2003–04 Household Income and Expenditure Survey data. The activity rate is defined as the share of youth working, looking for work, or in school.

Youth economic exclusion must also be studied in comparison with adults. Young people tend to have higher unemployment rates than adults because they are just beginning to look for work and may change jobs more frequently in an effort to find a good match for their interests and skills. Even so, the ratio of unemployed youth to unemployed adults (the relative unemployment rate among youth) in Syria, which stood at 4.3 in 2005 compared with 6.5 in 2002, is high compared with the worldwide average of 3.5.

Another way to examine relative youth unemployment is in terms of shares. In 2005 young people in Syria represented 61 percent of the total unemployed population, down from 78 percent in 2002. This is a big improvement in the relative situation among young people in Syria (the largest decline among countries with available data in the Middle East). However, Syria still has among the highest shares of unemployed youth in the region, indicating that unemployment in Syria remains very much a youth problem.

It may seem contradictory that youth unemployment rates in Syria are lower than the regional average, while youth unemployment shares (and relative unemployment rates) are higher. The reason for this is that Syria has one of the lowest adult unemployment rates in the region, very close to the world average of 4 percent. Add to this the fact that first-time job seekers in

Syria represented 78 percent of the unemployed in 2005, and we can conclude that unemployment in Syria is primarily a labor market insertion problem. Once people start working, they tend to stay working.

Despite evidence of substantial improvements in labor market outcomes for youth, several concerns remain. First, youth unemployment shares and relative unemployment rates are quite high, indicating a difficult transition to regular employment among young workers. Second, long-term unemployment is often used as an indicator of economic exclusion, and young Syrians endure long wait times for jobs.

Not only might higher unemployment spells increase exclusion, they also have a negative impact on future labor market outcomes because youth can "unlearn" by "not doing."[14] According to findings from the School-to-Work Transition Study, over 75 percent of unemployed young people surveyed had been searching for work for over a year.[15] Search times were similar across levels of educational attainment but appeared to be shorter among postsecondary school graduates. Also, there were no significant gender differences in the share of the unemployed who had been searching for more than a year.

Thus, as in other Middle Eastern countries, youth unemployment spells in Syria are measured in years, not months. What is not clear is the extent to which long unemployment spells are the result of a mismatch between the skills of workers and needs of employers, a lack of jobs in general, or the result of queuing for public sector jobs, as has happened in other countries of the region such as Egypt and Morocco.[16] That unemployment spells are extensive among youth at all levels of educational attainment suggests a combination of occupational mismatch and weak labor demand.

In sum, unemployment rates among Syrian youth are high compared with the worldwide average but not with the region. However, the share of youth among the unemployed is the highest in the region. These basic indicators point toward youth economic exclusion as a potential problem in the country, but labor force participation and activity rates suggest a more complicated reality. Nearly all young men are actively engaged in the transition from school to work. That few young men are discouraged from looking for work and nearly all are employed by the time they reach age 30 suggests that economic exclusion may be taking place with respect to good jobs, not simply jobs. There is also an important gender dimension, with young women less than one-third as likely as young men to participate in the labor force and more than twice as likely to be unemployed, suggesting potential barriers to labor market entry among young women.

Factors Influencing Youth Unemployment

Supply and demand pressures play a key role in explaining employment trends in Syria, as do institutional factors such as public sector employment policies.

Labor Supply

One of the principal factors potentially driving the high rates of youth unemployment over the past decade appears to be high labor supply pressures. Between 1983 and 2003 the number of youth in the labor market increased by about 5 percent a year, nearly doubling the young labor force over those two decades. As more and more young people entered the labor force, they naturally had difficulty finding jobs in general and high-quality, high-wage jobs in particular. The labor supply growth rate among youth has been dropping and is expected to have reached less than 1 percent in 2008. Thus, to the extent that labor supply pressures are contributing to high rates of unemployment among youth, their effect is transitory and not a cause for long-term policy intervention. But short-term intervention is required to ensure that today's unemployed youth do not become tomorrow's unemployed adults.

A second factor driving labor supply trends is an increase in female labor force participation rates (figure 8-2). Those rates doubled between 1980 and 2005 but started from very low initial rates. The annual increase in female labor force participation was about 0.5 percent a year. Even with this increase, women account for only 15 percent of the labor supply.[17] But because women gravitate toward specific occupations, it is likely that the higher participation of women in the workforce has affected the employment prospects of women in female-oriented occupations, helping to explain the observed gender differences in unemployment rates.

A mitigating factor affecting youth unemployment rates is international migration. Emigration by Syrian youth to other countries means less competition for jobs in Syria, for both youth and adults. Although data limitations prevent a detailed examination of this issue, some estimates exist. The destination of Syrian emigrants is dependent on educational attainment and skills. Those with higher skills head mostly to the Persian Gulf countries and some emigrate to Europe and North America. Less skilled workers tend to work in Lebanon, usually for only a few months of the year.[18] The number of Syrian migrant workers in Lebanon is thought to have

Figure 8-2. *Estimates and Projections of Economically Active Syrian Youth, by Gender, 1983–2018*

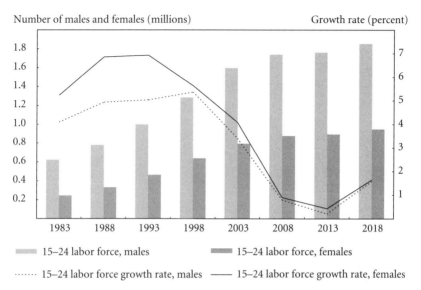

Source: International Labor Organization, Economically Active Population Estimates and Projections (EAPEP) database, 5th ed. (2006).

been about 350,000 in early 2005, but demand is dependent on the volatile political situation in that country.

Another factor that affects the size of the labor force and unemployment is educational attainment. An increase in average enrollment rates at all levels of schooling can reduce labor force participation. For the effect to be permanent, however, governments must find ways of increasing economic growth and job creation in occupations that require higher levels of education.

Labor Demand

As noted earlier, the Syrian government is in the middle of a major economic reform effort to move the country from a state-controlled economy to a social market economy. It has removed barriers to private sector entry for most industries; regulations of the private sector are being pared down; and legislation to reform the country's rigid labor laws has been introduced. Despite these efforts, Syrian reforms have not been as extensive as those seen in other countries.

One major reform was introduced in 2000, when the government revised its key investment law (Law No. 10) to provide additional incentives for export industries, firms that locate in less industrialized regions of the country, and companies willing to hire large numbers of workers and register them with the social services agency. Although these incentives may possibly strengthen the private sector, they may not increase employment because less than 6 percent of the total number of registered workers in the industrial private sector worked for firms that operated under the investment law before it was revised. As of 2006, 60 percent of registered workers were employed by small firms registered under Law No. 47.[19]

Syria has made significant progress in some areas related to the ease of doing business; for example, the number of procedures and the number of days required to start a business have fallen significantly since 2006 and are now below the Middle Eastern average.[20] A reduction in the highest corporate tax bracket from 65 percent to 35 percent in 2003 has been associated with a positive effect on investment.[21] Still, administrative and tax policies remain cumbersome and time consuming. Such bureaucratic obstacles have encouraged or forced many entrepreneurs to operate in the informal economy.[22]

Despite progress made in reforming the business environment, more should be done. Such reforms are a moving target as countries compete to attract foreign investment. For example, increasing labor market flexibility is a key factor in improving the business environment as well as in encouraging private firms to hire young inexperienced workers. The Syrian government has drafted legislation that would increase labor market flexibility but has yet to pass the law. As such, its global ranking in the World Bank's "Employing Workers" index fell from 89th in 2006 to 122nd in 2009, as other countries proceeded to implement such reforms.[23] The Syrian government has delayed the passage of labor laws for good reason; it is trying to improve social safety nets ahead of introducing the reforms. However, delays are surely affecting its global competitiveness.

Public Sector Employment Policies

Although the flat wage structure resulting from the low returns to education may encourage students to drop out of school, Syrian youth appear to seek higher education partly to gain employment in the public sector. Young people in Syria have a strong preference for public sector employment. Indeed, the share of employment in the public sector increases steadily and dramatically with the level of educational attainment, from 12 percent of illiterate men and 3 percent of illiterate women to 81 percent of men and 78 percent of women with university degrees. For young women, public sector employment actually peaks at 87 percent among graduates of postsecondary intermediate institutes.

In terms of higher levels of educational attainment, employment in the public sector comes at the expense of employment in the formal and informal private sectors, but the negative association is stronger for the informal sector. For young men, employment in the informal sector falls steadily from 53 percent of illiterate paid workers to 2 percent of university graduates. For young women, the decline is even sharper, from around 90 percent for illiterate young women to nearly 8 percent among university graduates.

In 2003 over 80 percent of unemployed young people in Syria (aged 15 to 29) indicated that they were interested in public sector jobs, and nearly 60 percent indicated that they were interested in jobs exclusively in the public sector. By comparison, only 34 percent were interested in private sector jobs, and only 9 percent wanted jobs exclusively in the private sector. Only 14 percent were interested in self-employment or owning a business. Unemployed young women were more interested than young men in public sector employment and less interested in self-employment or owning a business. Nearly 90 percent of unemployed young women were looking for public sector jobs, and 70 percent were looking for jobs exclusively in the public sector.[24] Kabbani and Al-Habash find that preference for public sector jobs increases with age and educational attainment.[25] Young men are motivated in their job search by family need, whereas social norms influence the employment choices of young women. The difference between the predicted public and private sector wages for unemployed youth is also associated with public sector job preference, especially among women.

Young people are attracted to public sector jobs because they offer higher benefits and greater job security than jobs in the private sector. Dismissal of public sector employees is virtually impossible once they are granted a "fixed contract," which occurs after they have completed a year-long training period.[26] Young women are especially attracted to public sector jobs because of the more flexible working hours and the generous benefits and maternity leave policies. For young women, public sector jobs are also considered more socially acceptable, because the private sector is associated with higher levels of workplace discrimination and stigmatized as such. There is also evidence that young women tend to earn higher hourly wages in the public sector.[27] Most young men also prefer jobs in the public sector, but hourly wages for them are on par with the private sector. The main benefit seems to be job security and benefits.

In line with its economic reform agenda, the Syrian government has begun developing public sector employment retrenchment policies and has allowed private sector competition in many sectors that were previously state dominated. The government has taken steps to strengthen the private sector and encourage entrepreneurship to increase the capacity of the private sector to absorb young labor market entrants. However, the government has also raised public sector wages repeatedly since 2000, and public sector compensation packages continue to be more attractive than those in the private sector for most groups, especially young women.[28] Introducing retrenchment policies without bringing public sector wages and benefits into alignment with the private sector may actually result in higher unemployment rates among young people, as evidenced by the experiences of other Middle Eastern countries.[29]

One factor often associated with lower levels of youth employment and higher rates of youth unemployment is the minimum wage. In Syria, the minimum wage has historically been set at a lower rate in the private sector than in the public sector. It has been increased three times since 2002. The latest increase, in 2006–07, raised the minimum wage for the private sector to 4,805 Syrian pounds per month (around $100) and brought the two sectors into alignment. Compared with other Middle Eastern countries, the monthly minimum wage in Syria is low.[30] However, at current levels, the minimum wage would have been binding on 28 percent of full-time paid employees in 2003–04. Given compliance problems in the private sector, a higher minimum wage is likely to increase the size of the informal sector. Paradoxically, the biggest impact the minimum wage may have is on public finances and unemployment, because it will increase the attraction of government jobs among low-skilled workers.

Starting a Business and Access to Credit

One alternative to paid work is starting a business. Successful start-ups not only potentially improve the livelihoods of young entrepreneurs but also create job opportunities for others. According to the 2003–04 HIES, by age 29, over 36 percent of young men in Syria were self-employed or had their own businesses. But years of heavy regulation of private sector activities have contributed to an adverse business climate in the country. In 2009 the World Bank ranked Syria 124th out of 181 countries in the ease of doing business.[31] Syria's ranking on the minimum amount of capital needed to start a business (relative to income per capita) is especially low. Access to credit also remains a serious problem in Syria, where it ranks next to last in the world.

The regulatory framework of the Syrian banking system remains undeveloped, impeding the development of the already weak private sector. Among public sector banks, conditions for approving loans are prohibitive, and loan ceilings fall below the financing needs of most borrowers, especially youth. For example, Commercial Bank, arguably the most important lender to businesses, offers loans to established businesses but practically none to start-ups, which are more likely to encompass youth-led endeavors. Although private banks were allowed to open and operate in Syria beginning in 2003, their services are still limited. As with public banks, private banks in Syria require high levels of collateral, mainly to mitigate the risk of defaults. Collateral requirements range from 100 to 150 percent of loan amounts, and interest rates range between 10 and 11 percent. Furthermore, banks are not able to effectively use collateral to cover bad loans, making them reluctant to offer credit. As a result, only a few well-established investors gain access to financing while the newest and neediest small investors do not. Limited access to financing from banks narrows the choices available to young people in starting businesses or in taking out personal loans to purchase a house, often a key condition of marriage in Syria.

In sum, formal institutions in Syria do not adequately promote youth inclusion. Despite remarkable progress in educational attainment and equitable access, the education system has not been successful in transferring skills demanded in the labor market. The legal framework presents special challenges for youth. Rigid labor laws and regulations make private businesses reluctant to hire young people. High wages and benefits in the public sector contribute to job seekers lining up for public sector jobs. The doubling of the minimum wage between 2001 and 2006 may make government jobs even more attractive if the private sector fails to abide by and pay the higher wage rates. Finally, young people who decide to become self-employed or to start their own businesses face a weak business climate, especially in terms of the capital needed to start a business and limited access to credit through formal sources of finance.

Exclusion and the Influence of Family and Society

Personal attitudes, family circumstances, and social influences all potentially play a role in the economic exclusion of youth in Syria. Gender issues are particularly relevant here.[32]

Personal attitudes and choice play an important role in determining unemployment and labor force participation. Entry into the labor force and acceptance of a job are choices that many young Syrians have to make, especially young women. However, care must be taken in interpreting unemployment and labor force inactivity as voluntary exclusion. Le Grand and Barry advise caution when analyzing voluntary exclusion because the quality of choices available and the information that the decisions are based on may not warrant considering the exclusion to be truly voluntary.[33] Further, a group that excludes itself voluntarily may not be able to return to normative roles in society.

In considering the influence of personal attitudes in defining a set of alternatives for youth, we begin with a look at their priorities. Nearly 40 percent of young men but only about 12 percent of women report work as the most important goal in their lives. By contrast, more than 50 percent of young women but just 25 percent of young men rank family and marriage as their most important goal in life. An almost equal percentage of men and women placed education as most important.[34]

At a superficial level these results help explain the differences between labor force participation and inactivity rates for young men and women. However, the priorities of young people are certainly influenced by their families and the environments in which they are raised and socialized. Traditionally, a woman's position in the Middle East has been characterized by her engagement in the private sphere as a mother and wife. While this view has been changing, young women still prioritize marriage and family, and traditions and social norms in Syria remain an important determinant of division of labor on the basis of gender. For example, most young women and their families expect husbands to be the breadwinners, so many young wives choose to exit the labor force after marriage while many others exit in deference to their father's or husband's wishes. Indeed, housework and child care responsibilities are reported as the main reasons for inactivity among 44 percent of women who are neither in school nor in the labor market.[35] In addition, about one-third of inactive young women indicated that the primary reason for their inactivity was family refusal to allow them to work or to search for work. This represents our first piece of empirical evidence of economic exclusion along social dimensions. Less than 10 percent of economically inactive young women cited lack of jobs as a main reason for their inactivity.

Family influence and circumstances are also important factors in studying youth unemployment in Syria. Young Syrians rely heavily on family connections to secure employment, housing, and credit in preparation for marriage. The availability of strong family support structures may also contribute to high youth unemployment rates by allowing young people more time to find good employment opportunities.[36] Young people from low-income households have little choice but to work to support themselves and their families. Those from middle- or high-income families can afford to be more selective in their labor market choices and to wait for good jobs. Thus, unemployment among young people is not only decided by labor market conditions and employment availability but also by personal choices linked to family circumstances.

Family and social connections are important elements in looking for and finding work. More than 90 percent of young people report that they rely on help from family and friends in looking for work. The second most frequently used job search strategy was visiting establishments directly, with 87 percent indicating that they used this method.[37] These results highlight the limited use of more formal institutions and methods in searching for a job, such as public employment offices or the media. On the demand side, few private companies list vacancies with public employment offices (although they are required by law to do so) because of the widespread belief that the offices propose job candidates for vacant positions based on connections rather than on qualifications.[38]

Among those who completed their transition from school to work, meaning that they found a job with a long-term contract or did not claim a desire to change jobs, a majority (54 percent) found their current job through friends and family.[39] The second most common strategy for finding a stable job was through a training institution (21 percent), followed by visiting the establishment directly (9 percent). Other methods, including more formal job searches through media outlets or government employment offices, accounted for only 2 to 3 percent of successful transitions. The importance of informal networks in the job search process in Syria suggests that young people without such connections have fewer chances of obtaining employment and are likely to be economically excluded. This fact has important implications for young women. A young woman may decide to go against her family's wishes and look for a job. But the task becomes much more difficult if she needs their help and connections to secure one. However, as discussed above, labor force participation rates among young women increase dramatically with the level of educational attainment. Indeed, receiving an education that is useful and relevant to available job opportunities appears to be more than simply a mitigating strategy; rather, it is the primary strategy that, if successfully completed, could overcome network shortcomings and other barriers to social and economic inclusion.

In sum, young people in Syria rely heavily on family and social connections to find and obtain stable employment. Young people who lack such connections are at a disadvantage in finding work, especially good jobs. For young women, there is evidence of some measure of voluntary exclusion from the workforce; a majority indicated that their main goal in life is family and marriage. But family refusal was the second most common reason given for economic inactivity, behind housework and child care. As such, young women experience familial and social pressures to stay out of the labor force, which may be compounded if access to employment through informal networks is withheld. It is difficult to separate voluntary from involuntary exclusion in such cases, because the two are related in complex ways that cannot be easily disentangled. Nonetheless, educational attainment appears to provide a considerable measure of economic inclusion, especially among young women.

Conclusion

Unemployment rates among youth in Syria were estimated at 19 percent in 2005, down from 26 percent in 2002, around the time when major economic reforms were initiated to move the country from a state-led to a social market economy. While lower than the regional average, the youth unemployment rate in Syria is higher than the worldwide average of 12 percent. Furthermore, this rate is 4.3 times the adult unemployment rate, and youth represent 61 percent of the unemployed population. While both indicators were lower in 2005 than in 2002 (when the unemployment ratio was 6.5 and the share of youth among the unemployed was 78 percent), they were high compared with regional and worldwide averages. These findings suggest that despite substantial gains in youth employment outcomes, youth economic exclusion remains a serious issue in Syria. There is also an important gender dimension, with young women less than one-third as likely as young men to participate in the labor force and more than twice as likely to be unemployed, suggesting potential barriers to labor market entry for young women.

Many of the economic factors associated with youth employment outcomes seem to be transient. These include demographic trends and female labor supply pressures. However, structural factors also appear to be embedded in the economic and social institutions of the country. These include a weak education system that perpetuates skill mismatches; public sector employment policies that provide high wages and benefits, contributing to queuing for government jobs; rigid labor laws and regulations that make businesses reluctant to hire young workers; and a weak business climate, especially in terms of the large amounts of capital needed to start a business and limited access to credit.

Social factors appear to be an important element in the economic exclusion of youth in Syria. Young people rely heavily on family and social connections to look for and obtain stable jobs. But educational attainment also can buy a measure of economic inclusion. Moreover, taking personal initiative seems to be rewarded. Indeed, that nearly all young men are employed by the time they reach the age of 30 suggests that economic exclusion may not be taking place so much with respect to finding a job as with respect to finding a good job (stable, high wage, high benefits). For young women, there is evidence of some measure of voluntary exclusion from the workforce. A majority indicate that their main goal in life is family and marriage. But family refusal to allow young women to work is the second most common reason for economic inactivity.

In sum, the economic situation of young people in Syria has improved in the wake of government reform efforts. However, much more needs to be done to help create an environment where young people can reach their full potential. Future reform efforts should include the removal of institutional barriers that perpetuate youth economic exclusion and support for access to public and private educational resources that provide knowledge and skills relevant to a social market economy.

Data limitations restrict our analysis to the period between 2003 and 2005. While most of the core issues regarding youth exclusion are not likely to have changed substantially since this time, we are mindful that recent developments are likely to have had an effect on the situation of youth. Recent labor force surveys suggest that the unemployment rate among youth in Syria continued to fall in 2006 to under 18 percent, before rising to 19 percent in 2007. The upward pressure on youth unemployment rates is likely to continue in the face of the global economic crisis, which is expected to reduce foreign direct investment flowing to the country, reduce remittances, induce return migration from aboard, and contribute to a slowdown in the rate of economic growth. In this context, the burden is on the government to maintain the pace of those economic reforms that can encourage private sector activity and investment.

Notes

1. We adopt the most widely used definition of youth: those between the ages of 15 and 24, noting that some young people begin their transitions to work and adulthood at earlier ages and some (such as university graduates) at later ages. We expand the range of ages under analysis when there is a need and data are available.

2. Robert Barro and Jong-Wha Lee, "International Data on Educational Attainment: Updates and Implications," Working Paper 42 (Harvard University, Center for International Development, 2000).

3. UNESCO Institute for Statistics, *Global Education Digest 2008: Comparing Education Statistics across the World* (Montreal), www.uis.unesco.org.

4. World Bank, *The Road Not Traveled: Education Reform in the Middle East and North Africa* (Washington: 2008). The education Gini coefficient is based on the distribution of average number of years of schooling across the population. A value of 0 indicates perfect equality and a value of 1 indicates perfect inequality.

5. Nader Kabbani and Noura Kamel, "Youth Exclusion in Syria: Social, Economic, and Institutional Dimensions," Middle East Youth Initiative Working Paper 4 (Wolfensohn Center for Development at the Brookings Institution and the Dubai School of Government, 2007).

6. Djavad Salehi-Isfahani and Navtej Dhillon, "Stalled Youth Transitions in the Middle East: A Framework for Policy Reform," Middle East Youth Initiative Working Paper 8 (Wolfensohn Center for Development at the Brookings Institution and the Dubai School of Government, 2008); Kabbani and Kamel, "Youth Exclusion in Syria."

7. The 2005 School-to-Work Transition Survey (SWTS) was developed by the International Labor Organization (ILO) and was administered by the Syrian Central Bureau of Statistics (SCBS) to 2,000 young people aged 15 to 24 in November 2005. The SWTS is not nationally representative, so we do not use it to derive prevalence estimates. But the data are sufficiently representative for studying issues of youth exclusion.

8. Henrik Huitfeldt and Nader Kabbani, "Returns to Education and the Transition from School to Work in Syria," Working Paper Series 2007-1 (American University of Beirut, Institution of Financial Economics, 2007).

9. World Bank, *The Road Not Traveled.*

10. International Monetary Fund, "Syrian Arab Republic: Selected Issues and Statistical Appendix" (Washington: 2003); Huitfeldt and Kabbani, "Returns to Education and the Transition from School to Work in Syria."

11. Some sources refer to "inactive" as being synonymous with "not in the labor force." In this chapter, we find it more conceptually appealing to use "inactive" to mean neither in school nor in the labor force.

12. The 2003–04 HIES is a nationally representative survey administered by the SCBS to 30,000 households. We use it to generate disaggregated statistics on youth unavailable through published sources.

13. ILO, *Global Employment Trends for Youth* (Geneva: 2008).

14. Amartya Sen, "Social Exclusion: Concept, Application, and Scrutiny," Social Development Papers 1 (Manila: Asian Development Bank, Office of Environment and Social Development, 2000).

15. Annual Syrian labor force surveys do not gather information about unemployment duration; however, an analysis of unemployment rates by year after expected graduation shows that they decline rapidly with age, especially for university graduates. Questions about unemployment duration were asked in the 2005 School-to-Work Transition Survey. While the SWTS is not nationally representative, its key employment outcomes are not that different from official estimates.

16. Ragui Assaad, "The Effects of Public Sector Hiring and Compensation Policies on the Egyptian Labor Market," *World Bank Economic Review* 11, no. 1 (1997): 85–118; Brahim Boudarbat, "Employment Sector Choice in a Developing Labor Market," Department of Economics Working Paper (University of British Columbia, 2004).

17. Nader Kabbani and Zafiris Tzannatos, "Labor and Human Resource Development," in *Syrian Country Profile*, edited by Samir Aita (Cairo: Economic Research Forum, 2006).

18. "Annual Transfers from Syrian Labor in Lebanon at USD 1.5-2 bn," *Syria Report* (Paris: Middle East Information and Communication Agency, April 2005).

19. Kabbani and Tzannatos, "Labor and Human Resource Development."

20. World Bank, *Doing Business 2009* (Washington: 2008).

21. "A New Income Tax Law Is Issued," *Syria Report* (Paris: Middle East Information and Communication Agency, December 2003).

22. Kabbani and Tzannatos, "Labor and Human Resource Development."

23. World Bank, *Doing Business 2009.*

24. Nader Kabbani and Leen Al-Habash, "Raising Awareness of Alternatives to Public Sector Employment among Syrian Youth," ERF Working Paper 387 (Cairo: Economic Research Forum, March 2008).

25. Ibid.

26. Law No. 50, article 17.

27. Nader Kabbani, "The Preference of Syrian Youth for Public Sector Jobs," Middle East Youth Initiative Policy Outlook 2 (Wolfensohn Center for Development at the Brookings Institution and the Dubai School of Government, 2009).

28. Ibid.

29. Assaad, "The Effects of Public Sector Hiring and Compensation Policies on the Egyptian Labor Market"; Boudarbat, "Employment Sector Choice in a Developing Labor Market."

30. Nader Kabbani and Ekta Kothari, "Youth Employment in the MENA Region: A Situational Assessment," Social Protection Discussion Paper 534 (Washington: World Bank, 2005).

31. World Bank, *Doing Business 2009.*

32. We make use of data from the 2005 SWTS to examine some of the topics in this section.

33. Julian Le Grand, "Individual Choice and Social Exclusion," CASE Paper 75 (London School of Economics, Centre for Analysis of Social Exclusion, 2003); Brian Barry, "Social Exclusion, Social Isolation and the Distribution of Income," CASE Paper 12 (London School of Economics, Centre for Analysis of Social Exclusion, 1998).

34. SWTS 2005.

35. Ibid.

36. Niall O'Higgins, "Trends in Youth Labor Market in Developing and Transition Countries," Social Protection Discussion Paper 321 (Washington: World Bank, 2003).

37. SWTS 2005.

38. Kabbani and Tzannatos, "Labor and Human Resource Development."

39. Alissa Sufyan, "The School-to-Work Transition of Young People in Syria" (Geneva: ILO, 2007).

RAGUI ASSAAD, GHADA BARSOUM, EMILY CUPITO,
and DANIEL EGEL

9

Addressing Yemen's Twin Deficits: Human Development and Natural Resources

With over 75 percent of its population under age 25, Yemen's population is one of the youngest in the Middle East. And unlike many countries in the region where the youth bulge has already peaked, the share of youth in Yemen's total population will not begin to diminish for many years to come. Under the right conditions, a large youth population can foster economic growth and stimulate social development, but Yemen's challenge of turning its youthful population into a demographic dividend is daunting because of deficits in human development and natural resources, deteriorating economic and political conditions, and social and institutional roadblocks that impede youth from reaching their potential.

The human development challenge facing Yemen today is highlighted by its poor performance across a range of development indicators. Yemen ranks 153rd out of 177 countries in the United Nations Development Program (UNDP) human development index and 140th on combined gross enrollment in primary, secondary, and tertiary education. Yemen also faces one of the largest gender gaps in the world in regard to human development. In addition, it ranks as the country with the fifth-largest gender gap in gross primary education enrollment rates. [1]

These human development challenges are compounded by severe limits on essential natural resources such as water and arable land and by a mountainous topography that makes the costs of transporting goods and resources very high. Water resources are being depleted more quickly than they can be replenished, and the limited amount of arable land must be subdivided among a rapidly growing rural population. Even oil resources, which have

211

provided a major source of income for Yemen in recent years, are projected to be exhausted within the next twenty years. Furthermore, Yemen's topography makes it difficult for the state to provide adequate levels of public services as the population is highly dispersed across a large number of hard-to-reach settlements.

The macroeconomic and political conditions in Yemen are also important contributing factors to the country's human development deficit. Indeed, since its formation in 1990 following a prolonged struggle between the northern Yemen Arab Republic and the southern People's Democratic Republic of Yemen, this nation has endured many severe economic setbacks. In 1991, shortly after unification, Yemeni citizens lost their preferential visa status in Saudi Arabia when Yemen declared sympathy for Iraq during the first Gulf War. Nearly 1 million migrants, equivalent to 8 percent of the total population of Yemen, were forced to return to Yemen. This had dramatic negative consequences for the country, with both the government and individuals deprived of the remittances from these migrants, which had been an essential source of income, and a massive influx of unemployed workers inundating the labor market.

The Gulf War marked the beginning of a long period of decline for Yemen. In 1994 Yemen suffered through a civil war that destroyed much of the productive capacity of the once vibrant southern coast.[2] Since 1994 frequent kidnappings have limited the development of tourism in Yemen, and the bombings of the USS *Cole* in 2000 and the French supertanker *Limburg* in 2002 both dramatically reduced the utilization of Aden's modern container port and discouraged investment in Yemen. Indeed, since the Gulf War, poverty and unemployment have increased, educational attainment has fallen, and inflation has skyrocketed.[3] The effects of these setbacks are still very present in Yemen today.

Finally, social and institutional factors play an important role in Yemen's human development deficit. Conservative social norms limit girls' access to education, restrict women's employment opportunities, and encourage them to marry early and bear a large number of children. Long-standing policies to protect the Yemeni middle class, including policies that resulted in a bloated bureaucracy and provided lifetime job security to government employees, have hampered the development of the private sector and reduced employment opportunities for youth. An educational system accustomed to providing graduates with the credentials needed to join the bureaucracy is ill-suited to a dynamic economy led by the private sector, producing a mismatch between the skills taught in the school system and those demanded by the labor market. Social assistance programs in this resource-poor country historically have had limited outreach and impact. Finally, the chewing of *qat*, the leaves and shoots of the plant *Catha edulis*, is a major pastime activity among Yemenis, including the young generation. This habituating stimulant has serious adverse consumption, productivity, and health consequences. Qat cultivation also depletes scarce water resources and crowds out the production of essential food crops and agricultural exports.

These factors combine to exclude a large portion of the youth population in Yemen. Young Yemenis have a high incidence of illiteracy, limited access to basic education, and weak prospects for employment. Their exclusion has lifelong impacts, making it difficult for them to access the resources and support they need to participate productively in society.

Resource Constraints, Demography, and Population Growth

Yemen has always been a nation of scarce resources: the water supply is particularly meager, and the country's difficult topography means that much of the land is not arable. Yemenis have long lived in careful balance with these resources, developing creative ways of using them in a sustainable manner. However, the recent surge in population, the use of new technologies, the rise of urbanization, and weak policies regarding resource management have all tipped this careful balance. Yemen is now exploiting its resources—especially water, oil, and land—much faster than they can be replenished, setting the country up for future crises. Moreover, high fertility rates continue to increase the population pressures on these already scarce resources.

An extremely water-scarce country, Yemen has an estimated 2.1 billion cubic meters of annually renewable water resources that must be divided among 20 million people; that works out to a mere 105 cubic meters of water per person per year.[4] The worldwide average is 7,500 cubic meters per person, and the regional average in the water-scarce Middle East is 1,250 cubic meters per person. To be food self-sufficient, a country must have at least 1,000 cubic meters per person, meaning that Yemen has about one-tenth of the water it needs to be food self-sufficient in the long term.[5] The World Bank estimates that Yemen's water use exceeds its renewable allotment by almost 1 billion cubic meters per year.[6] Yemen's aquifers drop by about 6 meters each year and are expected to run dry in fifteen to fifty years.

Oil is a critical contributor to the Yemeni economy. The income from oil has helped keep many Yemenis from falling below the poverty line and has supported social programs such as the Social Welfare Fund. However, Yemen's oil supply is being quickly depleted. In 2000 oil contributed 17 percent to real GDP, but by 2005 this contribution had dropped to 12 percent. Production is expected to decline by 2 to 3 percent annually, with an eventual depletion in the 2020s.[7]

Land resources are also scarce in Yemen. After a long history of sustainable land usage, recent population growth, urbanization, a focus on marketable crops, and a lack of land maintenance have radically compromised these efforts.[8] Yemen has 1.66 million hectares of arable land, of which 64 percent is cultivated. The United Nations Population Fund estimates that the per capita allocation of land was 0.07 hectares in 2004 and will fall to 0.03 hectares per person by 2034.[9]

The increasing population is placing unprecedented pressures on already limited natural resources. High fertility rates in Yemen coupled with declining mortality rates have resulted in a high, steady annual rate of population growth of about 3 percent.[10] Yemen's birth rates did not begin to decline until the 1990s, substantially later than in other Middle Eastern countries. Because populations continue to grow for many decades after fertility begins to decline, Yemen can expect no relief from its bulging population in the near future.

High fertility rates and declining mortality rates have buoyed Yemen's 15- to 24-year-old population, which will make up a steady 20 percent of the population for the foreseeable future. As figure 9-1 shows, recent declines in fertility will not affect the share of the youth population for many decades. Even as the proportion of the population aged 0 to 14 falls during the next four decades, the youth population will continue to constitute a large, steady proportion of the population. With the overall population of Yemen expected to triple by 2050, so too will the youth population.

Young families in Yemen begin childbearing early and space their children closely together, leading to a high national fertility rate. According to the 2003 Arab Family Health Survey, the total fertility rate for Yemen from 1998 to 2003 was 6.2 children per woman, which was just below the peak of 6.7 children per woman reached during the mid-1990s.[11]

Fertility patterns show large regional differences. Unsurprisingly, total fertility rates are greater in rural areas (6.7 children per woman) than in urban areas (4.5 children per woman). But regional differences are strong even after controlling for urban-rural differences. In fact, the urban regions of some provinces have fertility rates as high as or higher than their rural counterparts.

Figure 9-1. *Population Age Structure in Yemen, 1950–2050*

Percent of total population

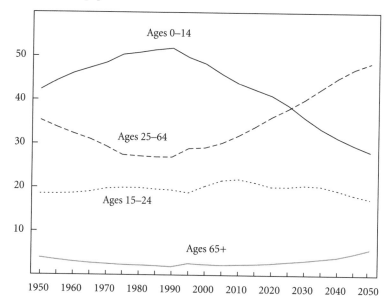

Source: UN Population Prospects, 2005 revisions using medium variant population projections.

These high fertility rates make the challenges facing youth all the more difficult. As long as fertility rates remain high, the population will continue to boom, spreading thin an already strained supply of resources. The high fertility rates also pose a direct challenge to youth as they begin to form their own families. Young parents who must care for the immediate needs of large families often lack the resources to invest in themselves. These parents might find it difficult or impossible to take low-paying jobs that would boost their human capital or to save financially for their futures. It may also reduce their ability to invest in their children. Young women who marry early and have high rates of fertility face limited opportunities in other areas of their lives, such as employment or education. The expectation of high fertility also hurts young women: employers are hesitant to hire them for fear they will soon leave their jobs to raise their large families.[12] Furthermore, high fertility, especially at young ages, poses health risks to young women and may hinder their ability to work.

Education

Yemen's constitution guarantees all citizens the right to an education, yet Yemen has some of the poorest education indicators in the world.[13] Enrollments are low, retention is poor, and illiteracy is widespread. These problems are pervasive throughout the country, but they disproportionately affect women, the poor, and rural residents. Ensuring young people's access to a high-quality education is a critical social investment. Poor educational attainment and low standards in education quality will produce a generation that is ill prepared to contribute economically, participate in society, and invest in the human capital of the next generation.

Yemen's Education System

After the 1990 unification of North and South Yemen, the newly merged Ministry of Education established a system that consists of nine years of basic education followed by three years of secondary education. Children are supposed to start basic education at age 6, but they are legally allowed to start anytime between the ages of 6 and 9 (10 in rural areas).[14] Most of the students enrolled in the Yemeni education system are in basic education. Only a small proportion of students pursue secondary education and an even smaller group pursues higher education.

After the completion of basic education, students who do continue their education can decide to enter general or technical secondary school. General secondary school lasts three years and is designed to prepare students for university. Technical secondary school lasts either two or three years, depending on the track the student chooses. Students who complete the three-year technical track or who have graduated from general secondary school are eligible to pursue a two-year technical higher education degree.

Technical and vocational education and training (TVET) includes both tracks of vocational secondary school as well as higher technical education. Less than 2 percent of Yemeni students are currently enrolled in TVET; however, this small group of students is extremely expensive for Yemen's government to subsidize.[15] The per-student cost of TVET is 5.6 times higher than the per-student cost of basic education.[16]

As in most education systems in the Middle East, entrance to university is determined by a student's score on an examination at the end of general secondary school. This test is based on rote memorization from textbooks. Little coordination exists between TVET institutions and universities. Students who attend vocational secondary school are not permitted to enter university, although general secondary school graduates may attend higher technical institutes.[17] Of the budget for higher education, nearly one-third is spent on providing scholarships for students to study abroad, perhaps indicative of the government's acknowledgement of the weaknesses of the domestic education system.[18]

The government of Yemen spends 19 percent of its total budget on education, which translates to 6 percent of GDP, a relatively large share for a low-income country. Although a large majority of funding—more than 80 percent—goes to general secondary education, the share of funding devoted to TVET and higher education is increasing.[19] Despite the relatively high level of funding, the Yemeni school system suffers from a lack of resources. Facilities are often overcrowded, especially in urban areas. Many rural students do not attend school because no schools are located within a reasonable distance.[20] Low levels of private school enrollment do little to alleviate the burden on the public school system.[21]

Educational Enrollment

While educational attainment among youth in Yemen is low, most youth attend school for at least a short time. A little more than one-fifth of youth report that they had never enrolled in school.[22] Never enrolling is almost exclusively a problem for girls: 35 percent of young women but only 5 percent of young men never enroll. Furthermore, the problem is much more pronounced in rural areas, where topography and dispersion of the population make it hard to reach all groups.[23] "Never-enrollment" rates for rural and urban women are 63 percent and 20 percent, respectively. There are also some region-specific variations in school enrollment. Enrollments are high for youth in Aden, Taiz, Ibb, Sana'a City, and the eastern parts of the country (Al Mahrah, Hadramaut, and Shabwah). Rates are low for women in the north and for rural youth in the west.

Many factors affect educational enrollment, including school proximity— many families do not send their children to school because there are no schools near them—cost, and the suitability of school facilities for girls.[24] Families with young girls are not necessarily opposed to the idea of their daughters receiving an education; rather their decisions are often based on logistical considerations, such as the absence of female teachers, coeducational classes, a lack of female-appropriate sanitary and recreational facilities, and the peril of solitary travel to the nearest school. These factors are particularly pronounced in rural areas, which have trouble recruiting female teachers and which lack the numbers of students necessary to justify gender-segregated classes or the construction of easily accessible schools. If some of these logistical circumstances change, more families might decide to enroll their girls in school.[25]

The government's attempts to increase enrollment of disadvantaged groups has witnessed limited progress. Female school enrollment increases by only 1 percent each year.[26] While enrollment has risen for children from wealthier backgrounds, enrollment of poor children fell between 1998 and 2005.[27]

Delayed Entry, Repetition, and Early Dropout

Young people in Yemen who do attend school often do so late, repeat grades, or drop out prematurely. Only 40 percent of youth start school at the recommended age of 6 years and more than 20 percent delay entry until age 8 or later.[28] Rural residents and girls are more likely to experience delayed entrance to school than are urban residents and boys. Delayed enrollment constrains educational attainment by cutting short the amount of time spent in school. High rates of grade repetition also constrain the educational attainment of Yemeni youth. These high rates reflect both the low quality of education and the lesser priority families often accord to education when more pressing needs arise.

One way to measure delayed entry and grade repetition is by analyzing overage rates for each grade level. For example, by age 8, 60 percent of Yemeni boys and more than half of Yemeni girls are overage for their grade level.[29] Overage rates increase for most groups as students get older, indicating that students either repeat grades or move in and out of education. Both phenomena illustrate that young Yemenis and their families view the opportunity cost of education as high and its benefit as relatively low.

Perhaps most detrimental to educational attainment, many young people who enroll in school drop out prematurely. Figures 9-2 and 9-3 show declining enrollment with age. The factors that cut short the educational trajectories of young people include gender and region.[30] Gender has a strong negative effect on length of education, particularly for girls in rural areas. Residing in an urban area has a strong positive effect on the educational attainment of young women, because urban areas are more likely to have female teachers and separate facilities for girls.[31] Furthermore, girls in urban areas are rarely required to travel long distances to reach their school buildings and may not be required to do as much domestic work, such as fetching water and firewood, as girls in rural areas. Figure 9-3 depicts the pronounced differences between urban and rural women in educational attainment through the basic and secondary levels.

Figure 9-2. *Share of Boys Enrolled in School, Yemen, 2005–06*

Share enrolled (percent)

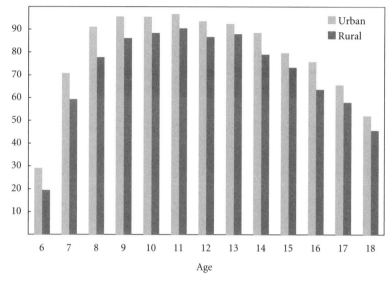

Source: Central Statistical Office, Republic of Yemen, *Household Budget Survey 2005/2006.*

Figure 9-3. *Share of Girls Enrolled in School, Yemen, 2005–06*

Share enrolled (percent)

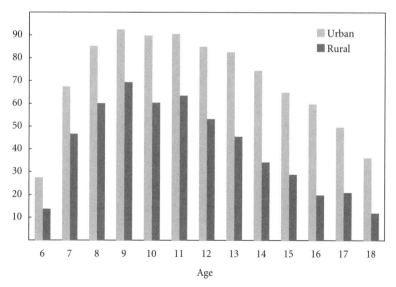

Source: Central Statistical Office, Republic of Yemen, *Household Budget Survey 2005/2006.*

The effect of parental education is dramatically gender specific. Mothers' educational attainment strongly affects their daughters' longevity in school but has little effect on the educational attainment of their sons. Conversely, fathers' education has a strong effect on boys but little effect on girls. Thus, policies that increase female education will have a positive intergenerational impact on girls, while policies that solely increase boys' enrollment will do little to foster future female enrollment.

Regional factors are important in determining the number of years of education, but these factors are particularly important for women. The north fares particularly poorly in terms of women's educational attainment, while women fare the best in Taiz, Ibb, and Sana'a.

Education Quality

Many students—especially women in rural areas—view education as irrelevant to their current and future work. Women in rural areas are expected to learn how to carry out domestic chores such as cleaning, cooking, caring for children, and fetching water and firewood. Thus, many families deem formal education for girls as a barrier that only delays the development of skills they will need in the future.[32]

In any case, the education system in Yemen fails even those who are ready and willing to learn. Overcrowding in schools is common, with urban areas having an average of 90 students per classroom.[33] Yemen's shortage of educational facilities has forced the Ministry of Education to admit 50 percent of its students into schools housed in unsuitable structures, including tents, caves, or the open air.[34] Further, as many as 60 percent of teachers of basic education are unqualified for their positions.[35] Teacher absenteeism rates are high, and teaching methods are limited to rote memorization from textbooks issued by the ministry rather than focusing on developing critical thinking or other job-related skills.[36] Because of these systemic deficiencies, the poor quality of education means that even youth with many years of schooling are gravely unprepared for the job market.

Employment and Livelihood

The three central aspects of employment and livelihoods in Yemen are participation in work and access to employment, formality and informality of the youth labor market, and wages and income. Migration, remittances, and the use of qat are also central to understanding both the opportunities and challenges that youth face.

Figure 9-4. *Share of Yemeni Youth Engaging in Market Work, 2005–06*

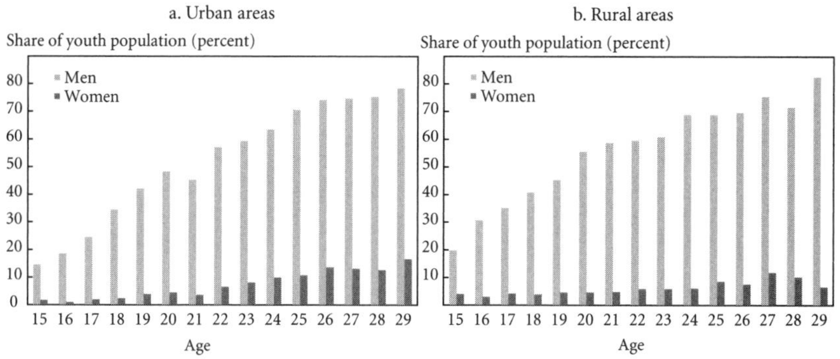

a. Urban areas

Share of youth population (percent)

b. Rural areas

Share of youth population (percent)

Source: Central Statistical Office, Republic of Yemen, *Household Budget Survey 2005/2006.*

Labor Force Participation

Two broad categories are used to analyze participation in the labor force by youth.[37] *Market work* includes agricultural and nonagricultural wage and nonwage work. *Nonmarket work* includes nonmarket subsistence and domestic work. Subsistence and domestic tasks have been included in the definition of work to capture the significant contribution of Yemeni women to livelihood activities.

Figure 9-4 shows the share of youth engaged in market work disaggregated by age, gender, and region. The low rates of market work for women are unsurprising in a country where women are much more likely to engage in domestic and subsistence work. However, young men are far from being universally engaged in market work.

Although the probability that women engage in market work is low, it increases significantly with age, with nearly 20 percent of urban women in their upper 20s reporting that they do market work. Market work among urban women is almost entirely nonagricultural, while rural women are engaged in primarily agricultural nonwage work. Market agricultural nonwage work consists of working on a family farm and contributing to the production of a marketable product such as grain, coffee, or qat. In many rural areas, and particularly among children and women, such work often includes taking care of livestock. Nonmarket subsistence work involves the production of products consumed directly by the household, such as milk or cheese, or the collection of firewood for cooking.

When the analysis is broadened to include all work activities, including unpaid domestic and subsistence work, young women of all ages in both urban and rural areas are more likely to be working than young men. This gap, which is particularly large among younger youth, reflects the important role that young women play in household-based subsistence and domestic activities.

While the majority of men who work are employed in market activities, a significant number of men are engaged in nonmarket work—especially younger men and those in rural areas. For example, over 35 percent of 15-year-old rural men report working the previous week using the broader definition of work (including market and nonmarket work), while 20 percent are engaged in market work only.

Several important factors affect young men's participation in work, including education, marriage, migration, age, and region.[38] First, young men who have some type of education are more likely to engage in market work than those who are illiterate. However, high school and university graduates are significantly less likely to be employed than graduates of either primary or lower secondary schools. While this finding likely indicates a lack of opportunities for these more educated individuals, it may also indicate that these youth have a higher reservation wage and are therefore more likely to remain unemployed as they search for the right job. The lower probability of employment for high school graduates may simply indicate that they are continuing their schooling.

Second, men who are married are much more likely to have market work than those who are not married. However, rather than indicating that marriage encourages men to find employment, this statistic reflects the importance of market work in making men eligible for marriage. Third, migration has a positive effect on the probability of market work for men, indicating that men likely move to a new area only if they know of an opportunity for employment. Fourth, the probability that men engage in market work increases with age, and the probability that they engage in nonmarket work decreases with age. This pattern suggests that young men are expected to contribute to subsistence and domestic chores within the household until they secure market work.

Last, there is strong regional impact on the probability that youth engage in market work, which demonstrates the high variance in employment rates across different regions of the country. Using multivariate analysis, region is shown to be the strongest predictor of market work among men.[39] For example, a large negative coefficient on the "Aden" variable indicates that men living in Aden are much less likely to be employed in market work compared with the control group, which is made up of the poor governorates of the north. Interestingly, the northern and western governorates, which represent the two poorest regions, have the lowest rates of male unemployment. The predominance of agriculture in these two regions compared with other regions suggests that this difference in the nature of the local economies may partially explain the low levels of unemployment in these two regions. However, because less than a third of total employment in the northern governorates and only 20 percent of employment in the western governorates are in the agricultural sector, this is unlikely to be the only explanation.

Education, marriage, migration, and region also have strong effects on female labor force participation. For women, education seems to be a measure of social class in addition to providing access to the labor market; highly educated women provide less subsistence and domestic work and more market work. Married women, unsurprisingly, are much more likely to be involved in domestic and subsistence work; they are typically the primary caregivers of children and hence often confined to the home. Market and nonmarket work are not typically substitutes for women, with women who work for pay also engaging in significant amounts of domestic work. However, the higher burden of domestic work for married women precludes significant levels of participation in market work.

Interestingly, similar to men, women who are migrants are significantly more likely to engage in market work. This result is unusual because it suggests that many women may be migrating in search of employment and not only for marriage, which is typically discussed as the central reason for female migration.

The variation in female participation in the labor force between urban and rural areas and across the regions of Yemen is indicative of the differing structure of the economies in different parts of the country. Young women in urban areas are less likely to engage in either market or nonmarket work. This difference likely reflects the lower subsistence and domestic work burdens in urban areas and the fairly limited opportunities for women to engage in market work outside of agriculture. Further, the higher rate of female participation in market work in the northern governorates may reflect the important role that women play in agricultural production in this region. However, only 8 percent of the women in the sample report engaging in market work, and there may be regional variation in the types of work that women consider to be market versus nonmarket.

While underemployment is a concern for youth in some developing countries, it does not seem to be prevalent among young Yemeni men. In both urban and rural areas, the average number of hours worked by men of all ages exceeds forty hours per week and approaches fifty for some age groups. Interestingly, women who do participate in market work average over thirty hours of work a week in urban areas and twenty in rural areas. This indicates that many of these women are working in full-time positions, rather than working part time to supplement family income.

Many Yemeni youth are active in the labor force while they are still in school, activity that has important implications for the development of human capital. Nearly 20 percent of male students aged 15 to 29 are actively working under the expansive definition of work, providing on average thirty-five hours of labor a week. A much higher two-thirds of female students aged 15 to 29 are working an average of twenty-six hours a week. To the extent that female labor likely represents domestic work and chores, the long hours worked by these women may have deleterious effects on the quality of their education. This too may be the case for young men, although there is a greater likelihood that they are able to gain a wider range of skills in a variety of work experiences outside the home.

Formality and Informality of Employment

There are few employment opportunities for youth in the preferred formal sector of the economy. Instead, youth are largely confined to informal employment, which provides limited job security and few opportunities for career advancement.

There are two different types of formality in paid employment. The first, and more restrictive, definition of formality includes only those positions that provide health insurance, a pension, or paid leave and is referred to as "formal wage and salary employment." Less than 10 percent of Yemeni youth have positions satisfying this definition. A second definition of formality provides a better description of the labor market and includes anyone working for a wage or salary.

Approximately two-thirds of men engaged in market work earn a wage or salary, suggesting some degree of formality in their employment. However, only 26 percent of employed men in urban areas and 17 percent in rural areas have formal employment and other benefits. The vast majority of these formal positions with wages and benefits are with the government or public sector, suggesting that the private sector has been unsuccessful in creating preferable formal positions that would attract highly skilled youth.

Although the proportion of young women engaged in market work is quite small, at under 8 percent, there is a striking difference between urban and rural areas. In rural areas, the vast majority of market work for women is nonwage work in agriculture. In urban areas, most female market work is wage and salary work, and about half of that is formal and includes benefits. However, nearly 89 percent of this type of formal employment for urban women is in government, once again showing the limited reach of private sector opportunities.

Domestic and International Migration

The share of migrants among youth is over 35 percent in urban areas for both men and women, and in Sana'a this share is nearly 60 percent. This high incidence of migration in urban areas reflects recent urbanization in Yemen as both youth and families move to urban areas in search of work. As expected, the incidence of migration into rural areas is low. But, interestingly, more than twice as many rural young women are migrants, likely reflecting the fact that women move to join their husbands' families when they marry.

Most migration of youth is from rural areas, although there is a significant amount of migration among urban areas and a bit of migration from urban to rural areas. Migration to Sana'a from other urban areas reflects the perceived benefits of the capital city in terms of access to employment.

Migrants earn significantly lower wages relative to the native-born population. However, they compensate for lower wages by working longer hours so that their net total earnings are not significantly different from the native-born population. This suggests that youth who migrate to urban areas have social networks that help provide access to employment markets.[40]

International migration is also common among Yemenis. Remittances from Yemenis who have migrated internationally have been an important source of wealth for the people of Yemen as well as for the government since at least the 1970s. The flow of remittances fell dramatically in the early 1990s, when Yemen's special labor relationship with Saudi Arabia changed. However, these flows have recovered somewhat, with nearly 600,000 Yemeni emigrants working throughout the Gulf region, the United States, and Europe. In 2007 total official remittances to Yemen amounted to 6.7 percent of GDP, making Yemen the fifth largest recipient of remittances relative to GDP in the broader Middle East region.[41]

Nearly half of households in rural areas and nearly two-fifths of households in urban areas receive remittances. Interestingly, youth-headed households are somewhat more likely to receive remittances, possibly because youth with parents working abroad can more easily afford to set up their own independent households.[42] Among youth-headed households that receive remittances, remittance flows surpass other sources of household wage income in Aden and the rural areas of the southern governorates of Abyan, Al Bayda, Ad Dali', Ibb, Lahij, and Taiz. In addition, remittances account for well over half of household wage income in Al Bayda, Ibb, Lahij, Sana'a, and Taiz.

Qat Production and Consumption

The production and consumption of the stimulant qat play an important role in the lives of Yemeni youth. Since the 1970s the cultivation of qat has risen dramatically and has provided an important source of rural revenue in the face of falling prices for grain.[43] Official consumption rates of qat are around 60 percent for men and under 30 percent for women.[44] However, several sources suggest that actual consumption rates are significantly higher.[45] One study estimates that 50–60 percent of women and 80–85 percent of men chew at least once a week, and the UNDP reports that 70–90 percent of men and 30–50 percent of women consume qat, although this latter number likely includes those who only chew on special occasions.[46]

Qat production may have a positive impact on rural incomes, but its consumption has a negative impact on Yemeni youth in two central ways. First, the consumption of qat among youth reduces productivity because significant amounts of time are spent both purchasing and consuming qat. Indeed, one estimate suggests that qat consumption reduces productivity by as much as 25 percent.[47] Many people consume qat while working in agriculture, retail, transportation services, or construction, which may negatively affect productivity at work.

Second, qat consumption places a sizable financial burden on youth and young families. Though there is little evidence that qat expenditures substitute for food expenditures, expenditures on qat are typically quite large and are likely substituting for other, more productive, uses for this money.[48]

Qat expenditures make up nearly 20 percent of total expenditures among households that consume it. Interestingly, qat expenditures are higher in urban areas, representing over 15 percent of total urban expenditures, compared with 10 percent in rural areas (although this difference may be driven by consumption of home-produced qat in rural areas). Qat expenditures, even in relative terms, increase with education. This increase occurs in part because incomes also increase with education; one study found a rise in the share of qat users for increasing income deciles.[49]

Family Formation

Marriage and family formation have historically been the indicators of the transition into adulthood in Yemen. However, the changing economic and social environment has introduced complications in the ability of youth to marry and have families. In particular, delays in the timing of marriage are frustrating men, and a lack of support for childbearing and rearing is creating new challenges for young families.

The rising age of marriage for young men in both rural and urban areas in recent years shows that young men are delaying this important transition. While postponement of marriage is a cause of unhappiness for young men, young women are also experiencing a similar delay, which is likely to have a positive development impact. Indeed, these women, who play a strong role in the education of the next generation, typically cut short their educational and personal development to get married. Thus delayed marriage, especially if it results in young women obtaining more education, is likely to be a boon for young women and the next generation, even if it causes angst among young men.

Most young wives in Yemen bear children frequently. Thus, reproductive health, prenatal care, and child outcomes for young mothers are central to the lives of female youth. Although the government of Yemen has made strides to improve access to women's health facilities, young women often struggle to find the support they need to create healthy families.

Yemeni Women: Early Marriage and Its Determinants

Most Yemeni women continue to marry at a young age, significantly earlier than men. According to the 2003 Arab Family Health Survey, the median age of marriage for women born in 1978 was 19 in urban areas and 18 in rural areas.[50] A 1992 family law prohibits the marriage of girls under age 15, but the law has never been effectively enforced and early marriage is still common.[51] In fact, marriages for children as young as 8 are still reported.

Rural women are particularly prone to early marriage, as seen in figure 9-5.[52] The gap between rural and urban women mostly disappears after accounting for differences in the levels of female education between rural and urban areas. This is not surprising as female educational attainment and age of marriage are linked in several ways. First, women who for other unobserved reasons are likely to marry later may simply remain in school longer to obtain higher social status. Second, most young women discontinue their education after marriage, either by choice or because their

Figure 9-5. *Median Age of First Marriage for Yemeni Males and Females by Birth Cohort*

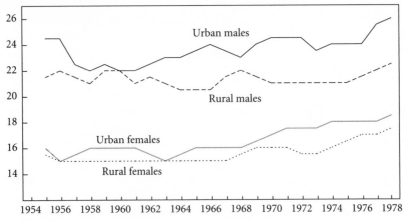

Source: Arab Family Health Survey, 2003.
Note: By using life table techniques, the figures shown above correct for the fact that a certain proportion of each cohort was not married at the time of the survey.

families or husbands do not allow them to continue. Finally, women who do complete either secondary school or university usually get married shortly after they leave school.

In addition to disrupting their education, early marriage has important implications for the health and livelihood of these young women. Early childbirth, especially during the teenage years, dramatically increases the chances of maternal and infant mortality.[53] According to the 2003 Arab Family Health Survey, the neonatal mortality rate for children born to teenage mothers in Yemen was 60 per 1,000 live births, almost twice as high as the rate for children born to mothers aged 30 to 34. The World Bank claims that a third of maternal deaths in the country can be directly linked to early marriage.[54] Furthermore, women who marry young maximize their childbearing years and thus increase their total fertility.

When coupled with men's age at marriage, early marriage for women becomes even more problematic because it often implies a large age gap between husbands and wives. More than 96 percent of Yemeni women marry men who are older than they are, and 50 percent of women marry men who are five or more years older. This age gap may create power imbalances within the household. Early marriage is also troubling because many Yemeni women have no say in who they marry. Of female youth married between 1998 and 2003, only about 75 percent agreed to the marriage. While it was uncommon for women to actively disagree with the marriage (less than 1 percent), 11 percent of the women reported that they were not asked for their opinion and 14 percent said they voluntarily kept silent.

Yemeni Men: Delayed Marriage and "Waithood"

Younger cohorts of Yemeni males, especially urban males, show signs of delaying marriage. The median age of marriage has gradually increased for both sexes in both urban and rural areas, with the age of marriage for urban males showing a significant jump among recent cohorts, as shown in figure 9-5. The median age of marriage for urban males born in 1960 was 22. This median has risen to 24 for cohorts born in 1966 through 1975 and to 26 for cohorts born in 1977 and 1978. In contrast, the median age of first marriage for rural males rose only slightly during this time period, from 21 to 23. While the increase in the marriage age for urban males in Yemen is not as large as in other parts of the Middle East, the increase is nonetheless significant.[55]

Education has a significant effect in determining marriage ages for these men. In contrast to females who delay marriage if they have more education, men tend to marry at a younger age the more they are educated. Education may signal to the bride's family the potential suitor's future wages. Furthermore, because education is tied to family background, men with more education are more likely to come from better-off families. This pattern is in sharp contrast with the situation in Egypt, for instance, where education significantly raises the age at marriage for men.

The strong difference in marriage ages for urban and rural males reflects a phenomenon common in other Middle Eastern countries in which men delay marriage while they attempt to establish themselves in the workplace.[56] Rural men in agricultural areas often marry young, following the norms of traditional agrarian societies. Their families assist them in making the transition to adulthood, since they too have followed the same patterns.

Men in urban parts of the country, however, find that their expectations for the future clash with the expectations set forth by a traditional culture. These men try to establish themselves by obtaining wage work, but they often have trouble finding steady work. Without certainty about their future, these men delay marriage as they wait for things to come together in their working lives, a period of anxious waiting that has been dubbed *waithood*.[57] As urban migration continues and the job market tightens, waithood will become an increasingly prevalent phenomenon in Yemen, with urban men struggling to establish themselves in a world different from that of their parents.

Regional effects play a strong role in determining males' marriage age. These effects are stronger than the effects for women, but they follow the same regional patterns. Men in the wealthier regions of the country, including Aden, Ibb, Taiz, and the eastern sections of the country, marry later than men in other regions.

Living Arrangements and Reproductive Health Services

In Yemen, marriage does not necessarily signal the start of an independent life, because many newlyweds do not form nuclear households but remain with their parents or move in with their in-laws. Over 60 percent of married young men live with their parents, and only 36 percent of married young men are heads of households. Somewhat surprisingly, there is little difference in living arrangements for rural and urban youth. These rates highlight the importance of the family in Yemeni society and hint at the scarcity of affordable housing and opportunities for employment outside of family networks.

Most young couples move in with the groom's family after marriage. The younger the groom is, the more likely it is that the couple will move in with his family. Roughly 60 percent of men who marry before age 30 live with their parents. Because young women tend to marry older men, only 40 percent of young women who marry before their 30th birthday live with their in-laws.

As noted earlier, young families in Yemen begin childbearing early and space their children closely, leading to the high national fertility rate. Women who have their first child at a young age often do not receive prenatal care. Only 57 percent of women who had their first child as a teenager received prenatal care, compared with 65 percent of women who were between 20 and 29 at their first birth and 80 percent of women who were over 30 at their first birth.[58] A large reason for the low rates of prenatal care is the lack of access to health facilities. Living in a rural area dramatically reduces a woman's chance of receiving prenatal care, regardless of age. Over 20 percent of young mothers in rural areas reported that they did not receive prenatal care because service was too far away or unavailable altogether. Only 5 percent of young mothers in urban areas reported the same problems. Another 13 percent of young mothers in both urban and rural areas reported that prenatal care was too expensive. In addition, a lack of qualified female physicians, especially in rural areas, limits access.[59]

The government of Yemen has publicly acknowledged women's health challenges and has made many attempts to reduce fertility in Yemen.[60] Family planning is a sensitive political issue, however, and many attempts at reforming population policies have been met with debate and opposition.

Policy Implications and Recommendations

The Yemeni government recognizes the enormous challenges of achieving greater youth inclusion in the face of huge increases in the youth population. It has adopted an integrated children and youth strategy to attempt to tackle the challenge. The full implementation of these strategies, however, is constrained by a severe shortage of resources and limited institutional and administrative capacity.

In February 2006 the government launched a National Children and Youth Strategy in collaboration with UNICEF and the World Bank, reflecting a commitment on the part of the Yemeni government to improve circumstances for youth. Yemen is the only nation in the Arab region to have set forth this type of strategy. The World Bank calls the strategy a "huge positive step" toward a better understanding of youth issues and the creation of plans to assist youth.[61]

The goals of the National Youth Strategy are to assess the status of children and youth in Yemen and to analyze the specific risks that affect each age group, especially in relation to achieving the Millennium Development Goals. The strategy also strives to identify policies that affect youth and to assess their effects, with a large focus of the strategy being to develop intersectoral collaboration.[62]

The National Youth Strategy has yet to have far-reaching effects in Yemen. The overall consensus among Yemenis is that the strategy is on the right track but will never be fully implemented because of capacity issues.

Basic and Secondary Education Development Strategies

Through the 2002 Education Development Strategy and the 2007 Secondary Education Development Strategy, the government of Yemen has declared its dedication to the improvement of the country's education system and in meeting the Millennium Development Goals for education.

The government has gone some way in implementing these strategies. In September 2006 Yemen abolished school fees for girls in grades one through six and for boys in grades one through three.[63] In theory, this should eventually increase the educational attainment of youth by reducing the never-enrollment problem. However, a School Fee Abolition Impact Survey conducted in 2007 determined that the abolition of fees had little effect on school enrollment for the poorest households.[64]

Also in 2007 the Ministry of Education adopted a conditional cash transfer program, with the goal of encouraging the retention of girls in grades four through nine. Any girl who is enrolled or who reenrolls in one of those grades is eligible to receive a transfer, conditional on maintaining at least an 80 percent attendance rate and a passing grade. The program was piloted in two governorates during the 2007–08 academic year.[65] While the impact of the cash transfers is yet to be assessed, the program is unlikely by itself to address the structural barriers to girls' education.

The lack of female teachers has been identified as one of the primary obstacles to school attendance by girls in rural areas, and the government has been trying to address this issue in multiple ways, including giving female teachers who are willing to locate in rural areas additional incentives such as housing benefits and salary premiums. These attempts have generally proven unsustainable because few female teachers remain in the remote villages for very long. Now, the government is attempting to qualify as teachers female secondary school graduates from the villages themselves, to the extent that such graduates are available.

Yemen's participation in the Trends in International Mathematics and Science Study (TIMSS) test in 2007 shows the Ministry of Education's commitment to monitoring and improving quality.[66] This participation increases the transparency of the nation's education system and perhaps puts pressure on the ministry to increase quality. Unfortunately, Yemen was one of the lowest-performing countries, with fourth graders scoring 224 in mathematics against a benchmark of 500. Interestingly, Yemen was one of eight countries where girls tested better than boys at the grade four level.[67]

The Technical Education and Vocational Training Strategy

The primary focus of Yemen's Technical Education and Vocational Training (TEVT) strategy is to shift from a supply-driven approach to a demand-driven orientation. The strategy's goals include diversification of offerings, establishing better links to labor market needs, devolution of managerial responsibility to the training-center level to allow for better responsiveness, and diversification of funding sources.

The TEVT system is currently very small, absorbing only 3.2 percent of secondary school enrollment. There are also concerns that the system is still essentially closed to some groups, namely, young women.

In the strategy, the TEVT system is slated for expansion, with the goal of reaching 15 percent of students in secondary and higher education. This expansion should be viewed with caution, because the Ministry of Technical Education and Vocational Training has started to establish TEVT facilities across the country with little regard to demand or expense. The ministry has promised to reform the system, but little progress has been made toward these reforms, although construction of new facilities continues at full speed.[68] Ensuring that the system is demand-driven and responsive to the needs of the market is likely to be a huge challenge given the existing incentives and organizational structure of training providers. [69]

Policy Issues Related to Employment and Livelihoods

Three types of policies are essential in addressing many of the difficulties youth face in their transitions to employment and successful livelihoods.

First, to expand the size of the private sector and create jobs, Yemen needs to continue to improve its ability to attract foreign investment. Some progress has been made in recent years, but the benefits will only be realized in the next five to ten years. As part of a new economic development program in 2006, Yemen received $5 billion in development aid, with over half coming from the countries of the Gulf Cooperation Council.[70] This program has improved investment laws and conditions for foreign investors in an effort to increase investment from countries in the Gulf and throughout the world.[71]

A major reason for low levels of foreign investment in Yemen in recent times is the uncertain security situation. The importance of security in attracting foreign investment is highlighted by the decline in foreign investment, particularly in the south, after the bombing of the USS *Cole* in 2000 and the *Limburg* in 2002. The frequent kidnappings of foreigners in the 1990s had a similarly negative impact on investment in the tourism sector in particular. Despite recent efforts to improve security, such as the banning of guns in cities, several fatal attacks on tourists have occurred recently in high-profile tourist areas such as Ma'rib and Shibam. Further, the attack on the U.S. embassy in 2008 in the usually secure capital of Sana'a is a strong reminder of the security difficulties that foreign companies may face if they choose to invest in Yemen.[72]

Second, policies designed to encourage private sector firms to formalize would be beneficial for both firms and youth. Because of their inability to offer candidates formal competitive benefits, many private sector firms currently find it difficult to attract the highest caliber of young people, which is essential for their success in a competitive international market. In fact, the government is nearly the sole provider of preferred formal positions. Thus, firms and youth alike would benefit from efforts to reduce the cost of formality for private sector firms through tax incentives, as has been done elsewhere in the region, or through partial subsidization of health care or pensions.

Third, policies that help reduce qat consumption would likely have a positive impact on the lives of many youth. Although President Ali Abdallah Saleh has made a significant effort to reduce qat by banning its use during official meetings and in government buildings and by publicly reducing his own qat consumption to only one day a week (Friday), youth consumption of qat still remains quite high and socially acceptable. While this role-model approach and the efforts of other organizations, such as the Combating Qat Damage Association, to publicize the negative health impacts of qat are one approach to reducing its consumption, they are unlikely to be sufficient. Indeed, combining these efforts with more active policies to at least reduce the frequency of consumption as well as to discourage qat consumption among the very young—many children begin chewing as young as age 4 or 5—would be advisable.

Conclusion and the Way Forward

Yemen faces enormous challenges in human development that especially affect its youth population. The government has signaled its awareness of these issues by being the only Arab country to have issued a National Youth Strategy. However, because of major resource and financial constraints and even more limited institutional capacity, this strategy has not been fully implemented. The following three broad recommendations can guide policymakers in dealing with issues affecting youth inclusion in Yemen. In addition, the role of development assistance is critical in helping Yemen overcome its twin human development and natural resource deficits.

First, use a holistic approach in assisting youth. The challenges facing youth are multidimensional and interdependent. Instead of focusing on single dimensions of youth exclusion, the government of Yemen and international donors should focus on strategies that assist youth in multiple ways and across multiple markets.

Second, improve access for women and girls. Women are often implicitly and explicitly discouraged from fully participating in the public sphere in Yemen. Education, health care, and the labor market need to become more conducive to female participation. Schools need to be made safer, more accessible, and, in general, more friendly to girls. More female doctors are needed to provide women with adequate health care, and firms must increase the hiring rate of women and strive to create more female-friendly workplaces. Policymakers should focus not just on the number of women participating but also on the percentage of women who are leaders and managers in these fields.

Third, focus on microinstitutional factors. The government of Yemen has focused on large-scale projects such as building schools or health facilities. While there is no doubt that Yemen needs more of these facilities, indiscriminate building of facilities will fail to assist many of Yemen's socially excluded youth unless the rules of the game change. On one hand, parents and youth must get the correct signals about what it takes to succeed in Yemeni society and must be empowered to act on these signals. On the other hand, service providers must get the right incentives to respond to the needs and wishes of their clients. This need implies a greater degree of competition among service providers and a reward system that depends on performance.

Finally, given the magnitude of the challenges facing Yemen and its twin deficits in human and natural resources, the country will need to receive considerable assistance from the outside world to ensure a brighter future for its youth. This assistance should come both from Western donors as well as from Yemen's oil-rich neighbors in the Arabian Peninsula. A large injection of development assistance on the part of Yemen's richer neighbors would be an excellent investment in regional stability. The neighboring Gulf countries should also consider adopting more open migration policies with respect to Yemeni labor to relieve some of the intense pressure on Yemen's limited arable land resources and its overcrowded urban labor markets.

Notes

1. United Nations Development Program (UNDP), *Human Development Report 2007/08, Fighting Climate Change: Human Solidarity in a Divided World* (New York: Palgrave Macmillan, 2007).

2. Nora Ann Colton, "Poverty Alleviation and Development in Yemen," paper presented at the Poverty and Governance Conference (Sana'a, August 1–3, 2001).

3. Mouna H. Hashem, "Poverty Reduction in Yemen: A Social Exclusion Perspective," in *Yemen: Into the Twenty-First Century: Continuity and Change,* edited by Kamil A. Mahdi, Anna Wurth, and Helen Lackner (Reading, U.K.: Ithaca Press, 2007).

4. Christopher Ward, "Practical Responses to Extreme Groundwater Overdraft in Yemen," in *Yemen: Into the Twenty-First Century,* edited by Mahdi, Wurth, and Lackner.

5. Ibid.

6. World Bank, "Yemen: An Integrated Approach to Social Sectors towards a Social Protection Strategy; Phase 1 Report" (Washington: Middle East and North Africa Region Human Development Department, 2007).

7. Ibid.

8. M. Mosleh Al-Sanabani, "Land Tenure and Resource Management in the Yemeni Highlands," in *Yemen: Into the Twenty-First Century,* edited by Mahdi, Wurth, and Lackner.

9. United Nations Population Fund (UNFPA), "The Population and Development and Future Challenges," paper presented at the Yemen National Population Conference (Sana'a, December 10–11, 2007).

10. Ibid.

11. Ministry of Health and Population, Republic of Yemen, and the Pan Arab Project for Family Health, *Yemen Family Health Survey* (2003) (www.papfam.org/pap-fam/yemen.htm). The Yemen Family Health Survey was conducted as part of the Arab Family Health Survey. The total fertility rate is defined as the average number of children a woman would have over the course of her childbearing years (age 15–49) if she followed the current age-specific fertility rates. See also United Nations Statistics Division, *Population Statistics 2005,* http://unstats.un.org/unsd/default.htm.

12. World Bank, "Yemen: An Integrated Approach to Social Sectors towards a Social Protection Strategy."

13. Mutahar A. Al-Abbasi, "The Education Sector in Yemen: Challenges and Policy Options," in *Yemen: Into the Twenty-First Century,* edited by Mahdi, Wurth, and Lackner.

14. Ministry of Education, Yemen National Commission of Education and Culture and Sciences, Republic of Yemen, "Education in Republic of Yemen: The National Report," paper presented at the international conference on education (Geneva, September 8–11, 2004), www.ibe.unesco.org/International/ICE47/English/Natreps/reports/yemen_eng.pdf.

15. Central Statistical Office, Republic of Yemen, *Household Budget Survey 2005/2006* (Sana'a).

16. Takako Yuki, "Distribution of Public Education Spending for the Poor: The Case of Yemen," *Asia Pacific Education Review* 4, no. 2 (2003): 129–39.

17. Ministry of Education, "Education in Republic of Yemen: The National Report."

18. World Bank, "Yemen: An Integrated Approach to Social Sectors towards a Social Protection Strategy."

19. Ibid.

20. Raufa Hassan Al-Sharki and others, *The Education Situation of the Girl Child in Yemen: Promoting Girls' Education in Order to Achieve Equal Opportunities* (Sana'a: Ministry of Education, Republic of Yemen, UNICEF, and ADRA, 2005).

21. Yuki, "Distribution of Public Education Spending for the Poor: The Case of Yemen."

22. Central Statistical Office, *Household Budget Survey 2005/2006.*

23. Social Fund for Development, *Annual Report* (Sana'a: 2001).

24. Central Statistical Office, Republic of Yemen, *Yemen Poverty Monitoring Survey 1999* (Sana'a).

25. Al-Sharki and others, *The Education Situation of the Girl Child in Yemen.*

26. Social Fund for Development, *Annual Report.*

27. World Bank, "Yemen: An Integrated Approach to Social Sectors towards a Social Protection Strategy."

28. Central Statistical Office, *Household Budget Survey 2005/2006.*

29. For the approach to calculating overage rates, see Harry Anthony Patrinos and George Psacharopoulos, "Socioeconomic and Ethnic Determinants of Age-Grade Distortions in Bolivian and Guatemalan Primary Schools," *International Journal of Educational Development* 16, no. 1 (1996): 3–14. See also Ragui Assaad and others, "Youth Exclusion in Yemen," Middle East Youth Initiative Working Paper (Wolfensohn Center for Development at the Brookings Institution and the Dubai School of Government, forthcoming 2009).

30. For more details, see Assaad and others, "Youth Exclusion in Yemen."

31. Al-Sharki and others, *The Education Situation of the Girl Child in Yemen.*

32. Ibid.

33. Social Fund for Development, *Annual Report.*

34. Ibid.

35. World Bank, "Yemen: An Integrated Approach to Social Sectors towards a Social Protection Strategy."

36. Ibid.

37. For more details, see Assaad and others, "Youth Exclusion in Yemen."

38. Ibid.

39. Ibid.

40. Ibid.

41. Dilip Ratha and Zhimei Xu, *Migration and Remittances Factbook 2008* (Washington: World Bank, 2008).

42. Youth-headed households are those where the head of the household is between the ages of 15 and 29.

43. Nora Ann Colton, "Political and Economic Realities of Labour Migration in Yemen," in *Yemen: Into the Twenty-First Century: Continuity and Change,* edited by Kamil A. Mahdi, Anna Wurth, and Helen Lackner (Reading, U.K.: Ithaca Press, 2007).

44. Estimated by comparing the self-reported qat usage rates among youth from the 2003 Yemen Family Health Survey and 2005–06 Household Budget Survey.

45. Milanovic, who uses the 1998 consumption survey for his analysis, reports 70 percent of households with at least one user, which is comparable to the 2003 data. See Branko Milanovic, "Qat Expenditures in Yemen and Djibouti: An Empirical Analysis," *MPRA Paper* 1425 (University Library of Munich, 2007) (http://mpra.ub.uni-muenchen.de/1425/1/MPRA_paper_1425.pdf).

46. John G. Kennedy, *The Flower of Paradise: The Institutionalized Use of the Drug Qat in North Yemen* (London: Springer Science & Business, 1987). See also UNDP,

Country Evaluation: Yemen; Assessment of Development Results (New York: UNDP Evaluation Office, 2005).

47. Government of Yemen, World Bank, and UNDP, *Yemen Poverty Assessment, Volume I: Main Report* (Sana'a: 2007).

48. Milanovic, "Qat Expenditures In Yemen and Djibouti: An Empirical Analysis."

49. Ibid.

50. This cohort is the focus because 1978 is the latest cohort for which reliable data are available.

51. Ilse Worm, "Women's Health and Politics in Yemen," in *Yemen: Into the Twenty-First Century,* edited by Mahdi, Wurth, and Lackner.

52. For this analysis, we used the 2003 Arab Family Health Survey to conduct a survival time analysis of the age at first marriage for cohorts of Yemenis born between 1954 and 1978. We then estimated a hazard model to determine the factors that correlate with early marriage. This model confirms our descriptive analysis, which showed rural females marrying earlier than urban females. For more details, see Assaad and others, "Youth Exclusion in Yemen."

53. Hoda Rashad, Magued Osman, and Farzaneh Roudi-Fahimi, "Marriage in the Arab World" policy brief (Washington: Population Reference Bureau, 2005).

54. World Bank, "Yemen: An Integrated Approach to Social Sectors towards a Social Protection Strategy."

55. Ragui Assaad and Mohamed Ramadan, "Did Housing Policy Reforms Curb the Delay in Marriage among Young Men in Egypt?" Middle East Youth Initiative Policy Outlook 1 (Wolfensohn Center for Development at the Brookings Institution and the Dubai School of Government, 2008); Djavad Salehi-Isfahani and Daniel Egel, "Youth Exclusion in Iran: The State of Education, Employment and Family Formation," Middle East Youth Initiative Working Paper 3 (Wolfensohn Center for Development at the Brookings Institution and the Dubai School of Government, 2007).

56. Djavad Salehi-Isfahani and Navtej Dhillon, "Stalled Youth Transitions in the Middle East: A Framework for Policy Reform," Middle East Youth Initiative Working Paper 8 (Wolfensohn Center for Development at the Brookings Institution and the Dubai School of Government, 2008).

57. Ibid. See also Navtej Dhillon and Tarik Yousef, "Inclusion: Meeting the 100 Million Youth Challenge," Middle East Youth Initiative Report (Wolfensohn Center for Development at the Brookings Institution and the Dubai School of Government, 2007); and Diane Singerman, "The Economic Imperatives of Marriage: Emerging Practices and Identities Among Youth in the Middle East," Middle East Youth Initiative Working Paper 6 (Wolfensohn Center for Development at the Brookings Institution and the Dubai School of Government, 2007).

58. Ministry of Health and Population and the Pan Arab Project for Family Health, *Yemen Family Health Survey* (Sana'a: 2003), www.papfam.org/papfam/yemen.htm.

59. Worm, "Women's Health and Politics in Yemen."

60. Ibid.

61. World Bank, "Yemen: An Integrated Approach to Social Sectors towards a Social Protection Strategy."

62. Republic of Yemen, *The National Children and Youth Strategy of the Republic of Yemen 2006–2015.* Executive Summary.

63. World Bank, "Yemen: An Integrated Approach to Social Sectors towards a Social Protection Strategy."

64. Ibid.

65. Ibid.

66. Ibid.

67. Ina V.S. Mullis and others, *TIMSS 2007 International Mathematics Report* (Boston College, Lynch School of Education, TIMSS & PIRLS International Study Center, 2008); Michael O. Martin and others, *TIMSS 2007 International Science Report.* (Boston College, Lynch School of Education, TIMSS & PIRLS International Study Center, 2008).

68. World Bank, "Yemen: An Integrated Approach to Social Sectors towards a Social Protection Strategy."

69. TVET in other countries, such as Egypt, is commonly known to be of low quality, and graduates have poor workplace opportunities.

70. UNDP, "MDG Profile: Yemen," MDG Monitor (www.mdgmonitor.org/factsheets_00.cfm?c=YEM&cd=887).

71. Meir Javedanfar, "Yemen's Economy: The Region's Untapped Potential," Middle East Economic and Political Analysis Company, www.meepas.com/Yemeneconomicopportunities.htm.

72. Yemen Polling Center, "Foreigners' Safety Yemeni Priority," http://yemenpolling.org/english/index.php?action=showDetails&id=46.

NAVTEJ DHILLON *and* DJAVAD SALEHI-ISFAHANI

10

Looking Ahead:
Making Markets and Institutions
Work for Young People

Countries in the Middle East are experiencing a demographic transition, characterized by an increasing share of youth in the total population. While this change in the age structure has enhanced economic growth in other parts of the world, in Middle Eastern countries it has led to high unemployment and social exclusion. This is one of the most critical economic development challenges facing the Middle East in the twenty-first century. By addressing the disadvantages of young people today, Middle Eastern countries can lay the foundation for greater long-term equity across income and gender.

The eight Middle Eastern economies presented in this book are diverse in terms of their dependence on oil rents, integration into the world economy, and political systems. However, they share common features: flawed education systems and a prolonged unemployment crisis. The recent upturn in growth in countries such as Iran, Jordan, and Morocco has failed to significantly improve the welfare of young people.

This chapter focuses on how countries are responding to the challenges faced by their young citizens and the major gaps in their current approaches. We argue that more investments in schools, training programs, and subsidies targeting young people, while well-intentioned, do not address the underlying causes of social exclusion. For a majority of Middle Eastern countries, we interpret the difficulties faced by young people as a consequence of failures in key market and nonmarket institutions. Economic and social policy should be designed to improve the institutional environment and create incentives that empower current and future generations. We outline ten institutional features that are most responsible for the challenges facing young people today. Reforms that address these institutional features will go far toward rectifying the root causes of youth exclusion and, by association, toward improving the transitions of young people.

Demographic Pressures: An Impetus for Policy Reform

When it comes to assessing the current state of reforms in the Middle East, there is lively debate on whether countries have made sufficient progress.[1] The limited reach of economic reforms in the Middle East has been attributed variously to the region's geography and natural resource endowments, its political structures, and even regionally shared cultural elements. However, as the eight country studies in this volume demonstrate, demographic pressures are emerging as an important force for reform that is increasingly difficult for most governments to ignore. As the proportion of young people in the population increases, so too does the scale of their exclusion and frustration, causing the political balance to shift toward change.

Today, the urgency of expanding economic opportunities for young people is widely recognized. During the period of economic revival from 2002 to 2008, Middle Eastern countries invested heavily to tackle the problems faced by young people. Responses have been remarkably similar across different economies. Investments in training, subsidies to employers, and promises of job creation for the young are now part of the daily political discourse in Middle Eastern countries.

In addition, many countries in the region have exhibited strong macroeconomic performance and have improved their investment climates during the past decade. These types of reforms have had an indirect but influential impact on shaping youth inclusion by enhancing the overall economic environment and fostering job creation. These policies include incentives for investment in labor-intensive projects, trade liberalization, tariff reductions, the adoption of international trade agreements, and improved investment laws and fiscal and monetary policies. Implementation of these policies has been uneven across the Middle East, but there is some evidence that growth in private sector employment in countries like Egypt and Jordan can be attributed to some of these macroeconomic policies.[2]

In the education sector, policies have focused on improvements through upgrading school infrastructure, constructing new schools, producing pedagogical material, recruiting and training teachers, and subsidizing education. Jordan has continued to modernize its education system through the introduction of information and communication technology (ICT) in the classroom and by revamping curriculum and pedagogy methods. Syria has revised school curricula to support the country's transition toward an economic model that relies more on private sector development. By and large, however, educational reforms have failed to effect real improvements in the quality of education.

To address unemployment challenges, countries have pursued active labor market programs providing services ranging from training and skills development to job matching. In addition, some countries such as Egypt, Iran, and Morocco have amended their labor laws to introduce greater flexibility in hiring and firing for employers. This has happened despite the existence of entrenched interests that are opposed to granting greater freedom to the private sector.

Even family formation has emerged as a target of public policies. Marriage funds and sporadic credit programs geared toward youth have responded to the immediate need to alleviate the costs of family formation, yet they have not led to a system of finance and credit that empowers young people to establish themselves through economically sound and sustainable means.

However, a major gap in these recent reform efforts is the insufficient attention policymakers have paid to the role of institutions and incentives for young people.[3] Transitions of young people are influenced by the markets of education, labor, credit, housing, and marriage. The distortions and rigidities in the institutions and the signals they generate end up reinforcing the continued exclusion of young people.

Because these markets are interconnected, the outcomes in one area are affected by the institutions in another. Consequently, the scope of policy in one sector goes beyond the sector itself and often beyond the markets that are normally associated with youth welfare.[4] For example, in the marriage market, the valuation of a groom's future earnings is, quite reasonably, related to the security of his job. Thus, norms in the marriage market may create an important social and political imperative for stronger job protection, often leading to an overwhelming preference for employment in the public sector. Reducing public sector employment without any parallel efforts to introduce widespread social protection measures could adversely affect young men's ability to marry, because they frequently lack alternative means for signaling their future prospects.

Generation Empowered:
Improving Institutions and Incentive Structures

Ten institutional features of Middle Eastern countries are key to unlocking the potential of this generation. These institutions determine the quality of human capital, thereby affecting the growth potential of Middle Eastern countries.[5] They also shape the distribution of the benefits of growth for young people and especially for young women. To promote inclusive development, it is critical to improve the incentive structures within these institutions. These ten features should be priorities for further research and reform.

First, the provision of education is dominated by the public sector. Most students (and all students from poorer families) attend public schools and universities. Because most countries have highly centralized education systems, governments have a monopoly in setting national quality standards for schools. Competition between schools and accountability to parents and students are poor. Because of the dearth of competition, teachers and school administrators face distorted incentives that in turn affect the quality of student learning. These weaknesses should be the focus of any reform effort.[6] The low quality of education affects the job readiness of youth, creating a mismatch between the skills that students develop through the education system and those needed by employers.

Second, grade promotion and university admissions are heavily determined by standardized tests. In several countries, such as Iran, Jordan, and Syria, entrance to universities depends on performance on a single national test— often a multiple-choice test that encourages rote memorization across all levels of the education system. University education is the destination of choice for nearly all students who go beyond the primary level of school, in part because a university degree is required for jobs in the public sector. As such, university admission policies have led to a set of distorted incentives that narrowly focus school curricula and student efforts on test preparation rather than on acquisition of a broad range of knowledge and skills. As a result, families across the Middle East spend billions of dollars on test preparation courses and private tutors for their children, a phenomenon that contributes little to long-term productivity.[7] Admission exams should be reformed to test a broader range of skills such as writing and critical thinking.

Third, disproportionate government investment goes to tertiary education, even though investments in primary education have the highest social returns. The demand for higher education means that Middle Eastern countries spend disproportionately more on upper secondary and tertiary education at the expense of primary education, which has higher enrollment rates.[8] The inefficient distribution of expenditures and excessive investment in higher education has long-term effects in reinforcing the lure of university education for securing government jobs. While this pattern of investment fits the structure of private returns to education, which are highest at the university level, it is not efficient when viewed from the perspective of social returns.[9]

Fourth, the large role of the public sector in employment leads to distorted learning incentives and encourages long waits for perceived good jobs. Government jobs are highly preferred among new graduates, in part because of the security and benefits that these jobs offer. As a result of public sector hiring and compensation practices, "good" jobs are perceived by parents and students alike as requiring a degree rather than investment in learning specific skills. While deep changes in the civil service code are not always politically practical and take time to implement, an intermediate step could include the introduction of assessments and interviews to evaluate key skills and personal traits rather than relying on diplomas and test scores. Written exams for prospective entrants and judicious use of recommendation letters from teachers and employers would begin to weaken the link between government hiring and university degrees and thus begin to reduce the negative grip of government employment on skill formation.

Fifth, tight regulation of private sector employment reduces employment prospects for young people. In most countries, labor laws impose heavy penalties on discretionary layoffs to protect workers from the vagaries of private employers.[10] These regulations on hiring and firing work to the benefit of incumbent workers and to the disadvantage of new entrants.[11] Strong employment protection raises the cost of hiring new workers and lowers job turnover. Furthermore, where private employment is heavily regulated, private employers behave like public employers, and because they have to offer job security in their hiring decisions, they give more weight to ex ante signals of productivity such as educational degrees and certificates. Recently, some countries have taken steps to relax their labor laws. However, these labor law reforms often benefit firms and can force young workers into short-term fixed contracts, undermining job stability. Therefore, comprehensive reforms that strike a balance between protecting workers and enhancing flexibility for firms are necessary. In addition, hiring policies in the private sector should be improved by requiring evidence of a wider range of skills rather than relying on official qualifications or personal connections. This reform would give private employers a greater voice in skill formation.

Sixth, a large informal sector limits the opportunities for human capital development. Early work experience influences skills development in two main ways. First, it allows young entrants to gain skills that are not taught in schools. Second, work experience signals these skills to future employers. However, informal firms are not in a good position to provide either type of work experience because, being informal, they are less inclined to invest in the firm's reputation, technology, and training. Governments should explore new instruments, such as training funds and vouchers, to encourage private training providers (nonprofit and for-profit) to target young people in the informal sector.

Seven, work conditions and social norms influence the employment choices of young women. Young women continue to experience hardship in their transitions from school to the workplace. One major factor is that social norms prohibit young women from taking certain jobs, especially in the informal sector or low-wage work. Small firms do not give women the same sense of security as larger and more established firms, especially in the public sector. In addition, private sector work often involves long hours, inflexible schedules, and few benefits such as maternity leave. Without imposing crippling costs on firms that would discourage them from hiring women, it is important to remove disincentives that women face in their participation in the labor force.

Eight, oil rents, remittances, and strong family support potentially affect young people's willingness to work and how they search for jobs. Those who decide to participate in the labor market (about 90 percent of men and one-third of women in the Middle East) often face a choice between waiting for desirable jobs in the formal sector or building a career through multiple short-term employment stints. An important determinant of the length of time a person is willing to wait for a job is the reservation wage, or the wage at which an individual is indifferent to working or not working. Various forms of transfers to the young, from the government or from within the family, raise their reservation wage and reduce their willingness to take up informal jobs that could teach them valuable skills. There is little understanding of reservation wages, their impact on the youth labor supply, and their implications for designing effective programs such as career counseling and job matching.

Nine, marriage customs and laws affect the transition to family formation. Inflexible social norms and expectations, such as the costs of marriage, place too much emphasis on economic security at a time when education and labor market outcomes are changing rapidly. Marriage contracts in the Middle East often include high up-front costs and serve as forward-looking agreements intended to secure the perceived welfare of women. Education and a government job are traditionally used to evaluate the future earnings and economic security of potential grooms.[12] However, with low returns to education and diminishing labor market prospects, the marriage market has not adjusted to enable young people to form families in the face of economic insecurity.

Ten, credit and financial institutions fail to help young people smooth their future consumption. Young people need access to credit to start businesses, purchase homes, and pay for the initial costs of family formation. This need often goes unmet, however, because they lack the collateral, steady jobs, or reputational capital required to obtain credit. In the Middle East, the greatest challenge for credit markets is the provision of housing finance for youth. Good credit market policies not only would contribute to a more widely shared growth but could also help facilitate youth inclusion. This is especially true for the growing majority of youth who live in urban or peri-urban areas across the Middle East and are aspiring to independent living arrangements after marriage.

Policy reforms should realize the role of institutions in effecting outcomes and should take into account the links among outcomes in education, employment, and family formation. Failure to do so can undermine the effectiveness of policy changes. As a number of previous examples show, prevailing institutions, especially in the labor market, are proving to be a roadblock to current education reforms. A recent World Bank flagship report on education in the Middle East makes a strong case for reform initiatives that address teacher and school incentives and raise public accountability, thereby shifting the focus of education policy in the region from inputs to incentives.[13]

But distortions in incentives are not confined to the education system. Labor market institutions across the Middle East signal rewards for skills and thus similarly distort the accumulation of human capital. These signals indicate high rewards for degrees and certifiable skills to secure public sector jobs and only weak rewards for a range of hard-to-certify skills that are of greater value to private employers. Therefore, reforms in education must also address the signals and incentives that emanate from the labor market. Reforms that focus on one set of institutions without considering related institutions are likely to prove ineffective.

In addition, ignoring institutions and incentives can create significant inefficiencies. For example, the lure of a university diploma as the pathway to a public sector job drives parents and students into learning strategies—from early childhood through high school—that do not foster productive global skills and that cost billions of dollars a year in private tutoring fees. This huge misallocation of time and resources could be better used toward skill development if proper reward structures were institutionalized in labor markets. As such, public policy would be more efficient and effective if institutions were aligned with stakeholder incentives.

Improving the institutional environment for young people is especially critical at a time when the Middle East is affected by the global economic slowdown.[14] The global downturn that began in 2008 raised protectionist pressures in many countries, and as a result, private sector–led reforms have become politically more difficult to implement. How Middle Eastern countries respond to the current crisis will determine whether their young citizens will be able to exploit the new opportunities that lie beyond today's ailing global economy. The time of uncertainty might make retrenchment or even reversal of liberalizing policies tempting, but institutionalizing greater protection and rigidity in key markets is likely to further marginalize young people in the long term.

Maxims for a New Policy Agenda

The reform of existing institutions is an ambitious agenda—and one that is likely to be shaped by politics. A number of actors will justifiably have an interest in the way reforms take shape, including representatives from governments, the private sector, and civil society organizations. The political economy of reform is better navigated by multiple stakeholders when guided by common principles.

1. First, "quick-fix" solutions can jeopardize the long-term goals of improving incentives. For example, many countries face urgent demands to create more jobs for skilled workers, but basing eligibility for employment-generation programs exclusively on education credentials bolsters existing distorted incentives for diplomas and degrees and worsens the mismatch of skills for future job market entrants.

2. Second, reforms should be geared toward using the region's large youth population to prepare Middle Eastern economies for the competitive global economy. As the youth bulge decreases in size in some countries, the opportunity is closing for many countries in the Middle East to maximize gains from their demographic gifts and to foster more effective uses of human capital.

3. Third, effective monitoring and evaluation must be streamlined into policy and program formulation and implementation in the region. Rigorous, independent impact evaluations are critical to achieving real progress in addressing the major challenges facing young people. Sound evidence promotes better understanding about what works, enhances cross-country sharing of best practices, boosts capacity in the region, and improves policymaking and public spending toward more effective youth development. To date, few projects aimed at young people have been (or can be) evaluated in terms of impact. Monitoring and impact evaluation, therefore, must be integrated in the design of programs and interventions so that "real-time" feedback can be received, mid-course corrections made and, the efficiency and effectiveness of expenditures assessed.

4. Fourth, in addition to evaluating the impact of specific programs, greater policy research is needed on the life courses and transitions of young people. Knowledge is lacking on how young people make use of their time during the period of "waithood" (the period of time spent waiting between schooling and employment) and how they interpret market signals. Other underexplored areas include the relationship between parental support and reservation wages of young people. These few examples underline the need for deeper research on the lives of young people across countries and over time.[15]

5. Finally, given that most countries across the Middle East face a shared set of challenges and are characterized by some combination of the ten institutional features described earlier in this chapter, progress will depend upon greater cooperation between countries. The variety of interventions that have already been tested in the region can provide for localized ideas and can generate learning across borders.

Prospects for Reform

In this final section, we consider the political feasibility of implementing reforms aimed at tackling the underlying causes of youth exclusion in the Middle East. Some of the policies, such as retrenchment of public sector hiring and education reforms, have been on the reform agenda for some time. The fact that they have not been fully implemented points to political constraints, especially in the area of labor market reform. Prospects for reform can be strengthened, however, by considering interdependence and sequencing of policy, engaging young people and parents as political allies, and committing to greater social protection.

Earlier, we argued that confining reforms to the education system alone is likely to have limited impact as long as schools, students, and parents continue to receive distorted signals from the labor market regarding the skills that are most valued by employers. Recognizing the interdependence between education and labor market reform allows policymakers to build on links between the two sectors. For example, to promote the acquisition of productive skills, specific skills training in schools can be combined with incentives for employers, such as a wage subsidy, to reward these skills. Interdependence also allows policymakers to start at the politically least controversial link and build momentum for reform in other areas. The political economy in specific countries will determine the sequence of reforms, such as whether to start with education or labor market reforms.

All reforms have trade-offs, and to mobilize wide support for change, a new and transparent discourse is needed between governments, parents, and youth. To date, the interests of older workers, especially when it comes to labor market reforms, tend to supersede those of young workers. This is because comprehensive reforms in education and the labor market undoubtedly arouse a wide array of opposing forces. Teachers' unions may oppose greater accountability, and workers' unions will oppose relaxing job protection rules. Fears of increased job insecurity in a new, globalized economy tend to create pressures for increased job protection rather than less.

Nonetheless, if political discourse can shift away from focusing on static benefits to prioritizing intergenerational gains, youth and parents can be mobilized as political allies within the reform process. A discourse that equates the protection of parents' jobs with the loss of future opportunities for sons and daughters can create a larger constituency for reform.

The reforms outlined here are difficult to achieve without commitment to social protection and social insurance. As Tarik Yousef has argued, this reform strategy requires renegotiating the social contract in the Middle East.[16] The heart of this new strategy involves replacing old job protection rules and regulations with social protection and social insurance policies. Political barriers to greater flexibility can be surmounted by simultaneously proposing social insurance schemes to allay general fears while enlisting the support of youth and their parents who seek a brighter future for their children.

Notes

1. See, for example, Alan Richards and John Waterbury, *A Political Economy of the Middle East* (Boulder, Colo.: Westview Press, 2007); Marcus Noland and Howard Pack, *The Arab Economies in a Changing World* (Washington: Peterson Institute for International Economics, 2007); and Paul Rivlin, *Arab Economies in the Twenty-First Century* (Cambridge University Press, 2009).

2. World Bank, *Doing Business 2009* (Washington: 2008); World Bank, *2008 MENA Economic Developments and Prospects: Regional Integration for Global Competitiveness* (Washington: 2008); World Bank, *2007 MENA Economic Developments and Prospects: Job Creation in an Era of High Growth* (Washington: 2007); Taher Kanaan and May Hanania, "The Disconnect between Education, Job Growth, and Employment in Jordan," in this volume.

3. Djavad Salehi-Isfahani and Navtej Dhillon, "Stalled Youth Transitions in the Middle East: A Framework for Policy Reform," Middle East Youth Initiative Working Paper 8 (Wolfensohn Center for Development at the Brookings Institution and the Dubai School of Government, 2008).

4. Ibid.

5. Ibid.

6. World Bank, *The Road Not Traveled: Education Reform in the Middle East and North Africa* (Washington: 2008).

7. See, for example, Ragui Assaad and Asmaa Elbadawy, "Private and Group Tutoring in Egypt: Where Is the Gender Inequality?" paper presented at the Economic Research Forum eleventh annual conference (Beirut, December 14–16, 2004); Aysit Tansel and Fatma Bircan, "Private Tutoring Expenditures in Turkey," Discussion Paper 1255 (Bonn: Institute for the Study of Labor (IZA), 2004); and World Bank, *The Road Not Traveled*.

8. World Bank, *The Road Not Traveled*.

9. High private returns, especially for higher education, have been confirmed by econometric studies of returns to education. See Ragui Assaad, "The Effects of Public Sector Hiring and Compensation Policies on the Egyptian Labor Market," *World Bank Economic Review* 11, no. 1 (1997): 85–118; Abdallah Dah and Salwa C. Hammami, "The Impact of Education on Households' Quality of Life in Urban Lebanon," Paper presented at the Economic Research Forum seventh annual conference (Amman, October 26–29, 2002); Henrik Huitfeldt and Nader Kabbani, "Labor Force Participation, Employment, and Returns to Education in Syria," paper presented at the eighth International Conference on the Economics and Finance of the Middle East and North Africa (Byblos, Lebanon, May 22–24, 2006); Aysit Tansel, "Wage Employment, Earnings and Returns to Schooling for Men and Women in Turkey," *Economics of Education Review* 13, no. 4 (1994): 305–20; and Aysit Tansel, "Public-Private Employment Choice, Wage Differentials, and Gender in Turkey," *Economic Development and Cultural Change* 53, no. 2 (2005): 453–77. Low social returns to education in the Middle East are confirmed by empirical cross-country studies that reveal no impact on

economic output from the increase in education. See Zeki Fattah, Imed Limam, and Samir Makdisi, "Determinants of Growth in the MENA Countries," in *Explaining Growth in the Middle East*, edited by Jeffrey B. Nugent and M. Hashem Pesaran (Oxford: Elsevier, 2007); and Lant Pritchett, "Has Education Had a Growth Payoff in the MENA Region?" Middle East and North Africa Working Paper Series 18 (Washington: World Bank, 1999).

10. See, for example, World Bank, *Unlocking the Employment Potential in the Middle East and North Africa: Toward a New Social Contract*, MENA Development Report (Washington: 2004); Tarik Yousef, "Employment, Development and the Social Contract in the Middle East and North Africa," technical report (Washington: World Bank, 2004); Mona Said, "Public Sector Employment and Labor Markets in Arab Countries: Recent Developments and Policy Implications," in *Labor and Human Capital in the Middle East: Studies of Labor Markets and Household Behavior*, edited by Djavad Salehi-Isfahani (Berkshire, U.K.: Garnet & Ithaca Press, 2001), pp. 91–145; Pierre-Richard Agenor and others, "Labor Market Reforms, Growth, and Unemployment in Labor-exporting Countries in the Middle East and North Africa," *Journal for Policy Modeling* 29, no. 2 (2007): 277–309.

11. For a more detailed description of labor market regulations in the Middle East, see World Bank, *Unlocking the Employment Potential in the Middle East and North Africa: Toward a New Social Contract.*

12. Salehi-Isfahani and Dhillon, "Stalled Youth Transitions in the Middle East."

13. World Bank, *The Road Not Traveled.*

14. Navtej Dhillon, Djavad Salehi-Isfahani, Paul Dyer, Tarik Yousef, Amina Fahmy, and Mary Kraetsch, "Missed by the Boom, Hit by the Bust: Making Markets Work for Young People in the Middle East" (Wolfensohn Center for Development at the Brookings Institution and the Dubai School of Government, 2009).

15. Navtej Dhillon and Tarik Yousef, "Inclusion: Meeting the 100 Million Youth Challenge," Middle East Youth Initiative Report (Wolfensohn Center for Development at the Brookings Institution and the Dubai School of Government, 2007).

16. Yousef, "Employment, Development, and the Social Contract in the Middle East and North Africa."

About the Authors

Aziz Ajbilou is the director of studies, cooperation, and legislation at the Ministry of Tourism, Handicraft, and Social Economy in Morocco. A statistician engineer, he has been a professor of higher education at the National Institute of Statistics and Applied Economics (INSEA) since 1985. From 2001 to 2006 Ajbilou was the director of the Centre of Studies and Demographic Research (CERED). He received a PhD in demography from the Catholic University of Louvain–La Neuve in Belgium and has written several scientific works on the topic of population and development. He is a member of the Association of Moroccan Demographers, the International Union for the Scientific Study of Population (UIESP), the Union for African Population Studies (UEPA), and the Maghreben Association for the Studies of Population (AMEP).

Samia Al-Botmeh is the director of the Center for Development Studies and a lecturer in economics and gender studies at Birzeit University in Ramallah, West Bank. She is also pursuing her thesis, "Gender Differentials in Labor Market Outcomes in the Occupied Palestinian Territory," as a doctoral candidate at the University of London, School of Oriental and African Studies. Previously, Al-Botmeh worked as senior researcher and coordinator of research at the Palestine Economic Policy Research Institute in Ramallah. She has published extensively on Palestinian economic affairs, labor markets, gender differentials in economic outcomes, and poverty in the West Bank and Gaza Strip.

RAGUI ASSAAD is professor of planning and public affairs at the Hubert H. Humphrey Institute of Public Affairs at the University of Minnesota. He was formerly the regional director for West Asia and North Africa at the Population Council. Assaad is editor of *The Egyptian Labor Market in an Era of Reform* (American University in Cairo Press, 2002) and has written numerous publications on labor markets, gender, and economics in the Middle East. Assaad is coauthor of "Youth Exclusion in Egypt: In Search of 'Second Chances'" (Middle East Youth Initiative Working Paper 2, 2007).

GHADA BARSOUM is currently a research associate at the Population Council, West Asia and North Africa office. She is the author of "The Employment Crisis of Female Graduates in Egypt: An Ethnographic Account" (Cairo Papers in Social Science, 2004) and "Who Gets Credit? The Gendered Division of Microfinance Programs in Egypt" (*Canadian Journal of Development Studies,* 2006). Barsoum is also coauthor of "Youth Exclusion in Egypt: In Search of 'Second Chances'" (Middle East Youth Initiative Working Paper 2, 2007). She received her PhD from the University of Toronto in 2005.

BRAHIM BOUDARBAT is an assistant professor of economics in the School of Industrial Relations at the University of Montreal, where he received his PhD in economics in 2003. Boudarbat previously worked for the Moroccan Department of Vocational Training, where he was in charge of studies on the employment of graduates. He has written several papers on the economic performance of immigrants, investment in and returns to human capital in Canada, vocational training, and youth employment in Morocco. His recent published papers include "Recent Trends in Wage Inequality and the Wage Structure in Canada," "Vocational Training in Morocco: Social and Economic Issues for the Labor Market," and "Job-Search Strategies and the Unemployment of University Graduates in Morocco."

JAD CHAABAN is assistant professor of economics at the American University of Beirut. He previously worked as an economist at the World Bank Country Office in Beirut. Chaaban has a PhD in economics from the University of Toulouse and an MBA from the Paris Graduate School of Management, European School of Management. He is the author of "The Costs of Youth Exclusion in the Middle East" (Middle East Youth Initiative Working Paper 7, 2008).

EMILY CUPITO is a consultant with the Population Council in Cairo. She is also the coauthor of "Inclusiveness in Higher Education in Egypt" (forthcoming 2009). She earned her master's in public policy from Duke University in May 2008. She holds a BA in economics and public policy analysis from the University of North Carolina at Chapel Hill. She is currently a Presidential Management Fellow with the Social Security Administration's Office of Retirement Policy in Washington.

NAVTEJ DHILLON is the director of the Middle East Youth Initiative and a Fellow at the Wolfensohn Center for Development at the Brookings Institution. Previously Dhillon served as a special advisor and speech writer to James D. Wolfensohn and worked at the World Bank. Dhillon's research focuses on development economics and in particular the transitions of young people. He has written widely on the social exclusion of young people in the Middle East, and his work has been featured in the *New York Times*, *Wall Street Journal*, *Guardian*, *Independent*, *The National* (United Arab Emirates), and additional regional newspapers. He also has been interviewed by BBC World Service, Public Broadcasting Service, and Al-Jazeera.

PAUL DYER is a research associate at the Dubai School of Government, where he focuses on youth and labor markets in the Middle East and North Africa. He has written extensively on demographics, labor market policy, and the regulatory environment for business, particularly in the countries of the Gulf Cooperation Council. Dyer received a master's in Arab Studies with a concentration in economics and development from Georgetown University, where he was the Sheikh Sultan bin Mohamed Al Qassemi Scholar. Before joining the Dubai School of Government, he worked with the World Bank for four years as a consultant in the Office of the Chief Economist, Middle East and North Africa Region.

DANIEL EGEL is a doctoral candidate in the Department of Economics at the University of California, Berkeley. His research interests are applied microeconometrics and development economics. He is currently working as a consultant with the Social Fund for Development in Yemen. Egel is coauthor of "Youth Exclusion in Iran: The State of Education, Employment, and Family Formation" (Middle East Youth Initiative Working Paper 3, 2007).

MAY HANANIA is a consultant specializing in public policy research, analysis, and report writing on behalf of think tanks, public agencies, and academic institutions. Her research focuses on issues critical to the development process in Jordan, primarily in the areas of education, innovation, entrepreneurship, employment, and youth. She received a BA, cum laude, from Harvard University and a master's in public policy from Harvard University's Kennedy School of Government.

NADER KABBANI is the director of research at the Syria Trust for Development, a nonprofit nongovernmental organization headquartered in Damascus. Before joining the Syria Trust, Kabbani was an assistant professor in the Department of Economics at the American University of Beirut. He holds a PhD in economics from Johns Hopkins University. Kabbani has been a consultant to the World Bank, the European Training Foundation, the Food and Agriculture Organization, and the United Nations Program on Youth. He has published numerous articles in edited volumes and international journals, including the *Journal of Human Resources* and *Teachers College Record.*

NOURA KAMEL holds an MA and a BA in economics from the American University of Beirut. Her research interests include labor economics, welfare studies, education, and public policy and reform. Recently she coauthored an International Labor Organization policy note on "The Impact of the Financial and Economic Crisis on Arab States: Considerations on Employment and Social Protection Policy Responses" (2009).

TAHER KANAAN is managing director of the Jordan Center for Public Policy Research and Dialogue. A graduate of Cambridge University, he has written widely on economic development in the Middle East. Kanaan was previously a consultant to the World Bank and has held senior executive positions in the United Nations Conference on Trade and Development, the Arab Fund for Economic and Social Development, and the Industrial Development Bank of Jordan. He served the state of Jordan as a member of parliament in the Upper House, secretary general of the Higher Council for Science and Technology, minister of planning, minister of state for development affairs, and deputy prime minister. Kanaan currently serves on the boards of trustees of the Economic Research Forum of the Arab Countries, Iran, and Turkey (ERF); the Center for Arab Unity Studies; the Institute of Palestine Studies; and the Arab Anti-Corruption Organization.

DJAVAD SALEHI-ISFAHANI is professor of economics at Virginia Polytechnic Institute and State University and a nonresident guest scholar at the Wolfensohn Center for Development at the Brookings Institution. He is also a member of the board of trustees for the Economic Research Forum for the Arab Countries, Iran, and Turkey. Salehi-Isfahani previously served as visiting professor at the Institute for Research in Planning and Development in Iran and was an economist at the Central Bank of Iran. He wrote "Human Resources in Iran: Potentials and Challenges" (*Iranian Studies*, 2005), "Fertility, Education, and Household Resources in Iran" (JAI Press, 2001), and "Demographic Factors in Iran's Economic Development" (*Social Research*, 2000), among other works.

EDWARD SAYRE is an assistant professor of political science, international development, and international affairs at the University of Southern Mississippi. He received his PhD in economics from the University of Texas at Austin in 1999. Sayre has written several journal articles, book chapters, and research monographs on the Palestinian economy, with an emphasis on the Palestinian labor market. Sayre was previously a visiting research associate at the Palestine Economic Policy Research Institute (MAS) in Jerusalem from 1996 to 1997 and has also taught at Kenyon College and Agnes Scott College. He is a member of the board of directors for the Middle East Economic Association, where he has served since 2002.

TARIK YOUSEF is dean of the Dubai School of Government and a nonresident senior fellow at the Wolfensohn Center for Development at the Brookings Institution. Yousef specializes in development economics and economic history with a particular focus on the Middle East. He has held the positions of associate professor of economics in the School of Foreign Service at Georgetown University and Sheikh Al Sabah Chair in Arab Studies at Georgetown's Center for Contemporary Arab Studies. Yousef received his PhD in economics from Harvard University. His current research interests include the structure and dynamics of labor markets, the political economy of policy reform, and development policies in oil-exporting countries.

Index